AUSTRALIA'S WILDERNESS HERITAGE

VOLUME 1
WORLD HERITAGE AREAS

PENELOPE FIGGIS   GEOFF MOSLEY

PHOTOGRAPHY
LEO MEIER

Published in association with the Australian Conservation Foundation

WELDON
PUBLISHING

SYDNEY • HONG KONG • CHICAGO • LONDON

A Kevin Weldon Production
Published by Weldon Publishing
a division of Kevin Weldon & Associates Pty Limited
372 Eastern Valley Way, Willoughby, NSW 2068, Australia
First published 1988
Reprinted 1989

© Copyright Kevin Weldon & Associates 1988

The illustrations on the slipcase and cases of this publication were
especially commissioned from noted artist Rosemary Ganf.

Additional text: C. Warren Bonython, David Dale
Managing editor: Sheena Coupe
Design and art direction: John Bull, The Book Design Company
Layout and assembly: Stan Lamond, Lesley Workman
Maps: Mike Gorman, Stan Lamond
Production manager: Dianne Leddy
Production consultant: Mick Bagnato

Typeset in Australia by Savage Type, Brisbane
Printed in Australia by The Griffin Press, Adelaide

National Library of Australia Cataloguing-in-Publication Data
Australia's wilderness heritage. Volume 1, World heritage areas.

Bibliography.
Includes index.
ISBN 0 947116 53 2.
ISBN 0 947116 55 9 (set).

1. Wilderness areas – Australia – Pictorial works.
2. National parks and reserves – Australia – Pictorial works.
3. Australia – Description and travel – 1976 – Views,
I. Meier, Leo, 1951–   . II. Figgis, Penny, 1951–
III. Mosley, J.G. (John Geoffrey), 1931–   . IV. Title: World
heritage areas.

333.78'2'0994

Pages 2–3: Uluru and Kata Tjuta reflect the colours of arid Australia.

Pages 4–5: Rainforest sweeps down to reef-protected beach, Daintree National Park.

Page 6: Dense rainforest undergrowth, Barrington Tops, New South Wales.

Page 7: Kata Tjuta, a deeply spiritual site to Aboriginal people.

Pages 8–9: Sunrise over the Australian Alps.

Right; The Southern Ocean breaks over Sugarloaf Rock, Leeuwin-Naturaliste
National Park.

NOTE ON THE MAPS

The following abbreviations have been used in the area maps:

AAT	Australian Antarctic Territory
CP	Conservation Park
CR	Conservation Reserve
FHR	Fish Habitat Reserve
FR	Flora Reserve
NP	National Park
NR	Nature Reserve
SP	State Park

The symbol ⬡ indicates that the area, or part of the
area, has already been inscribed on the world heritage
list. The boundaries on the maps for areas which have
not been formally nominated or declared world heritage
are in no sense formal boundaries. They are included
merely to indicate the broad area regarded as having
world heritage qualities.

CONTENTS

*T*horny devil (*Moloch horridus*).

*S*unset over the Stirling Ranges, southwest Western Australia.

13

Foreword

MESSAGE FROM THE PRIME MINISTER

In our first century of European settlement Australia seemed so endless and its population so sparse that the land was widely held to be indestructible. Sadly, such assumptions have proved false. Australia's priceless tree cover, for instance, was just 10 per cent when European settlement began. It is now only 5 per cent. More than 41 million hectares of forest have been lost.

Fertile soils and irrigation have made the Murray-Darling Basin the nation's most generous food basket. But there is a price. Some areas of the basin are suffering from increasing salinity, wetlands have been destroyed and red gum forests threatened. Salt, fertilisers and pesticides and changes to water and land management have caused much of the damage.

Australia's native creatures have suffered for many more reasons than soil degradation, but none of them redeeming. Some two hundred species have been driven to extinction since European settlement, or one for every year.

Such bleak revelations in the past decade have made Australians more sensitive to their environment and its unique flora and fauna. They have also grown considerably more circumspect about its future. The States responded to this new concern by doubling the national parkland to 22 million hectares. The Federal Government took the important further step of nominating eight of Australia's most important wilderness areas for world heritage listing.

To understand why these eight areas were chosen for special protection, and to appreciate the wealth of possibilities for future listings, you need look no further. AUSTRALIA'S WILDERNESS HERITAGE is a splendidly appropriate tribute to the beauty, diversity and fragility of the chosen wilderness areas, and their native animals.

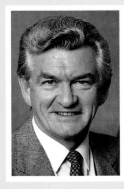

R.J.L. HAWKE

Left
A hidden valley in the heart of the Bungle Bungles, Kimberley, Western Australia.

Introduction

*N*ative conifers by the Artists Pool, Cradle Mountain, Tasmania.

The encouragement of people to think internationally, to regard the culture of their own country as part of world culture, to conceive a physical, spiritual and intellectual world heritage, is important in the endeavour to avoid the destruction of humanity.

The late JUSTICE LIONEL MURPHY in his judgment on the Franklin Dam Case,
1 July 1983

The ancient Greeks listed the Seven Wonders of the World but all except the pyramids have disappeared without trace. Now the concept has been revived in the form of a world heritage list, on which are inscribed those places of such exceptional interest and value that conserving them is considered to be the concern of all humanity. The idea is as breathtaking in its vision, and almost as simple, as the seven wonders. But there is one major difference. The ancient wonders were all the products of human endeavour; nature was considered hostile and something to be tamed. Today we find beauty in the wild, and the world heritage list includes outstanding natural areas as well as places of cultural significance.

Australia's Wilderness Heritage introduces the wonders of Australia's part of the world heritage. During the ten years in which the list has been developed, seven Australian areas have been included. Undoubtedly there will be more, and some of those already inscribed will be extended. Recognising that this is a dynamic process, *Australia's Wilderness Heritage* also describes other areas which the Australian Conservation Foundation believes have the potential to become part of the world heritage. For the entire continent, the list could eventually include twenty to thirty places, and the final chapter suggests a range of other possibilities.

What does listing really mean? How is an area chosen for inclusion on the world heritage list? World heritage areas, or 'sites', are natural or cultural properties which have been inscribed on the list by the World Heritage Committee, a Paris-based arm of UNESCO. This committee, and all the procedures relating to the identification and protection of world heritage areas, are provided for in the Convention Concerning the Protection of the World Cultural and Natural Heritage, which was adopted by the General Conference of UNESCO in 1972. The World Heritage Committee comprises representatives from twenty-one countries elected by the countries that have signed the convention. To date, 100 countries have ratified the convention, Australia being one of the first.

The core of the definition of world heritage in the convention is that the sites must be 'of outstanding universal value' from the points of view of art, history, science, anthropology, aesthetics or conservation. To establish the list, the committee has four criteria for natural sites and six for cultural sites.

A *natural property* must consist of an outstanding example of a major stage of the earth's evolution (such as an ice age); or be representative of significant ongoing geological or biological processes (such as the speciation of the flora and fauna in a rainforest); or include scenes of natural beauty; or contain the most important habitats of threatened species of animals and plants. It is not enough that a site is outstanding; it must be the best example of its kind. It must also meet conditions of integrity, with regard both to the naturalness of its condition and the measures in place for its protection.

A *cultural property* must represent either a unique artistic achievement or a masterpiece of creative genius; or have exerted a great influence on or contributed a unique testimony to a civilisation that has disappeared; or have been associated with outstanding events, ideas or beliefs; or be an outstanding example of a traditional human settlement that represents a certain culture.

The procedure for listing an area begins when it is placed on a tentative list of properties likely to be nominated over the next decade or so, and submitted to the World Heritage Committee. This is done by the country that is party to the convention (the 'state party'). It then follows this up with a specific nomination, which must be submitted by 31 December for consideration by the next meeting of the committee, usually one year later.

In Australia, nominations for the world heritage list are made by the Commonwealth (the state party), after vetting by the Australian National Commission for UNESCO. Until 1987 the Commonwealth did not nominate an area without the consent of the state in which it was situated. During the period before the nomination is decided upon, it is evaluated by internationally respected bodies — the International Union for Conservation of Nature and Natural Resources (IUCN) for natural properties, and the International Council on Monuments and Sites (ICOMOS) and the International Centre for the Study of the Preservation and the Restoration of Cultural Properties (ICCROM) for cultural properties. Extensions of a world heritage area can be made by submitting to the World Heritage Committee an addendum to the original nomination.

The first properties were entered on the list in 1978, and by 1988 there were 211 cultural and seventy-seven natural properties. Among the natural sites are the Grand Canyon, the Rocky Mountains, Serengeti Park, the Mesa Verde, the Galapagos Islands and Sagamartha National Park, near Mt Everest. The cultural sites include the Statue of Liberty, the Inca city of Machu Picchu, the pyramids of Egypt, the Taj Mahal, many of the great European cathedrals, including Chartres and Aachen, and the Palace of Versailles.

In Australia, Kakadu National Park Stage I, the Great Barrier Reef and Willandra Lakes were inscribed on the list at a meeting of the committee in the Sydney Opera House in October 1981. In 1982 Lord Howe Island and the Western Tasmanian Wilderness National Parks were inscribed. There was then a break until 1986, when the eastern Australian subtropical and temperate rainforests site in New South Wales was listed. In 1987 Uluru (Ayers Rock–Mt Olga) was added, and the wet tropics is almost certain to be added to the world heritage list at the end of 1988.

The World Heritage Convention is a unique form of cooperation and in some circumstances the World Heritage Committee can respond to requests for financial and other forms of assistance — the convention instituted a World Heritage Fund. Nevertheless, the principal obligation to world heritage areas rests with the local state party. Signatories to the convention recognise 'that the duty of ensuring identification, protection, conservation, presentation, and transmission to future generations of the cultural and natural heritage . . . belongs primarily to the State. It will do all it can to this end, to the utmost of its own resources . . .'

Each state party undertakes to set up conservation agencies, carry out research and training, and integrate the protection of heritage into other policies. Detractors of the convention who say that listing means handing over

Right

Cycad near the Hugh River, central Australia.

control to UNESCO are misinformed. Not only does the convention declare full respect for the sovereignty of the countries with world heritage properties, but it is the state party that decides whether to make a nomination, and the state party that must protect a listed property. There is no surrender of territory or rights, merely an acknowledgment that the area is held in trust for the world and will be protected accordingly.

The Australian situation is complex because, although the federal government has the responsibility for nomination and protection, most of the areas that are likely to become world heritage are administered by the states. Several states, including New South Wales and Victoria, have agreed that this is a proper role for the Commonwealth, but others have viewed it as unwarranted and fought against it. Queensland and Tasmania have complained that the Commonwealth has become involved with land-use decisions which have traditionally been made by the states alone.

The Commonwealth government is able to implement the convention chiefly through its responsibility for external affairs. In 1983, to strengthen its hand in doing this, it introduced the World Heritage Properties Conservation Bill. Its efficacy was made apparent when the Tasmanian government challenged the Commonwealth's prohibition of the construction of the Gordon-below-Franklin dam in the world heritage area in western Tasmania. A High Court decision confirmed that the Commonwealth's action was valid.

There are potential problems for areas that are considered by the federal government to be worthy of listing and are threatened, in some cases by a state government. Whether the federal government can protect an area in these circumstances has yet to be tested by the High Court, but it seems likely that it does have the power.

Which activities are permissible and which are not will depend very much upon the nature of the site and the justification for its listing. Most listed areas will be national parks or have equivalent protective status. The only kinds of development that are likely to be restricted are those that jeopardise the integrity of the property. For instance, in an area inscribed because of the significance of its forests, logging would be completely unacceptable. In a wilderness area, road construction would obviously be contrary to the aims of listing. The Commonwealth acted to stop the Gordon-below-Franklin dam because it would have drowned 114 kilometres of beautiful wilderness river, along with caves containing evidence of Aboriginal occupation 20 000 years ago. On the other hand, controlled fishing and tourism in the Great Barrier Reef does not conflict with the conservation of the coral reef ecosystem and at Willandra Lakes pastoral activities away from sensitive areas do not threaten the features that led to its listing.

Australia's involvement in the World Heritage Convention has already benefited conservation in Australia. But for it, the wilderness valleys of the lower Gordon and Franklin would have been drowned and the tropical rainforests near Cairns lost to the nation through logging. But the flow of benefits has not been all one-way. It is in Australia that the convention has been put to its severest tests. The decisions that have upheld its validity are considered to have strengthened the power of the convention as a whole. As well, some of Australia's nominations have shown the way to others. Kakadu and Uluru combine cultural and natural attributes in areas where Aboriginal traditional society lives on, and the concept of a world heritage area comprising many scattered parks, as in the New South Wales rainforest area, is new.

There is something irresistible about the biggest, the oldest and the greatest. But what about the other conservation areas, those that have not been given the accolade of 'world heritage'? Will the granting of such status to a select few areas mean that others will be neglected?

The answer to this depends upon the attitude of the entire community. The loftiest mountain and deepest canyon win widespread admiration, but this does not mean that lesser features have no interest. The one enhances the enjoyment and interest derived from the other. World heritage areas can help us to develop appreciation and respect for all heritage places. By definition, they are the best of their kind — but what one learns in the richest rainforest is applicable to all rainforests.

Tourism in Australia will obviously benefit from the World Heritage Convention. The increased flow of tourists can provide funds for protection and jobs for local people, sometimes to replace those lost with the closing of other industries. But there are drawbacks if the result is crowding and damage to the basic asset. Controls are obviously necessary, but if these are too severe the visitors' enjoyment will be reduced. Each world heritage area must be as large as possible so that management and the careful planning of visitors' accommodation and access systems have the best chance of success.

The test of effectiveness is twofold. Is integrity being maintained, and is the site contributing to human enjoyment and understanding? The world heritage area should be the best place to gain for ourselves insights into the history of the world — the world of humans and of nature. Each Australian world heritage site has a different part of the story to tell. In them we should be able to forget our immediate concerns and develop a longer term perspective on our life and that of others.

GEOFF MOSLEY

Magpie geese, Kakadu National Park.

Kakadu and Arnhem Land

Kakadu and Arnhem Land

The beautiful lagoons in Kakadu's wetlands are a haven for waterfowl.

*Our story is in the land
It is written in these sacred places
My children will look after these places
That's the law.*

BIG BILL NEIDJIE, Bunti Clan, Gagadju Language Group, 1982

Previous pages
The broken surface of the sandstone plateau guards many wildlife secrets.

National park/world heritage area
National park/proposed extension to world heritage area
Conservation zone/proposed extension to world heritage area

Proposed world heritage area

The eucalypt forest is sparse, the afternoon temperature soaring and the climb up the rugged slope of the escarpment increasingly difficult. The edge of the plateau is a broken maze of stone, its irregular channels choked with vegetation. But the view from the top is superb. On the right the red cliffs of the Nourlangie Rock–Mt Brockman massif enclose a huge natural amphitheatre, while away on the left the plains stretch to infinity, small flashes of light indicating distant lagoons.

This is a microcosm of the Gagadju country: part of the escarpment, fifty to 300 metres high, which runs over 500 kilometres from north to south, dividing the sandstone plateau of Arnhem Land from the rolling lowlands to the west; and in the Nourlangie Rock–Mt Brockman massif, one of the outliers of the plateau isolated by the escarpment's eastward retreat. Because it offered water and shelter and a range of environments, the escarpment, where the sandstone plateau meets the lower lying land with rivers and freshwater lagoons not far away, was an attractive habitat both for the wildlife and the Aboriginal people. Out of sight behind Mt Brockman are the estuaries and plains that fringe Van Diemen Gulf. The Alligator Rivers, which annually flood these plains, have their sources in the high country of the southeast, providing the link that unifies the region.

These are the landscapes of the 1 755 200 hectare Kakadu National Park, one of the largest parks in the world, but only a fraction of the area which the Australian Conservation Foundation believes should be inscribed on the world heritage list. The wider area includes the 220 700 hectare Cobourg Peninsula National Park to the northwest of Kakadu and the 8 million hectare Arnhem Land Aboriginal Reserve to the east. Both Kakadu and Cobourg are internationally significant pioneering attempts to combine the interests of the traditional Aboriginal owners with those of nature conservation.

A view over the lowlands from the eroded edge of the Arnhem Land
plateau. Erosion and weathering have created dramatic formations.

The main reasons why Kakadu was one of the first Australian sites to be listed are its rich wildlife, its role in protecting many endangered species, the existence of one of the world's greatest concentrations of pre-historic art, and its superlative natural scenery. The rock art, which records changing environmental conditions and lifestyles and includes paintings of great cultural and religious significance to the Aborigines, occurs at well over a thousand sites in caves and rock shelters at the foot of the escarpment and its outliers.

The oldest rocks of the Alligator River area are composed of Lower Proterozoic sedimentaries deposited about 2000 million years ago, subsequently metamorphosed by heat and pressure into schists, gneisses and granites, and then intruded with dolerite and phonolite. These rocks form the basement of the region but the event of greatest significance for today's landforms was the deposition in horizontal layers of the sandstone of the Kombolgie formation some 1800 to 1400 million years ago. This rock now constitutes the massive Arnhem Land plateau and its outliers, features of the Kakadu landscape.

The escarpment is not a continuous smooth line of cliffs. The rivers have cut it back to create narrow gorges, sometimes with magnificent waterfalls at their heads. Most impressive of all is the gorge of the East Alligator River, much of whose course is through the plateau. The lowland scenery is diversified by huge plateau remnants such as Mt Brockman–Nourlangie, the Djawambah massif and small outliers such as Obiri Rock and Cannon Hill. In the southern part of Kakadu, added to the park in 1987, a much folded and faulted area is dominated by a jumble of hills and by the valleys of the South Alligator and Mary rivers which follow major fault lines.

The plateau has a general elevation of 250–350 metres but in places it rises to just over 500 metres. Its surface is dissected along rectangular joint lines which appear from the air as a trellis-like pattern. It was

through this 'stone country' that the explorer Ludwig Leichhardt struggled in November 1845 and it is easy to imagine the party's elation when somewhere near Jim Jim Falls they came 'to the brink of a great precipice' and saw 'the extensive view of a magnificent valley opened before us'.

About a third of the plateau is bare rock and another third shallow sand supporting heath and spinifex. The remaining third is deeper sand in hollows and basins with oasis-like patches of evergreen myrtle (*Allosyncarpia ternata*). This tree, although thirty-five metres high and quite common, was not scientifically described until 1976, an indication perhaps of other botanical secrets hidden away in the plateau recesses.

The lowland region is undulating with a few rocky ridges. Drainage, often through extensive systems of billabongs and lagoons, is toward the Alligator Rivers and their major tributaries such as Magela and Nourlangie creeks. The vegetation includes belts of tall eucalypts dominated by stringybarks (*E. tetrodonta*) and woollybutts (*E. miniata*), savannah and grasslands. Paperbark forest dominated by melaleucas (*M. argentea* and *M. leucadendron*) fringes the rivers and swamps. At the junction of the lowlands and floodplains there are pockets of monsoon rainforest of considerable scientific interest.

The floodplains are inundated annually for two to six months by fresh water, the flooded Alligator Rivers merging with the tidal flats of the estuaries. Sedgeland and swamp are the dominant vegetation types here. The coastline, established at its present level some 6000 years ago, has three vegetation belts: a samphire zone; semi-deciduous forest on the dune ridge; and finally a tract of mangroves. Twenty-two species of mangroves occur in this area.

The weather becomes increasingly oppressive during October and November, to be broken by the northwest monsoon, which heralds the arrival of the wet season. The monsoon brings strong winds and high tides as well as heavy rain. The plains begin

*W*aterfalls occur when wet season rains tumble over the edge of the Arnhem Land escarpment.

28

*O*n the edge of a lagoon, eucalypts mingle with thicker forest.

to flood and the escarpment waterfalls change from trickles to thundering torrents. Elsewhere the dry, brown land bursts into life: within a month grass can be up to three metres high. Humidity reaches 80 per cent in January. No rain falls at Kakadu between May and September.

For richness of species and size of populations, the fauna of the Alligator Rivers region is matched in Australia only by the wet tropics of Queensland. Plantlife too is diverse and, although imperfectly studied, already numbers over 1000 species. But it is undoubtedly the fauna that most captures the imagination. Kakadu National Park has fifty-eight species of mammals, 275 species of birds, 100 species of amphibians and reptiles, and fifty species of fish.

Among the seventeen macropods the agile wallaby (*Macropus agilis*) is probably the most common. More restricted is the antilopine wallaroo (*Macropus antilopinus*). The black wallaroo (*Macropus bernardus*)

and the nabarlek or little rock wallaby (*Peradorcas concinna*) live in the rocky slopes of the escarpment along with the more common short-eared rock wallaby (*Petrogale brachyotis* sp.). Other marsupials of restricted distribution include Harney's marsupial mouse (*Antechinus bilarni*) and Woodward's rock rat (*Zyzomys woodwardi*).

The plateau is a particularly important habitat for birds, many of which are not found elsewhere. The rainforest and adjacent shrubbery are home to the banded fruit-dove (*Ptilinopus cinctus*), the white-lined honeyeater (*Meliphaga albilineata*) and an endemic subspecies of the helmeted friar bird (*Philemon buceroides ammitophila*). Other plateau habitats support the white-throated grasswren (*Amytornis woodwardi*) and the rock pigeon (*Petrophassa albipennis*). Lowland woodland supports such species as the hooded parrot (*Psephotus dissimilis*), the partridge pigeon (*Geophaps smithii*) and the Gouldian finch (*Erythrura gouldiae*).

Right

*P*aperbarks fringe a flooded swamp. These habitats are a vital refuge for waterfowl.

A jabiru feeds with egrets and other waterfowl on the pickings of a dry season wetland.

Geographically not so restricted but far more spectacular is the birdlife of the wetlands. In the Wet 2700 square kilometres may be inundated, and in the Dry the permanent waters are a refuge for waterfowl from all over northern Australia and nearby countries. The sight of thousands of magpie geese (*Anseranas semipalmata*) and other birds congregating on the wetlands at the end of the dry season is one of the most magnificent spectacles in the world. Wandering whistling ducks (*Dendrocygna arcuata*), green pygmy geese (*Nettapus pulchellus*), brolgas (*Grus rubicundus*), jabirus (*Xenorhynchus asiaticus*) and many others are part of this great

wildlife panorama. Because of their importance as waterfowl habitat Kakadu and Cobourg Peninsula are listed as wetlands of international importance under the Wetlands (Ramsar) Convention.

Even better known than the waterfowl are the region's crocodiles — the saltwater or estuarine crocodile (*Crocodylus porosus*) and the freshwater crocodile (*C. johnstoni*). A decade ago the numbers of saltwater crocodiles were declining due to uncontrolled hunting; today there are at least large numbers of young crocodiles, although commercial netting of barramundi is a threat to their survival to maturity. Also of interest among the reptiles is the Oenpelli

A juvenile pitted-shelled turtle.

python (*Morelia oenpelliensis*) and a large cave gecko (*Pseudothecadactylus lindneri*), restricted to the sandstone country.

The pitted-shelled turtle (*Carettochelys insculpta*), discovered at Kakadu only in 1973 and one of five species of freshwater turtles in the region, is one of several biological links with Papua New Guinea. Another is the primitive archer fish (*Protoxotes lorentzi*) which occurs only in the upper South Alligator River and Irian Jaya. Well known as a fine food fish is the silver barramundi (*Lates calcarifer*) which is the basis of a major fishing industry in the river estuaries as well as an important food source for Aborigines.

Aboriginal people once responded to their environment in a way that Europeans rarely understand. In many places the bond has been weakened or broken as Aborigines have been cut off from their traditional lands, but in Kakadu and Arnhem Land the link with the land they have lived in for 20 000 generations is still strong. This integral relationship naturally includes concern about any alterations of the important topographic features; such places are supposed to be inviolable.

At birth, tribal Aborigines acquire a personal 'dreaming' in which they are the reincarnation of an ancestral being. This creates rights and obligations in relation to the tracks followed by their ancestral beings and the topographic features they formed. Mt Brockman, for instance, is the sleeping place of the Rainbow Serpent.

The Top End of the Northern Territory is probably the point at which Aborigines entered Australia. The Dreamtime legends of the people of the region are all based on ancestral beings coming across the sea from the north. This was probably at its lowest level about 53 000 years ago. The oldest relic in the Kakadu area is a piece of ochre which dates back 23 000 years. An excavation at Malangangerr revealed the world's oldest edge-ground axe industry dating from 23 000 years ago. The most ancient wall paintings are estimated to be over 18 000 years old. Some are of great ceremonial significance to Aborigines because of their connection with the dreamings. Others show daily activities such as hunting and food sources.

George Chaloupka has classified the rock art of Kakadu into four main periods: pre-estuarine, estuarine, freshwater and contact. Pre-estuarine art is from the most recent ice age before the sea level rose to create the estuaries. The style is naturalistic and the subjects include animals that no longer exist in the area, such as the thylacine and

The escarpment and rocky outcrops provided galleries for thousands of
years of Aboriginal art, the beauty and diversity of which is now being recognised.

*D*ancing brolgas, Koolpin Creek. Other animals depicted have long since vanished from the area.

and the greater use of food items from this source such as waterbirds, magpie geese and waterlilies.

The contact period had begun by the sixteenth century, with visits by Macassan fishermen, and continued with the coming of Europeans, with their guns and horses. The Macassans visited the coast annually to catch and dry bêche-de-mer, arriving on the northwest monsoon winds and leaving when the wind changed to the southeast. They appear to have employed some Aborigines in their industry and introduced them to steel, smoking and dugout canoes. European discovery of the region began in 1625 when Jan Carstenz in the *Arnhem* sighted the land which came to bear his ship's name, but there was no permanent settlement until 1824 when Fort Dundas was established on Melville Island. From 1829, when Fort Dundas was abandoned, until 1849 Port Essington on Cobourg Peninsula was the main settlement.

*A*boriginal rock art at Kakadu records changing environments and lifestyles.

the Tasmanian devil. The stick-like depictions of humans characteristic of this style are known as 'Mimi art' since these paintings are said to have been the work of spirit people known as Mimi. The style is characterised by the frequent use of red ochre and the depiction of small groups of people, often hunting or fighting.

The rising of the sea level is indicated by the increased depiction of yams, which need high rainfall, and the Rainbow Serpent, which is associated with floods. Estuarine art reflects the completion of these changes as the sea invaded the lower valleys and the Aborigines became more dependent upon fish. During this period the distinctive and sophisticated X-ray art began to dominate.

The art of the freshwater period, still mainly in the X-ray form, records the conversion of the billabongs and lagoons on the subcoastal plain from salt to fresh water

Overleaf
*I*n their rock shelters, Aborigines were close to food sources. The holes are grinding hollows.

*W*eathering of the Kombolgie sandstone has created fantastic rock shapes, often of great religious significance to the Aboriginal people.

The settlers left but their impact continued. They had introduced water buffalo from Timor and the smaller Balinese cattle or bantengs. Although both ran wild, few of the bantengs survived. The buffalo, however, found an ideal environment in the coastal plains and spread so rapidly that by the 1880s a buffalo hide industry had begun. This became based in the Oenpelli region and employed many Aborigines, beginning the erosion of the traditional culture which has continued to this day.

An attempt in 1903 to set up a pastoral property on the Goyder River failed and the area became vacant crown land. As it was considered useless for grazing, parts of Arnhem Land were set aside as an Aboriginal reserve in 1920 and extended in 1931. Woolwonga followed in 1936. Church missions at Oenpelli, Yirrkala, Milingimbi and Roper River virtually controlled the Aborigines of Arnhem Land. With the

advent of mining in the 1950s and 1960s the reserves offered no protection, even when in 1968 the people of Gove strongly challenged the legality of the exploitation of their tribal lands.

In the 1950s twelve small uranium mines operated for a few years around El Sherana in the upper reaches of the South Alligator River. They had been abandoned by 1965 when the Northern Territory Reserve Board proposed the dedication of 638 550 hectares in the Alligator Rivers area as a national park. The proposal incorporated the 78 413 hectare Woolwonga Aboriginal Reserve which had received wildlife sanctuary status one year earlier.

In May 1969 progress seemed reasonable when the minister for the interior approved the park in principle. But a few months earlier a prospecting licence had been granted in the Nourlangie Creek area and pastoral leases at Mudginberri and

Right

*T*win Falls. In the Wet the rivers plunge over the escarpment, carving a path to the plains below.

*I*n the wet season, the rivers spread out over the coastal plains, merging with tidal waters. The future of the saltwater crocodile (*Crocodylus porosus*) is still threatened by habitat change.

Munmarlary covering 211 600 hectares of the coastal plains had been awarded to commercial buffalo meat interests.

In 1970 the Nabarlek, Ranger and Koongarra uranium deposits were discovered; Jabiluka followed in 1973. In 1975 the Commonwealth government gazetted but did not proclaim a Kakadu National Park and entered into an agreement for mining at Ranger. In the same year it set up the Ranger Uranium Environment Inquiry to consider both the future of the Alligator Rivers region and the wider question of uranium export. In its final report the commission recommended that at least one whole catchment should be included in the national park and that the most appropriate was that of the South Alligator River.

In 1977 mining at Ranger was officially sanctioned; it began in 1981. Mining also commenced at the smaller Nabarlek deposit near Oenpelli in the Arnhem Land reserve, although mining at the other two sites was temporarily embargoed. The Aborigines were given title to their traditional lands and Stage 1 of the national park was proclaimed in 1979, much of it comprising Aboriginal land leased for ninety-nine years to the director of the Australian National Parks and Wildlife Service. Part of the park was set aside for the tem-

Previous pages
*T*he East Alligator River forms the boundary between Kakadu and Arnhem Land to the east.

porary mining town of Jabiru. Stage 2 of the park was proclaimed in 1984. The Aborigines were not in favour of uranium mining but felt helpless to resist the offer of land rights and a share in mining royalties.

The question of mineral development at other sites remained unresolved until 1987 when the government legislated to ban mineral exploration and exploitation in all parts of stages 1 and 2. The price was a deferral of part of the third stage of the national park in the South Alligator River headwaters. This area had become the Gimbat and Goodparla pastoral leases in the early 1960s. Sixty-five per cent of the proposed extension was added to the national park in mid-1987 but 230 000 hectares along the South Alligator River were retained to allow exploration for gold, platinum and uranium to continue for five years in what was euphemistically called a 'conservation zone'. The granting of approval to mine would threaten the extensive wetlands downstream and would clearly be at odds with the concept of a whole catchment reserve for the park.

In northwest Arnhem Land two large wildlife sanctuaries, Murganella and Cobourg Peninsula, were proclaimed under Northern Territory legislation in the early 1960s. The Murganella sanctuary no longer exists but Cobourg (220 700 hectares) became a Territory national park in 1981. It has valuable wetlands, mangroves and monsoon rainforest and attempts to combine Aboriginal interests with nature conservation. There is also an extensive marine park of 229 000 hectares.

The setback in the South Alligator River is only one of the problems that have their source in the fundamental incompatibility of mining and conservation. The mine at Ranger has had difficulty in containing contaminated water within the 'restricted release zone' since the original projection underestimated the amount the mine would have to deal with. Jabiru township, which was supposed to be temporary, shows

*T*he sandstone plateau in the Arnhem Land Aboriginal Reserve.

A sparse eucalypt forest with dry grassy ground cover is typical of inland Kakadu.

every sign of becoming a permanent tourist centre and the Northern Territory government has proposed the building of an international airport close by.

Although only 2 per cent of the plants at Kakadu are exotic, they present major difficulties of control. An example is the thorny bush mimosa (*Mimosa pigra*), an introduced plant from South America. Mimosa grows in dense thickets and has the potential to occupy all the seasonally flooded habitats of Kakadu, upsetting drainage systems and wildlife. Biological controls are being tried but it is a race against time as each plant produces 10 000 seeds which are transported by water.

Of all the animal pests, the buffalo has caused the most disturbance. The extensive wallows and deep tracks known as buffalo roads were having a major hydrological impact and vegetation fringing streams was being rapidly destroyed as the buffaloes spread out. A campaign to eradicate the buffalo, partly related to brucellosis control, seems to be succeeding but feral pigs may be more difficult to control.

The number of tourists is growing rapidly and is now over 200 000 annually but the park management should be capable of limiting any adverse effects. Most of the traditional owners have returned to the park and a number of outstations have been established. Aborigines play crucial roles as rangers, environmental interpreters and guardians of the rock art. The establishment of the park is helping to counteract the negative social effects of mining. The experiment in joint control and management is still very young. Its degree of success will be important for considering the eventual extension of the world heritage site to include Cobourg Peninsula and the Arnhem Land Aboriginal Reserve.

GEOFF MOSLEY

The Great Barrier Reef

The Great Barrier Reef

*T*he clown fish is immune to the poisonous tentacles of the anemone.

*T*he Great Barrier Reef is perhaps the most important, certainly one
of the most beautiful and significant, gifts Australia has given the
world by nominating it as a World Heritage possession.

JUDITH WRIGHT, *Reader's Digest Book of the Great Barrier Reef*, 1984

Previous pages
*L*ady Musgrave Island and surrounding reef in the southern Bunker Group.

Some five kilometres off the north Queensland coast near Cape Tribulation lies a tiny sand cay. It must be one of the loveliest places on earth. No more than a hundred metres long, it looks like the desert island of a million cartoons. Someone has even tried to plant a single coconut on the highest point to complete the picture; the wind-torn palm about a metre high just survives. From the cay, the white rim of the mainland beaches is barely visible; above them, the coastal range rises steeply to defined peaks. The rainforest that covers the slopes looks grey-blue from this distance.

In sunlight, the sand of the cay is dazzling white; around it the sea moves from aquamarine to pure turquoise to the dark royal blue of deeper waters. But the range of lovely blues above water is no match for the brilliance beneath — the tiny electric blue damsel fish, the iridescent stripes and spots on the many species of butterfly and angel fish and the blue of the plentiful Linckia sea star. Close packed like an Escher design, a school of perhaps three hundred silvery blue and yellow hussars move as one creature, slowly rising and falling as they negotiate the maze of coral forms that make up the hundred-metre-wide fringe of reef on the windward side of the cay. This living garden of hard and soft corals is home to thousands of living things — fish, clams, starfish, shells, anemones, sponges, crabs, turtles — many of which appear to be dressed for an underwater mardi gras, so absurd and brilliant are their colours and patterns. People who spend even a few hours exploring this world become reef conservationists for life.

The Great Barrier Reef, the most famous of Australia's world heritage areas, was declared in 1981. In it Australians have a precious heritage — the greatest collection of coral reefs in the world. Coral reefs are to the marine world what rainforests are to the terrestrial. Like the forests they are extremely rich in species and certainly constitute the most diverse marine ecosystem on earth. As custodian of the Great Barrier Reef, Australia has direct responsibility to protect one of the most complex natural systems in the world.

The reef stretches for some 2000 kilometres along the east coast of Queensland; it begins near the mouth of the Fly River in the Gulf of Papua and ends at Lady Elliot Island, just north of Fraser Island at a latitude of 24°s. The marine park, which covers 348 700 square kilometres and encompasses most of the reef, extends from the latitude of Cape York in the north to Lady Elliot Island. The outer reef varies in its distance from the coast from thirty-two kilometres off Cape Melville to 260 kilometres near Mackay.

The name 'Great Barrier Reef', given by Matthew Flinders in 1802 and long accepted, is inaccurate in two ways. The singular term does little to convey the reef's complexity. Although it is often referred to as a single structure, in fact the world's largest, it is made up of over two thousand reefs, which vary enormously from tiny coral cays to large complexes covering more than 100 square kilometres. The term 'Barrier' is also misleading as, according to nomenclature devised by Charles Darwin, it refers only to offshore wall reefs which shelter a shallow lagoon between a reef and a mainland. The Great Barrier Reef incorporates many other reef types, including the fringing reefs that have developed off the mainland and around many of the islands and coral cays.

It is also important to note that the term Great Barrier Reef encompasses a huge marine province which takes in other ecosystems apart from coral reefs. These include the 540 high continental islands, the sand cays, the mangrove forests, seagrass beds and the soft sea bottoms between reefs.

The unquestioned place of the reef on the world heritage list arises principally from its status as the richest marine habitat on earth, supporting an extraordinary diversity of lifeforms which both create and depend on the reef. Many of these species exist nowhere else. Almost every marine organism is richly represented: there are over 1500 fish species alone, 400 species of coral and 4000 species of molluscs. A similar diversity is found among other major marine groups like crustaceans, echinoderms, anemones and marine worms. Some rare and endangered species, like the dugong (*Dugong dugon*), the green turtle (*Chelonia mydas*) and the loggerhead turtle (*Caretta caretta*), have vital strongholds within the reef environment.

*N*orth of the Daintree River rainforest meets reef.

*T*he mangrove is a vital component of the reef.

*T*he endangered green turtle (*Chelonia mydas*).

The marine park can be divided into three major sections. The northern sector, from Cape York south to Mossman, is quite narrow and shallow (with depths generally less than thirty metres), and hemmed by an outer wall reef on the edge of the continental shelf. On this outer wall are distinctive ribbon reefs running parallel to the edge of the shelf. Inside the outer reef lie a wide variety of patch reefs, some large platform reefs and low wooded isles where mangroves have colonised coral cays, creating specialised environments. Perhaps the best known sites in this remote region are Lizard Island and the Low Isles, where some of the earliest research into the reef's ecology was conducted.

_L_izard, Palfrey and South islands. The islands have fringing coral reefs and a giant clam garden.

_S_pectacularly coloured angel fish are among the loveliest of the reef's fish species.

The Reef Province includes complex reefs, continental islands, sand and coral cays, mangrove forests and sandy seabeds. *Above:* Agincourt Reef; *below:* Noble Island, near Lizard Island.

The central sector, which covers the reef south to approximately Mackay, is somewhat deeper, with depths up to sixty metres, and much wider. Its chief characteristic is a series of widely separated platform reefs which are generally a considerable distance from the coast. However, numerous fringing reefs surround the islands in this region, which contains many of the major tourist destinations of the reef — Green Island, Dunk Island, the spectacular mountainous continental island of Hinchinbrook, and the beautiful Whitsunday Passage with its well-forested islands and holiday resorts.

*T*he small vegetated coral cay of Green Island is a popular tourist destination.

*W*hitsunday Passage, where fringing reefs surround rugged forested islands.

A diver examines a sponge
on the reef wall.

*S*mall fish species hover near
the sheltering corals.

A platform reef in the vicinity of Cairns. The exquisite blues of coral reef
waters indicate a lack of plankton.

In the southern sector the continental shelf becomes considerably deeper — up to 145 metres in parts. The reef also continues to widen to its extremity of some 300 kilometres. This area has a great variety of reef types, including the unique remote Pompey complex, where violent currents carve through the reefs, creating sheer-sided walled channels up to a kilometre wide. Further south are the Swain reefs, which are markedly different, being composed of closely packed patch reefs studded with sand cays. At the southern end of the reef, from Gladstone to the official 'last island', Lady Elliot, the continental shelf progressively narrows. The most southerly major island groups, the Bunker and Capricorn islands, include a number of vegetated coral cays, among them the popular tourist resort of Heron Island.

The tail fluke of a diving humpback whale. Heron Island forms the backdrop.

Two characteristic colonisers of corals cays: the pandanus with *Argusia argentia* beyond.

Above: Hoskyns Reef, showing the grooved coral baffle which lessens the reef's exposure.
Below: Turtle tracks on Wreck Island, Capricorn Bunker Group.

Although this huge and complex phenomenon was created by living organisms, the present reef is actually a comparatively recent development in geological time. Estimates vary but it seems probable that the reef began to grow on the Queensland continental shelf some 18 million years ago with many parts as young as 1 million years. It began as the Australian continent drifted north into warm clear tropical waters which provided the right environment for corals — perhaps from the Coral Sea — to colonise and begin spreading. From about 2 million years ago to 8000 years ago reef growth was affected by numerous major changes in sea level as a result of increases or decreases in glaciation. During high sea levels the reef experienced growth but died as levels dropped. The modern reef has grown only in the last 6000 to 8000 years, since the sea level stabilised. It rests on the foundations of reefs that grew during former periods of high sea level.

The main reef builders are the coral polyps. Soft as living creatures, they secrete small cups of limestone. Corals as we recognise them are colonies made up of thousands of individual polyps. The living corals are a thin veneer on a substratum of limestone formed by the dead coral skeletons cemented together by the limestone secretions of coralline algae.

The extended polyps of the hard coral, *Tubastrea aurea*.

The brilliant colours of gorgonian fan corals.

Although coral is central to the construction of reefs the vast range of reef shapes and types provide evidence that other factors, such as tides and currents, wave action, winds and storms, have all played a significant part in the creation of the Great Barrier Reef.

The 400 living coral species that make up the surface layer of the reef create fantastic agglomerations: there are boulders, platforms, trees, mushrooms, pincushions, plates, giant brains, forests of antlers, even corals that look like piles of freshly cooked pappadums. The analogy with a garden, although hackneyed, is inevitable. Not only do many coral forms look like plants, but at night when the carnivorous polyps of the hard corals come out to feed on tiny reef organisms, their exquisite colours and the delicate form of their extended tentacles closely resemble flowers.

As well as the hard corals, the reef contains many species of soft corals which lack the solid limestone skeleton of the hard corals. These vary from the ethereal tree shapes of the *Dendronephthya* genus to comparatively dull and rubbery-looking species. Among the most distinctive of the soft corals are the sometimes bizarre, often lovely, gorgonian sea fans and whips.

Given the fascination of the reef's fauna, it would be easy to underestimate its less spectacular flora. However, the plants of the sea are an essential component of the functioning whole. Particularly important are the minute single-celled zooxanthellae, which live in vast numbers in the actual tissue of the polyps. The capacity of the corals to produce calcium carbonate, and hence reefs, is attributed to the complex symbiosis between the corals and these algae.

Other species of algae are food sources for a range of animals, including turtles, dugong, many sea urchins, crustaceans, molluscs and many fishes. Seagrasses are also marine plants of immense importance, being the major food source for the potentially endangered dugong as well as providing food for other marine animals including turtles. Plants contribute indirectly to the food chain of many other organisms as they break down and decay.

Plants also play a vital part in the development of the reef's landmasses. In the life of the Great Barrier Reef, literally millions of sand cays must have formed, only to disappear as wind, currents, storms or tides swept the accumulated sands elsewhere. Nevertheless, some cays do stabilise; some even become islands. A succession of plant communities is the key factor in this process. The sand cay is gradually covered by

Pisonia grandis forest on Rocky Island.

hardy salt- and wind-tolerant species which break down and together with birds' guano provide the nutrients that allow the next stage of plants to take root. With time, the island develops a range of plant communities — succulent herbs, vine thickets, even forests. The primary forest tree of the Great Barrier Reef sand islands is *Pisonia grandis*, a large-leafed, vigorous tree which creates enchanting closed-canopy forests — cool, sun-dappled refuges from the elements.

'As the world's most species-rich marine ecosystem, the Great Barrier Reef is home to an overwhelming variety of fauna. To the non-scientist at least, the most dramatic impact is created by the fishes, with their extraordinary shapes, brilliant patterns and extravagant colours. The reef fishes range

The beautiful harlequin tusk fish (Choerodon fasciatus).

from gobies, a few millimetres long, to the large predators — sharks, marlin and massive cod species.

Many of the most beautiful of the reef fish are small or medium-sized. The lovely iridescent blue damsel fish (Pomacentridae) is one of the prettiest of the smaller fish, hovering in schools just above the corals. The many species of butterfly fish (Chaetodontidae) and angel fish (Pomacanthidae) provide some of the reef's most dazzling designs — horizontal, vertical, diagonal and random stripes in brilliant blues, yellows, greens and whites. With their almost square bodies, pointed snouts and short fanned tails, they are for many people the classic reef fish.

Among the most common fish in the shallower reef regions are the gaudy parrot fish (*Scarus* spp.), which make up in extravagance of colour what they lack in elegant design. They share with many other

A colony of brown boobies on Fairfax Island.

*P*arrot fish can crush coral with their 'beaks'.

reef species the strange habit of changing sexes. Nor could anyone miss the aptly named clown anemone fish (*Amphiprion percula*), with its flounced costume of brilliant orange edged in black with broad bands of white. Among the most frequently encountered reef fish, it lives within the protective arms of reef anemones, especially *Radianthus rilleri* whose tentacles are poisonous to other species.

Other vertebrate animals of the reef and its associated ecosystems are the reptiles — the turtles, crocodiles and sea snakes; the mammals — the whales, dolphins and dugong; and the many species of birds that inhabit the cays and vegetated islands. The reef provides vital breeding grounds for many of these animals. The breeding sites of the green and loggerhead turtles, for example, are considered to be of world importance in conserving these species, and the world's largest remaining herds of the vulnerable dugong graze on the seagrasses and breed in these waters.

Huge breeding colonies of seabirds have established themselves on various cays and islands, thriving on the abundant food in the clear reef waters. The cays of the southern Capricorn Group are especially important nesting sites. The numbers are impressive: on North West Island in the north of the Capricorn Group there are colonies of 750 000 wedge-tailed shearwaters (*Puffinus pacificus*) and 160 000 black noddies (*Anous minutus*) plus smaller colonies of other species.

The invertebrates of the reef are predictably abundant and quite fantastic in form and colour. All the major groups are generously represented: there are literally thousands of species of shells, anemones, sea urchins, starfish, sea worms, sea slugs, sponges, octopus, crabs, lobsters, sea snails, shrimps, sea cucumbers and numerous other less well known marine invertebrates, all contributing to the kaleidoscope of life on the reef.

The names 'slug' and 'worm' hardly conjure up images of breathtaking beauty, yet both these major groups of marine invertebrates are as lovely as anything in the whole natural world. Perhaps the most spectacular of the sea slugs is one of the many nudibranchs, the fabulous Spanish dancer (*Hexabranchus sanguineus*) which when disturbed swims by twisting and turning its body and swirling its scarlet-orange 'cape' fringed in white.

In contrast, the infamous crown-of-thorns starfish (*Acanthaster planci*) is not a

*A*n undisturbed Spanish dancer nudibranch.

A crown-of-thorns starfish is caught by a giant triton.

pleasant sight. This sea star, which reaches sixty centimetres or more in diameter, turns inside out to spread the membranes of its 'stomach' over a patch of coral which it then proceeds to digest and absorb, leaving only a dead white skeleton. Large numbers mean virtual destruction of the coral in the infested zone. In recent decades millions of crown-of-thorns starfish have descended on particular areas of reef and left them barren wastelands. Given that one female is capable of producing an estimated 20 million eggs a year, the scale of the threat is immense. Scientists remain deeply divided over the cause of the population explosion — particularly as to whether it is a natural phenomenon or one caused by humans — and hence about the remedial action, if any, that should be taken.

The controversy about the crown-of-thorns is part of the wider question of human impact on the Great Barrier Reef. Aboriginal people have lived on the shores of the reef and used its resources for at least the 8000 years that the current reef has existed. Coastal Aborigines accumulated profound knowledge of the reef and its marine life. The creatures of the sea were central to the culture of these people, who performed ceremonies to ensure that the abundance continued. It is unlikely that Aboriginal use of the reef had any negative impact, given the relatively small numbers of the population, the immense area over which they roamed and the simple technologies they employed.

*T*iny fairy basslets (*Anthias* sp.) hover about gorgonian fan coral.

Even the reef's vast area has not protected it from the impact of twentieth-century society. Because of the limitations of our knowledge it is not always possible to tie down cause and effect, as the continuing debate over the crown-of-thorns starfish exemplifies. However it seems unquestionable that direct exploitation, particularly commercial fishing and the harvesting of shells, and indirect impacts, such as runoff of pesticides and herbicides, and silt from onshore agriculture, are causing damage at least on a local level.

Legally the reef is fairly well protected. After years of vigorous campaigning by conservationists and scientists the Great

Barrier Reef Marine Park Act was passed in 1975 and by the end of 1983 most of the reef, excluding the Torres Strait island region, was declared as a marine park. The park is managed jointly by the Commonwealth Great Barrier Reef Marine Park Authority and the Queensland Fisheries and National Parks and Wildlife services, which undertake its day-to-day management. The reef is divided into zones in which complex management plans are developed after public consultation. Conservation is a major object of the plans but the park is not exclusively for conservation and all 'reasonable uses' are allowed for, including commercial fishing. The long

*T*he diver enters a world of infinite enchantment.

*T*he Cape Tribulation road slashes through rainforest.

diction. With the increasing popularity of the reef as a destination for international tourists, these threats will require close monitoring by all those concerned for the reef's future.

Onshore activities also remain potential threats. The effects of siltation and chemical residues from land-based agriculture and industry are poorly understood but may be serious. There is evidence from overseas that fringing reefs are extremely vulnerable to onshore disturbance. The

battle to prevent oil drilling appears to have been successful and the conservation future of the reef looks comparatively good.

However, concern still arises from the fact that Queensland retains control over all the continental islands and coast on which many of the larger tourist resorts are located. Unsympathetic development, removal of vegetation, disturbance of turtle and bird nesting sites, dredging of lagoons, filling in of mangroves, destruction of coral for boat access or even in one case an airport, damage to fringing reefs from excessive trampling or effluent pollution — these are just some of the problems over which the park authority has limited or no juris-

future of the species-rich fringing reefs that abut the spectacular rainforests between the Daintree River and Cooktown is particularly doubtful, threatened by the heavy siltation that has resulted from the construction of a coastal road through steep country on highly erodable soil.

Given what is at stake — the richest marine ecosystem on earth, with all the beauty, excitement, knowledge and even potential products for the direct benefit of humans — there is no room for complacency and a vigorous watching brief must be maintained to ensure the continued protection of this great wonder of the natural world.

PENELOPE FIGGIS

Willandra Lakes

Willandra Lakes

*A*n isolated grove of cypress pines (*Callitris glaucophylla*) at the edge of Lake Mungo.

*The Willandra Lakes belong not only to the heritage of all
Australians, but they merit world heritage status as a unique document
of ice-age environment and testimony to the antiquity of
Aboriginal Australians.*

PROFESSOR K. J. MULVANEY and DR J. M. BOWLER, *The Heritage of Australia*, 1981

Previous pages
*T*he Walls of China, Mungo National Park.

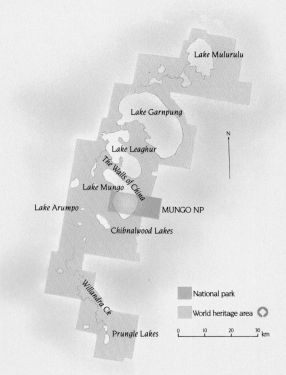

Around the lake perimeter among groves of trees the campfires glowed, lighting the branches above and the dark faces already gathered. In the last light the nearby lake reflected the soft pinks and ochres of the sky. Children still played noisily on the sandy beach, occasionally falling or being pushed into the shallow waters to emerge shining, laughing. A large flock of ducks took flight at the noisy splashing.

The afterglow faded, leaving the sky inky blue with early stars coming into focus. Pleasant smells of cooking meat and fish, and the companionship of the fireside, kept the chill wind at bay.

The plentiful food was divided — large fish, armfuls of mussels, yabbies, dark green emu eggs and, slowly roasting in the coal hearth, its great legs extending skyward, a large kangaroo. The kangaroo had been caught by hunters out on the sandplains beyond the forested shores of the huge lake. Now the stories of the day's hunt were told and the animals honoured in songs and tales of how they came to be.

This idyllic scene must be close to the reality of how Aboriginal people lived around the shores of Willandra Lakes in New South Wales some 35 000–40 000 years ago during the last ice age. The prolific remains of this ancient people and their lifestyle make Willandra Lakes unquestionably one of the most important archaeological sites in the world.

The Willandra Lakes world heritage region covers 3700 square kilometres of semiarid country in the southwest of New South Wales. The region contains a system of Pleistocene lakes, formed over the last 2 million years, with adjacent dunes or lunettes which were a major site of human occupation before the lakes dried out some 15 000 years ago. The area gained international recognition after the discovery in the late 1960s of human skeletal remains, tools, shell middens and animal bones in the sand dunes that fringed the ancient lake shorelines. Radiocarbon dating established that these materials were some of the earliest evidence of modern man (*Homo sapiens sapiens*) in the world.

The outstanding value of the site is the remarkable survival over the ages of landforms and layers of sediments, which provide a unique opportunity for researchers to interpret their materials preserved within the context of their original environment. The survival of these landforms in a largely unmodified state has international importance for the understanding of geomorphic and climatic processes in ancient times. The lake system was nominated for inclusion on the world heritage list in 1980 by the New South Wales government and became a registered site in 1981.

There are five large interconnected dry lake basins in the Willandra system and fourteen smaller basins, varying from six to 350 square kilometres in area. Today they are flat plains vegetated by salt-tolerant low bushes and grasses. From north to south the major lakes are Mulurulu, Garnpung, Leaghur, Mungo, the Arumpo complex, the Chibnalwood Lakes and the Prungle Lakes. Most are fringed on the eastern shore by a dune or 'lunette' formed when prevailing westerly winds swept up sand and, when the lakes were dry, clay particles on the downwind side of the lakes.

The most dramatic of these lunettes and the main focus of attention for the world heritage region is the lunette of Lake Mungo. The dunes rise up surprisingly steeply from the lake shoreline to reach a height of some thirty-six metres above the lake floor. The lunette extends for thirty-three kilometres around the eastern shore of the lake. Its major attraction comes from the processes of wind and water erosion which have shaped the sands and clays into a surreal landscape of weird shapes. From a distance, the entire landform creates the impression of a white wall; hence one explanation for the name 'the Walls of China'.

*T*he crescent-shaped dune or lunette that fringes the eastern shore of Lake Mungo. The dunes are a rich source of archaeological materials.

A stone scatter site at southern Lake Leaghur. To the scientist, such sites are evidence of human activity and part of the jigsaw of life in the ice age.

Below

*U*ndated human bones from Lake Garnpung. Some of the earliest evidence of modern humans is found at Willandra.

The archaeology and geomorphology of this extraordinary lake system are the major reasons for its international value. As an archaeological site the Willandra Lakes are without parallel in Australia.

In 1968 Jim Bowler of the Australian National University began research on the eroding lunettes. The dramatic discovery of human remains was made the following year — dramatic because they soon proved to be the earliest human remains in Australia and among the oldest remains of fully modern humans on earth. Bowler's team discovered two human burial sites — Mungo I and Mungo 3. They were found at the southern end of Lake Mungo among other evidence of occupation such as hearths, stone tools and food remnants.

Mungo I consisted of the remains of a young woman who had been cremated. The bones had then been smashed and buried. The significance of the finding was not only its great age but the elaborate nature of the burial which suggests a complex ritual life in remote times that may have been handed down largely unchanged to modern Aboriginal society. Dated at 26 000 years before the present, this was certainly the oldest recorded cremation site in the world. Immediately, this discovery gave the region international significance and, it is said, 'turned Australian prehistory upside down'.

Numerous other discoveries of tools, stone artefacts and midden contents confirmed the occupation of the region during the last ice age. In 1974 Bowler again made a major discovery — this time, the intact skeleton of a modern male. He had clearly been buried according to ritual practices as his bones and the surrounding earth were stained red with powdered ochre. Since these discoveries the fragmented remains of 133 other burial sites

The Lakes region is rich in animal bones (*top*) and shell middens (*above*), as well as human skeletal remains and tools.

Below

A researcher works on a hearth site, gathering evidence for the study of changes in the earth's magnetic field.

*W*ind and water erosion has created the fluted towers that
characterise the Walls of China.

have been recorded. One site, labelled WLH–50, is thought to be older than either Mungo 1 or Mungo 3. The more robust nature of the skull remains has led to speculation that the individual may have been a descendant of the more ancient *Homo erectus* people of Java and that two quite different peoples may have inhabited the Willandra area.

During the research of the past fifteen years, hundreds of sites of stone artefacts, fireplaces and faunal material have been recorded, about a third of which date to an ice age environment. These artefacts provide an outstanding opportunity for modern archaeologists to reconstruct the everyday life of ancient humans.

Evidence so far points to an extraordinary continuity of occupation over vast periods of time. The life of ancient Mungo man appears to have been similar to life along the great inland waterways as described by explorers in the early years of European settlement. This in turn attests both to the antiquity of Aboriginal culture and the adaptability of Aboriginal people to a semiarid environment.

During the last ice age, when the lakes were full, the people camped along the lake shore, where they ate a wide range of food. They collected freshwater mussels, and caught yabbies, the golden perch and Murray cod. They may, like their modern descendants, have snared these fish in nets of knotted rushes and collected them in pools as the lakes dried up. They also hunted a variety of marsupials, which probably included now extinct 'super-roos' (*Procoptodon*), standing three metres high, and large emus. These animals were cooked in hearths or coal ovens, often using clay or calcrete heat stones.

Right

*T*he sculptured beauty of eroded sand. The Walls of China lunette is gradually moving eastward under the prevailing westerly winds.

The Mungo people also exploited plant resources, particularly as the lakes began to dry and food was less abundant. Grindstones or mortars with which wild seeds were ground into flour were used extensively over the last 5000 years. One discovery in a Pleistocene site dates to 18 000 years ago, a date compatible with the earliest seed-grinding economies in the Middle East.

While the artefacts themselves are of enormous interest, the real significance of Willandra arises because these objects have been found within a landscape that is uniquely capable of giving them meaning because it has remained essentially unaltered. Peter Clark, an archaeologist who has spent six years researching the area, has said: 'The landscape context of the archaeology is perhaps the single most outstanding heritage attribute of the Willandra. Without it, archaeological sites and their interpretation mean very little.'

During the last ice age, which began approximately 60 000 years ago, the waters of the Lachlan, rising in the eastern highlands, overflowed into the Willandra basins which millions of years before had been covered by sea. Over time the shores became more vegetated and were able to support rich plant and animal life.

The lakes were fed by Willandra Billabong Creek, a tributary of the Lachlan, and at times of maximum level they overflowed through an outlet channel which joined the Murrumbidgee west of Balranald. The fact that these long-dry watercourses are still part of the landscape confirms the stability and longevity of the geomorphology. The entire landscape of dry watercourses, lakes and dunes provides many insights into how a non-glaciated zone responds before, during and after an ice age.

The landform feature that has excited the most interest is certainly the crescent-shaped dunes on the lakes' eastern shores.

*W*illandra Billabong indicates what the channels that once fed and connected the lake system looked like in the ice age millennia.

*I*ntricate water-carved patterns in Lake Mungo lunette.

The forces of temperature, wind and water have shaped the land into a
rich variety of patterns and textures.

*T*he sand blows of Willandra are composed of materials from all the age layers.

The ancient shorelines are stratified into three major layers (or units) of sediments which were deposited at different stages of the lakes' history. The earliest sediments, from before 50 000 years ago, are found in the orange-red Gol Gol unit (named after a nearby pastoral station). Above are the sediments of the Mungo unit — clays, clean quartz sand and soil that were deposited along the lakes' edges when the lakes were full of deep, relatively fresh, water, between 50 000 and 19 000 years ago. It is principally in these layers of fine white beach sand and soils that the oldest evidence of Aboriginal occupation has been found.

The upper or youngest layer is the Zanci unit which is composed largely of wind-blown clay particles heaped up on the lunettes during periods of fluctuating water levels before the lakes finally dried up. Despite some erosion of the top layers, what remains is a fossil landscape that pro-

vides a key to understanding the inter-relationships of landscape and climatic changes as well as how ancient humans interacted with their environment.

The vegetation of the area today is typical of much of the semiarid zone. Four broad vegetation types are found: mallee woodland, rosewood–belah woodland, chenopod shrublands of the lakebeds and lunette vegetation, as well as mixed mallee/rosewood–belah woodland.

Four main tree species characterise the mallee woodlands, which are largely found on the dunefields. Mallees are small, multistemmed eucalypts well adapted to arid conditions. The main species of mallee are congoo (*Eucalyptus dumosa*), pointed mallee (*E. foecunda*), lerp mallee (*E. incrassata*) and yorrell (*E. gracilis*). Herbs, grasses and the formidable spinifex (*Triodia irritans*) grow under the mallee overstorey. Blackbox (*E. largiflorens*) grows in lowlying

*T*his harsh landscape is the product of an ancient environment of lakes
that supported human life for thousands of years.

areas that collect run-off after heavy local rainfall. Rosewood (*Heterodendron oleifolium*)–belah (*Casuarina cristata*) woodland is found principally on the flat or undulating sand plains. This type of woodland has many species in the understorey, particularly chenopod shrubs.

The great flat plains, the beds of the ancient lakes, are now covered with salt-tolerant chenopod shrubs, including many species of saltbushes (*Atriplex*), bluebush (*Maireana*) and copperburrs (*Sclerolaena*). While chenopod shrublands are not unusual, their occurrence on lakebeds is of considerable scientific interest.

Lunette vegetation is considered a distinct category even though it is dominated by chenopod shrubs. The shrubs are less dense than on the lakebeds and the lunettes also support quite substantial stands of rosewood as well as the sandhill wattle (*Acacia ligulata*) and butterbush (*Pittosporum phylliraeoides*). In the southern section of the

world heritage area the two major woodland types become so intermixed that clear differentiation is difficult.

Perhaps the most important value of the vegetation arises from its role in stabilising the landscape and hence maintaining its sediment strata. Accelerated wind and water erosion resulting from vegetation disturbance could well destroy much of the area's unique value. This is especially true of the artefact-rich lunettes and lake margins.

A large number of animal fragments have been found throughout the world heritage area. The richest of the deposits is located between lakes Garnpung and Leaghur. Although research has been limited, to date fifty-five species have been identified, made up of thirty-five mammals, seven birds, five reptiles and amphibians, one crustacean, two fish, five molluscs and snails.

Forty of these animals — among them the 'Tasmanian' devil and the hairy-nosed wombat — are no longer found in the region. Eleven are totally extinct, including the thylacine or Tasmanian tiger and six species of Pleistocene fauna — four species of kangaroo, a large wombat-like animal or diprotodontid and a large stocky emu. The timing of their extinction remains uncertain and may have been earlier than 30 000 years ago. The diprotodontid was a huge animal as big as a hippopotamus. Its remains have been found elsewhere in eastern Australia but this is the most westerly occurrence to date. Fragments of the heavily set extinct kangaroo, *Procoptodon goliah*, have been found at a number of sites in the interlake zone. The solidly built emu-like bird (*Genyornis newtoni*), whose eggs were probably gathered and eaten by the ancient people of the lakes, disappeared some 20 000 years ago.

Apart from these ancient species of megafauna, many other species that are now extinct may have died out in recent times because of the destruction of their habitat with the coming of sheep grazing and the introduction and proliferation of feral animals such as goats and rabbits. This is especially true of the bettongs, native rats, mice and bandicoots.

Twenty-two species of mammals have been recorded at Willandra, of which bats compose the most important group. There are nine species of bats and populations of the echidna, the red and grey kangaroo, the dunnart and several other small marsupials. While none of these animals is restricted to the region, the greater long-eared bat (*Nyctophilus timoriensis*) and the little pied bat (*Chalinolobus picatus*) are uncommon.

The great survivors — the reptiles and amphibians — are thought to be much the same today as in the distant past. A 1984–85 study identified a total of forty species. Unfortunately the survival of these creatures may not continue to be secure

*T*he red kangaroo (*Macropus rufus*) is believed to have moved into the semiarid zone with the coming of settlers and more reliable water sources.

because of habitat change. Six species are now regarded as threatened fauna: the jewelled gecko (*Diplodactylus elderi*), Burton's snake-lizard (*Lialis burtonis*), various species of blue-tongued lizard (*Ctenotus atlas, C. brooksiiridis, Tiliqua occipitalis*) and Gould's goanna (*Varanus gouldii*).

Today the bird life of the Willandra region is similar to that in many other semi-arid areas of Australia. The bird list for the area now stands at 137 species. The most conspicuous are the flamboyant parrots and cockatoos and the noisy gatherings of brilliant little finches. Rare or endangered species which have been recorded in the region include the peregrine falcon (*Falco peregrinus*), pink cockatoo (*Cacatua leadbeateri*) and black-winged currawong (*Strepera versicolor melanoptera*). Two species, the malleefowl (*Leipoa ocellata*) and the Australian bustard (*Ardeotis australis*), are on the threatened list.

The fish, shellfish and crustaceans, which middens tell us formed such a major part of Aboriginal diet long ago, still exist, thousands of generations later, in inland waterways. The two fish species, the Murray cod (*Maccullochella peeli*) and the golden perch (*Macquaria ambigua*), are still regarded as excellent eating fish.

The human history of the region is not restricted to an ancient episode. In the top layers of sediment there is abundant evidence of occupation in the last 10 000 years. The presence of glass among Aboriginal artefacts is evidence that Aborigines lived in the area up to white contact *circa* 1840. Little is known about the Aboriginal history of the region thereafter, although the Burke and Wills expedition in 1861 recorded people living in the vicinity of the southern lakes.

European settlers began to move into this remote dry region around the 1850s when the navigation of the Murray and Darling rivers and regular boat services made the region somewhat less isolated. The land was harsh, subject to recurrent droughts and in the 1880s overrun with rabbits in plague proportions. After both

A male malleefowl (*Leipoa ocellata*) working to maintain its huge incubation mound. This species is now threatened.

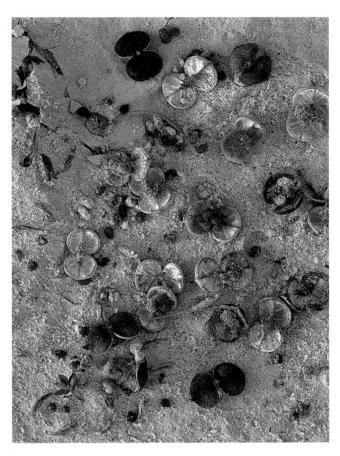

*F*allen seedpods at Lake Mungo. Only the hardiest plants survive in this environment.

world wars the region was opened up by the soldier settlement programs which provided incentives to returned soldiers to take up holdings. Only in very recent times have technological developments such as radio, television, telephone and improved roads and transport broken down some of the hardship and isolation of outback life.

Only a limited area, about 8 per cent of the world heritage site, is gazetted as a national park. The Mungo National Park covers about two-thirds of Lake Mungo and includes most of the more spectacular parts of the Walls of China. The rest of the area remains under some thirty-two pastoral leases within eighteen pastoral properties administered by the Western Lands Commission.

Potential conservation problems arise principally from the fact that much of the region is still pastoral land and hence subject to grazing, and also from the presence of considerable numbers of feral animals.

Growing tourist interest is creating new problems in the region.

The hard hooves of grazing sheep can trample and smash archaeological material. This is most likely to occur where stock concentration points such as watering areas are located close to actual or potential archaeological sites such as the lunettes or shorelines. Management measures including the relocation of watering points could alleviate the problem.

Erosion is an intrinsic part of the scenic and scientific value of Willandra. However, aggravated erosion is a conservation problem for the region. Erosion can break down the relationship between artefacts and their location and greatly reduce the knowledge that can be yielded from the finding.

Grazing sheep certainly alter vegetation and can disturb the stability of the environment. However, the populations of feral animals, especially the rabbit, are of particular concern. Rabbits tend to concentrate in the areas of greatest geomorphic and archaeological importance. Their grazing and burrowing severely affect vegetation, reduce the stability of the soil and disturb the stratigraphy of the sediments.

Loss of vegetation due to stock and feral animals can also affect native fauna. In these arid areas watering points, whether man-made or natural soaks, are vital to wildlife and yet are invariably the most heavily damaged areas. Therefore rabbit control and measures to avoid erosion and vegetation loss on lunettes and other sensitive areas will be priorities of a comprehensive management plan which should be brought into effect in 1988. It seems likely that areas of the region will remain under pastoral usage for some time; cooperative management between landholders, the Western Lands Commission and the parks service will therefore be essential to protect this fascinating landscape which can tell us so much about how humans coped with their environment over the ages.

PENELOPE FIGGIS

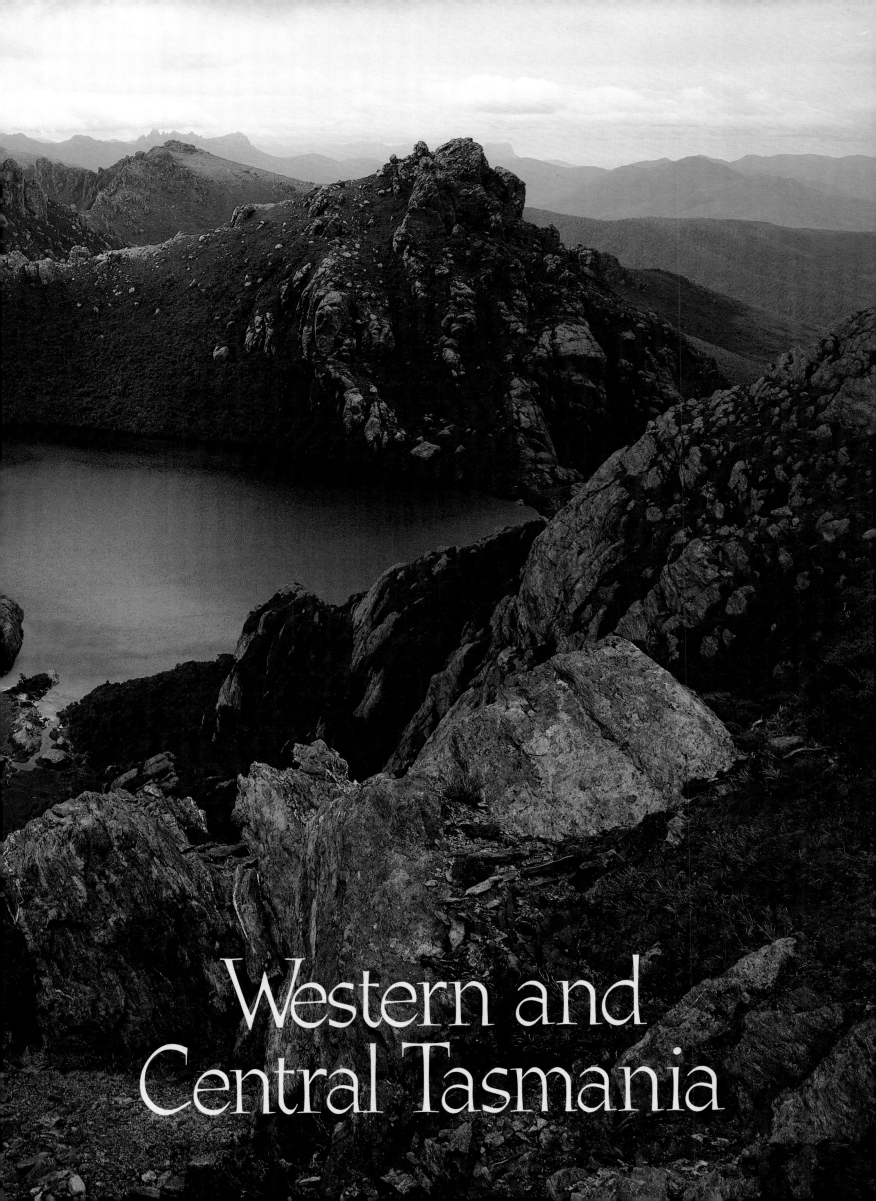

Western and
Central Tasmania

Western and Central Tasmania

*I*sle du Golfe seen from Prion Beach in the Southwest National Park.

*K*eep this treasure and hand it on to posterity so that those who come
after you will learn about beauty, about awe, about wonder, because
it is in the southwest of Tasmania that you will have a chance to solve
the mystery at the heart of things.

PROFESSOR MANNING CLARK, Hobart, June 1980

Previous pages
*T*he glacially fretted skyline of the Western Arthurs from above Lake Oberon.

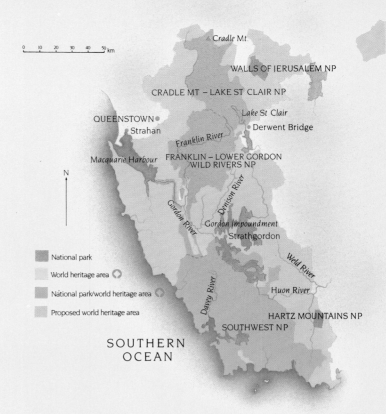

The map shows the following labels:

Cradle Mt.

WALLS OF JERUSALEM NP

CRADLE MT – LAKE ST CLAIR NP

Lake St Clair

QUEENSTOWN
Strahan
Derwent Bridge

Franklin River

Macquarie Harbour
FRANKLIN – LOWER GORDON
WILD RIVERS NP

Gordon River

Denison River

Gordon impoundment
Strathgordon

Weld River

Huon River

Davey River

National park
World heritage area
National park/world heritage area
Proposed world heritage area

HARTZ MOUNTAINS NP
SOUTHWEST NP

SOUTHERN
OCEAN

N

0 10 20 30 40 50 km

There is no more wonderful experience than a visit to a wilderness area. At the first smell of the forest or river, and the realisation that you are alone with the bush, everyday worries begin to disappear. As you find your way through the primitive landscape you can feel the environment's pulse, an experience no book or map can ever teach.

Most wilderness areas are dominated by one main physical feature such as a mountain range, a river valley or a desert. What is so distinctive about western Tasmania is the opportunity it offers to experience a wide variety of country: mountains, valleys, plains, lakes, rivers, forests, open areas and hundreds of kilometres of coastline. In this diverse land you can go wherever the fancy takes you for weeks on end. The impression that this was what the world was like before humans began to tame and divide the land with farms, towns and roads is particularly strong in the southwest. It is not surprising, then, that for several decades the region has been a mecca for bushwalkers.

When the region was nominated for world heritage listing it was described as 'the last great temperate wilderness remaining in Australia and one of the last remaining in the world'. Although the area met a record seven out of ten possible criteria applicable to world heritage sites, its most significant attribute is wilderness, a fact reflected in the title conferred by the World Heritage Committee — 'Western Tasmanian Wilderness National Parks'. Wilderness is an overarching quality that links and integrates the distinctive features of the area — the landforms and the post ice age mix of rainforests, sedgelands and eucalypts.

As more and more people came to enjoy the Tasmanian wilderness it was vanishing before their very eyes. Over the last twenty-five years development has halved its extent; its relentless pressure was sorely felt most recently in the eastern area where logging and associated roads were rolling the wilderness back ever westward. Today only the central part of the wilderness is fully protected, much of what was once wilderness has been lost, and the battle is now over whether the remainder should be protected or destroyed.

*I*ntruded granite at South West Cape. This wild coast has been
the site of many shipwrecks.

The protected area in the core of the world heritage site comprises the Southwest National Park (442 240 hectares), the Franklin–Lower Gordon Wild Rivers National Park (181 075 hectares) and the Cradle Mountain–Lake St Clair National Park (131 920 hectares). The boundaries are largely those of political convenience and the areas left out of the world heritage site are every bit as significant internationally as those included. Extensive areas have been proposed as world heritage both west and east of the existing site. To the west is the Eldon Range and the country south of Macquarie Harbour. To the east, starting in the north, there is the Central Plateau, including the Walls of Jerusalem National Park (11 510 hectares), the area around the Prince of Wales and Denison ranges north of Lake Gordon, and the eastern fringe of forests all the way from Wyld's Crag to South East Cape.

Not surprisingly, considering its exposure to the westerly airstream of the 'roaring forties', western Tasmania is second only to the wet tropics for the amount of rainfall and, bearing in mind its lower temperatures, is certainly the wettest region in Australia. All parts of the area have over 200 days with rain annually, but it is the cloudiness, the high wind and the changeability, as depression after depression rolls through, that give western Tasmanian weather a reputation to match its rugged terrain and daunting vegetation.

The main landform in the western part of the region is a series of parallel northwest-to-southeast aligned ranges separated by broad valleys. They are made of 700-million-year-old sandstones of Precambrian age which have been metamorphosed into resistant whitish quartzites and schists and sharply folded and uplifted many times. The valleys have been created where rivers along the line of the strike have eroded their way into the underlying soft strata.

There are younger limestone outcrops of Ordovician age at many locations, some of the caves being among the deepest in Australia. Even more important for the making

Right
*G*laciation was responsible for the creation of
Dove Lake and the sharp and distinctive
peaks of Cradle Mountain.

of Tasmanian scenery was the dolerite intrusion that occurred in the Jurassic period (about 165 million years ago). A layer of dolerite, in the form of molten lava up to 300 metres thick, was squeezed between the Permian and Triassic rocks to become the main rock of the Central Plateau. Its great thickness is most magnificently displayed in the vast escarpment known as the Western Tiers. With the Triassic rocks stripped away by erosion, dolerite forms the surface of most of the plateau and the highest parts of many of the peaks further west, such as the Eldons, Mt Picton and Precipitous Bluff.

In the Oligocene (30 million years ago) faulting further emphasised the northwest-trending structure, creating the Macquarie Harbour graben. The final touches were applied during the ice ages. At least three phases of advance have been recognised. During the last cooling (30 000–12 000 years ago) an icecap formed on the Central Plateau with the outlet glaciers spilling out into the Mersey, Forth and the Franklin–

*T*he great ravine, Franklin River. Powerful rivers have cut through the western ranges to create steep and rugged gorges.

Gordon area, increasing the erosive force of the rivers.

To the west and south the glaciers were smaller; one can see by the position of the lateral moraines on the flanks of the Arthur Ranges that they only just reached the plains. From them poured large amounts of outwash material, at one point creating a barrier behind which formed the shallow Lake Pedder. The glaciation sharpened the crests of the ranges and created scores of cirque lakes. Frenchmans Cap (1443 metres) and Federation Peak (1224 metres), both popular with rock climbers, are the mountain monarchs of the region. Lake St Clair, fifteen kilometres long and 161 metres deep, occupies the trough gouged out by a piedmont glacier. Even more spectacular are the lakes — over 4000 of them — that formed among the debris exposed when the icecap melted.

As the temperature increased again and the sea level rose over 100 metres, it invaded the coastal areas to create Port Davey and Macquarie Harbour. Hills on the coastal plain were isolated and became the Maatsuyker Islands.

Many other features owe their existence or dramatic features to the effect of water or freezing. Periglacial action, for instance, shattered the columnar dolerite into apron-like screes of giant brown boulders, known locally from their distant appearance as 'ploughed fields'.

*T*he quartzitic main face of Frenchmans Cap, framed by native conifers.

Right
*B*eech forest, once widespread in southern Australia, seen here on the northeast ridge of Mt Anne.

A lake sits high in one of the hollows created by cirque glaciers, Frankland Range.

Millions of years of downward cutting as the land was uplifted created deep gorges in the rivers that crossed the ranges; the extremely narrow Gordon Splits and the Irenabyss on the Franklin are only two of the better known. The Franklin is the best rafting and canoeing river in Australia. The caves in scattered limestone outcrops were deepened by the great volume of water produced when the ice melted — Anne-a-Kananda Cave near Mt Anne is 373 metres deep. The Salisbury River north of Precipitous Bluff flows over the sixty-metre-high Vanishing Falls and then disappears underground for several kilometres.

What sets this region apart from most of Australia except the wet tropics is not just its ruggedness but the conspicuous presence in the landscape of the direct descendants of the Gondwanan flora — the mesophyll temperate rainforest flowering plants and the even older conifers or gymnosperms. The more recently evolved eucalypt-dominated sclerophyll flora has certainly invaded the area and gained a good

*R*apids above the Irenabyss, Franklin River.

Right
*T*he tall, palm-like pandani (*Richea pandanifolia*) appears misplaced near frigid Lake Tahune.

foothold, and sedgeland covers one-third of the world heritage site, but the native conifers and rainforest species still dominate large parts of the landscape. The region's vegetation has acted as a barometer for recording the effect of changes in temperature on the plants of the area since the end of the ice age.

At the height of the last cold period, about 18 000 years ago, tundra similar to today's sedgeland covered most of the area and rainforest survived in only a few sheltered spots, but in the warm period (between 10 000 and 5000 years ago) rainforests spread quickly over most of the region. From 5000 years ago to the present, the climate has been less equable and fire

*S*assafras (*Atherosperma moschatum*), a rainforest species. The shining toothed leaves have an attractive flavour when crushed.

*W*eindorfers Forest. The name commemorates the founder of the Cradle Mountain–Lake St Clair National Park.

has been more frequent, due in part to burning by Aborigines. This aided the expansion of the sedge and eucalypts at the expense of the fire-sensitive rainforest. The vegetation pattern is still evolving, mainly in response to fire, and since most of the endemics are in the rainforests, fire is the main threat to their existence.

The rainforest is dominated by myrtle beech (*Nothofagus cunninghamii*) and sassafras (*Atherosperma moschatum*), and includes three of Tasmania's eight endemic conifers — the celery-top pine (*Phyllocladus aspleniifolius*), the slow-growing Huon pine (*Lagarostrobos* [*Dacrydium*] *franklinii*) and the King Billy pine (*Athrotaxis selaginoides*). Both the Huon pine and the King Billy live for 1500 years and more if protected against fire. Rainforest is the climatic climax of the region and often grows as an understorey to eucalypt. Without fire to create the conditions needed for regeneration, rainforest will replace the eucalypts.

The subalpine moorland over 1000 metres supports many plants that are not found in similar areas on the mainland. Most distinctive of all are the coniferous shrubberies of dwarf endemic pines (such as *Diselma archeri* and *Microcachrys tetragona*) and the cushion-forming plants (such as *Abrotanella forsterioides* and *Donatia novae-zelandiae*). In the higher areas, stands of King Billy pine and pencil pine (*A. cupressoides*) take the place occupied by snow gums in the Australian Alps. The prickly-leaved scoparia (*Richea scoparia*) is another common endemic plant of the tops. Its relative the forest grass tree or pandani (*Richea pandanifolia*) occurs mainly in high-altitude forests, adding an exotic touch to the flora. It is one of the largest members of the heath family, its palm-like stem reaching up to nine metres.

The wilderness explorer in southwest Tasmania is likely to meet all these vegetation types. The usual way in is through the tall eucalypt zone but beyond the Craycroft River most of the country is sedgeland dominated by buttongrass

A rare glimpse of the orange-bellied parrot (*Neophema chrysogaster*) at its nesthole. Breeding is restricted to two areas.

(*Gymnoschoenus sphaerocephalus*). Trees and shrubs are largely found in sheltered valleys and in corridors along river and stream courses. Walking over clumps of mature buttongrass is not easy but it is even more difficult to cross the forested areas which are usually well guarded by wet scrubs including bauera (*Bauera rubioides*) and the well-named horizontal scrub (*Anodopetalum biglandulosum*), whose growth form creates a close interlocking tangle of branches.

The fauna of this region is not as rich as that of eastern Tasmania but because of the area's wilderness some previously more widely distributed species can still be found here. Like elements of flora, some are of Gondwanan origin.

The orange-bellied parrot (*Neophema chrysogaster*) now breeds only in the sedgelands near Bathurst Harbour and south of Macquarie Harbour. There is a colony of Australian fur seals (*Arctocephalus pusillus doriferus*) on a small island south of Maatsuyker Island, and native fish are common in many of the streams. For many years hope was entertained that the Tasmanian tiger or thylacine (*Thylacinus cynocephalus*) would find sanctuary in the wild west coast but, in spite of several alleged sightings, there is no proof that the animal still exists.

International interest is now more likely to focus on the fauna of the lakes. Several varieties of syncarids, a primitive form of crustacea, are found only in the mountain lakes of Tasmania, the most famous being the Tasmanian mountain shrimp or anaspides (*Anaspides tasmaniae*). Elsewhere in the world this creature is known only from 200-million-year-old fossils. An urgent effort to salvage biological knowledge from the threatened Lake Pedder environment from 1966 to 1972 resulted in the discovery of seventeen endemic species, including a new species of a new genus, *Allanaspides helonomus* (also a syncarid). Because of the insights they offer into the evolution of the higher crustacea, the syncarids are as interesting to zoologists as the platypus and the echidna. The high western lakes of the Central Plateau — such as Lake Meston and Lake Adelaide — are particularly undisturbed and offer great opportunities for new discoveries.

During the last advance of the ice Aborigines occupied limestone caves in the valley of the lower Franklin River and other karst areas in the southwest. Archaeological finds in more than twenty caves over the last decade, but chiefly to date from Kutikina Cave, have provided evidence to indicate that the caves were first used about 20 000 years ago. At Judds Cave in the Craycroft Valley and Ballawinne Cave in the Maxwell River Valley there are paint-

*K*utikina Cave was home to Aborigines for over 6000 years during the last glacial period.

*T*he marsupial Tasmanian devil (*Sarcophilus harrisii*), now extinct on the mainland, is still common in Tasmania.

ings and inscriptions that probably belong to the same period.

At this stage Tasmania was linked to the Australian mainland, temperatures were some 7° Celsius lower than at present and glaciers occupied the sides of the ranges. The caves appear to have been the most southerly human habitations in the world at this time. Occupation of the caves ended between 14 000 and 13 000 years ago, perhaps because the resurgence of the rainforest following the warming of the climate made the area less accessible. The improvement of the climate also greatly reduced the extent of the land area and cut off Tasmania once more from the mainland.

After the end of the ice age the Aborigines of western Tasmania seem to have concentrated their activities on the coastal areas, while continuing their regular hunting trips inland. Land was fired both to make travel easier and to encourage game, and from 5000 years ago this and the drier conditions acted to reduce the rainforest and create the present vegetation mosaic.

At the time of European contact the Toogee band in the southwest numbered about three hundred. They lived in dome-shaped huts in the winter and used catamarans to cross rivers and reach the Maatsuyker Islands for sealing. The Aborigines were tricked into being removed from the west coast by Augustus Robinson

Right

*P*encil pines (*Athrotaxis cupressoides*) covered with icicles at Meander Falls, Great Western Tiers.

Clearfelled area in the Picton Valley, once part of the southwest wilderness.

in 1833–34, even though they were not in conflict with Europeans — surely one of the saddest events in the whole tragic story of Aboriginal repression in Australia.

In the centre of Tasmania the stock of the Europeans intruded on the hunting areas of the Big River people. Summer grazing on the Central Plateau began in the 1820s and by 1900 an estimated 350 000 sheep and 6000 cattle were being summered there. The Central Highlands further west were used only for the trapping of wallabies and possums. Burning off by the graziers, hunters and later prospectors reached a new height, devastating the subalpine vegetation.

Unlike the stability of the Aboriginal period, European occupation took the form of short-lived phases, each one lasting until the resource had been used up. The cutting of Huon pine began at Macquarie Harbour and Port Davey in 1815–16. The piners worked their way up the rivers, until by 1879 most of the trees had been cut out.

Ancient forest wilderness of beech and sassafras, Weld River, now threatened by logging.

Bay whaling had a similar history and had finished by the turn of the century. Fortunately the open areas of the southwest were considered to have a low agricultural potential and the Lands and Surveys Department enforced a strong policy against alienation — probably the single most important step taken by government to assist the survival of the area as wilderness.

Mining began in the second half of the nineteenth century and mine workings affected several parts of the region, including Port Davey (tin), the Central Highlands (copper) and Adamsfield (osmiridium). The cutting of timber for the mines near Queenstown had a significant effect but it was the extension of logging into the forests behind the towns of the south coast that was the most damaging aspect of forest use.

In the years after the Second World War, Tasmania increasingly sought its economic salvation by producing cheap hydro-electric power as an inducement for industry. The free rein given to an environmentally insensitive Hydro-Electric Commission meant that it was destined for a

*L*ake Pedder before its needless flooding. Its restoration would reflect changing values.

head-on collision with the conservation movement. This came with the Gordon power scheme; the level of the Great Lake and Lake St Clair had been raised and Lake Pedder flooded out of existence before the commission was stopped.

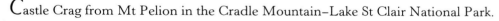

*C*astle Crag from Mt Pelion in the Cradle Mountain–Lake St Clair National Park.

Right

*C*ushion plants grow in a tightly packed mound in the Walls of Jerusalem National Park.

A landing stage on the Gordon River for the conservation protest camp, 1982–83.

Tasmania was a pioneer in the development of a state-wide system of scenic areas and one of the earliest was the Cradle Mountain–Lake St Clair reserve of 64 000 hectares proclaimed in 1922. An Austrian immigrant, Gustav Weindorfer, recognised its superlative beauty and led the successful campaign for the reserve. Interestingly it was a Lithuanian, Olegas Truchanas, who in the early 1970s led the struggle to try to have the decision to inundate Lake Pedder reversed. This campaign failed, even though the lake was the centrepiece of a national park proclaimed in 1955.

The reaction to the loss of this wilderness gem with its unique freshwater biota involved a strengthening of the Commonwealth role in conservation and a toughening of the resolve of the conservation movement to resist the plans for the second stage of the power scheme in the lower Gordon. Olegas Truchanas was gathering photographic material for this struggle when he drowned in the Gordon in January 1972.

The second stage involved the flooding of over 100 kilometres of wilderness river valleys in the heart of the rainforests of the lower Gordon–Franklin country, including

Kutikina Cave. Tension mounted as the campaign progressed; Manning Clark's words quoted at the beginning of this chapter were spoken at a pro-conservation rally in Hobart. Two and a half years later the conservation movement had set up a widely publicised blockade on the Gordon River and Xavier Herbert's message of support which referred to the blockaders as 'you brave hearts going into battle' captured the belligerent mood. Altogether 1272 blockaders were arrested. Finally the area was saved when part of the region was hastily added to the world heritage list and a new federal government, elected in March 1983, blocked the dam construction.

The attention paid to fighting the second stage of the hydro-electric power scheme resulted in relative neglect, for a time, of the threat to the southern forests. The roads and other works associated with the two stages of the power scheme had nearly

*D*e Witt Island in the Maatsuyker Group, Southwest National Park.

*T*he Meander River rises in the Great Western Tiers.

halved the extent of the wilderness, and protection of the forests was now vital to prevent any further loss of the region's most valuable resource. In 1987 the federal government halted logging and instituted an enquiry into the world heritage values of the southern forests and the Lemonthyme forest in the Forth Valley.

Other parts of the region which should be added to the world heritage site are included in the South West Conservation Area, which does not have the same degree of protection as the national parks. Most of the Central Plateau, which has close links with the Mersey and Forth valleys, is also not fully protected. South of the Walls of Jerusalem National Park there is the Central Plateau Wildlife Sanctuary but to the east the Central Plateau Protected Area has a lesser status.

There are many other problems. As yet there is no management plan for the protected areas as a whole and wilderness values could be damaged by insensitive tourist developments. Roads built for the abandoned hydro-electric power scheme need rehabilitating and it would make good sense to rescue Lake Pedder and its once-famous beach so that it occupies its rightful place as one of the highlights of the world heritage area. A Commonwealth–state consultative committee was established in the aftermath of the Franklin decision, but it will require the continuing vigilance of the conservation movement to complete the job of extending world heritage protection to cover all the wilderness areas and ensuring that management befits its pristine character and great stature.

GEOFF MOSLEY

Lord Howe Island

Lord Howe Island

*T*he rocky pyramid of Balls Pyramid, seen from Mutton Bird Point.

*W*hen I was in the woods amongst the Birds I cd. not help picturing
to myself the Golden Age as described by Ovid . . .

ARTHUR BOWES, Surgeon of the *LADY PENRHYN*, 1788

Previous pages
*M*t Lidgbird and Mt Gower from Malabar Hill, looking over the lagoon.

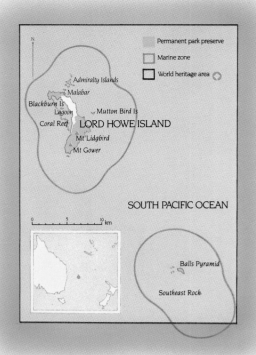

With an area of 1455 hectares, Lord Howe Island is one of the smallest areas ever included on the world heritage list on the basis of natural qualities; it is akin in this respect to a great cultural site such as a cathedral. And that is perhaps how we should regard Lord Howe Island and its fantastic companion spire of Balls Pyramid — as great natural cathedrals demonstrating that values of international significance can be found in a very small compass.

Officially the Lord Howe Island Group was inscribed on the list because of its exceptional natural scenery and its habitats containing endangered endemic species but, like many other world heritage areas, there are bonuses. The volcanic rocks that form the island, and the coral that has developed in the sea close by, both have unique features. The islands support extensive colonies of nesting seabirds, and scientist and amateur alike will find interest in the adaptations of the plants and animals which have colonised this land in the few million years since it was in a state of fiery eruption. Although introduced animals have destroyed much of the native fauna, the mountainous main island is still heavily vegetated. Its ruggedness and, ironically, its small-ness have saved it from many destructive pressures, and a great deal of value remains to be conserved.

The Lord Howe Island Group lies in the South Pacific Ocean 770 kilo-metres northeast of Sydney at approximately the same latitude as Kempsey in northern New South Wales. It is administered as part of New South Wales and is included in the federal electorate of East Sydney. The area inscribed on the world heritage list in 1982 includes an ocean buffer zone between latitude 31°25′s and 31°50′s and longitude 159°00′e and 159°20′e, a total of 1463 square kilometres.

Lord Howe Island itself is a narrow crescent shape, twelve kilometres long and varying in width from 2.8 to 0.6 kilometres. On the western side, cradled between the cliffs of the upland areas that form the horns of the crescent, is a six-kilometre-long lagoon. There are several groups of smaller islands, the most spectacular of which is Balls Pyramid.

*P*hotographing wildlife in the lagoon. The coral reef enclosing the lagoon at Lord Howe is the world's most southerly.

Situated in the track of the warm south equatorial current, and with atmospheric conditions dominated for most of the year by high pressure systems, the group's climate can best be described as subtropical. In spite of a general equability there is a definite seasonal rhythm in both temperature and rainfall; diurnal temperatures range from 17–25° Celsius in the hottest month to 14–18° Celsius in the coldest. Rainfall averages 1700 millimetres per annum, with most falling in winter. Windiness is characteristic but the tropical cyclones that plague north Queensland have lost most of their strength by the time they reach Lord Howe.

A major part of Lord Howe Island's attraction is that it has remained a quiet holiday place in a world in which the term 'resort' increasingly means frenetic activity based on artificial amusements. Most of the activities in which visitors engage are related to the natural environment. The idea of Lord Howe as an earthly paradise is most likely to be associated in visitors' minds with the view from one of the northern vantage points in the Malabar Hills over the sandy beaches of the reef-fringed lagoon, usually brilliant opalescent, to the towering bulk of the often cloud-wreathed Mt Lidgbird and Mt Gower.

*T*he tops of the southern mountains are often enveloped in cloud. From Mt Eliza the entire length of the island is in view.

*R*ough seas pound the base of Balls Pyramid. Destruction of the volcanic
rocks by incessant wave action has reached a more advanced stage here
than at nearby Lord Howe.

Balls Pyramid, twenty-three kilometres southeast of Lord Howe, is a worthy finale to the scenic splendour of the group. Only 1100 by 400 metres at its base, it rises to an awe-inspiring 551 metres. It is doubtful whether any more impressive stack, and certainly none so solitary, exists anywhere in the world. This island is rarely visited because of the difficulty of landing and was not climbed until 1965. Current policy is to discourage landings because of the danger and the disturbance to wildlife.

The mountain features of Lord Howe Island are remnants of a large shield volcano which developed on the western edge of the Lord Howe Island Rise some 6.9 million years ago. The rise is an underwater plateau extending 2000 kilometres north-west from New Zealand. At its western edge is a 1000 kilometre chain of underwater mountains, or 'seamounts', which probably resulted from submarine volcanoes as the crustal plate moved over hot spots. Lord Howe Island is the southernmost and youngest of this series but it is about twice as old as Norfolk Island 900 kilometres to the northeast. All the seamounts in the chain, except for Lord Howe Island and Balls Pyramid (which are parts of the same seamount), have been eroded away to below sea level by wave action. The different stages of destruction of the Lord Howe Island and Balls Pyramid fragments illustrates well the process that has eliminated the other former islands along the rise edge.

Right

*T*he dark green ledges of Balls Pyramid support a
range of plant and animal life.

Calcarenite or dune limestone, which occurs mainly in the settled area, was formed from windblown fragments.

developed on the wavecut platform. Calcarenite, a soft rock that occurs in the lowland area, was formed from the dissolving and cementing effect of rainwater on calcium carbonate in shelly material. Large numbers of dead marine organisms were blown on to beaches and dunes on the island when the wavecut platform was exposed during periods of low sea level. Included in the horizontal layers of the calcarenite are the bones of the giant horned turtle (*Meiolania platyceps*) which probably became extinct at the beginning of the last glaciation.

A plastic cast of one of the many fossil skeletons of the giant horned turtle (*Meiolania platyceps*) found in the calcarenite.

Geologists postulate that the horizontal sequence of basalt in southern Mt Lidgbird (777 metres) and Mt Gower (875 metres) is all that remains of lava which formed in a large caldera towards the end of the half million years or so during which the volcanoes were active. The basalt hills at the northern end of the island belong to the initial island-building period but were later intruded with dykes. The exposure of nearly 900 metres of unweathered volcanic rock is of great geological interest.

Wave action has already reduced Lord Howe Island to about a fortieth of its original area and half its height, the former extent being indicated by the fifty metre submarine contour.

The lower-lying central parts of the island that join the volcanic uplands are made up of debris from the erosion of the volcanic mass, and from the marine life that

Basaltic dykes, which occur along the north coast, were introduced into older volcanic rocks during the period in which Mt Gower and Mt Lidgbird were formed.

Right
The crest of the northern hills, viewed from the summit of Mt Eliza.

110

The waters around the Lord Howe Island Group contain an interesting mix of subtropical and temperate lifeforms. The true coral barrier reef which creates the lagoon on the western side of Lord Howe Island is the southernmost in the world. Because it is at the extreme temperature limit for coral reefs, there are many fewer species of coral and fish than in the southern part of the Great Barrier Reef. The reef plays a key role in protecting both the warm-water lagoon and the central part of the island whose weak rocks could otherwise be exposed to the full erosive effect of the southerlies.

The island environments offer a wide variety of conditions for plant growth. Patches of dry forest in the sheltered lowland areas, such as the western slope of Intermediate Hill, contrast strongly with the miniature cloud forest on the damp summit of Mt Gower where tiny mountain palms form a dense mix with mosses, ferns, orchids and many other endemic plants.

Cloud forest on the peak of Mt Gower, home of the Lord Howe Island woodhen.

*T*hickly vegetated talus slopes below the sheer volcanic cliffs of Mt Gower.

John Pickard has described seven different structural alliances from closed forest to short grass, nineteen plant alliances and twenty-five associations. Most of the island's vegetation could be described as subtropical rainforest.

The colonisation of the island following the volcanic upheavals has probably been assisted by periods of lower sea level when a chain of islands stretching towards New Caledonia and New Zealand provided stepping stones for migration. An indication of the sources of the flora is given by the 129 plant genera shared with Australia, 102 with New Caledonia and seventy-five with New Zealand. There are 180 angiosperms or flowering plant species, of which fifty-seven are endemic. Twenty-one of the moss species are also unique to the group. Some of the endemics are probably the result of speciation on the island.

*T*he banyan has a remarkable ability to spread by dropping aerial roots
from its branches to form subsidiary trunks.

There are three endemic palm genera, including *Howea* (formerly *Kentia*) with two species, and seventeen endemic ferns. The thatch palm (*Howea forsteriana*), which was used for roofing by the first settlers, proved to be a successful indoor plant and there has been a longstanding export of its seeds. The other two palms, both upland species, are the big mountain palm (*Hedyscepe canterburyana*) and the little mountain or moorei palm (*Lepidorrhachis mooreana*). Of the endemic ferns the most interesting are the four species of the genus *Cyathea*. There are several other unusual plants including the banyan (*Ficus macrophylla* ssp. *columnaris*), an endemic subspecies of the Moreton Bay fig, which has a huge potential for growth because of the way its roots drop down from the horizontal branches to form new trunks. One banyan was reported to cover over a hectare in the last century.

A close competitor for bizarre appearance is the endemic screw pine (*Pandanus forsteri*). Its long roots form tent-like props up to ten metres high.

Two of the island's plants are among the few tree-sized members of their families. Fitzgeraldii (*Dracophyllum fitzgeraldii*), with an attractive white spiky flower, is the tallest member of the heath family Epacridaceae, and the pumpkin tree (*Negria rhabdothamnoides*), which reaches eight metres, is probably the tallest of the Gesneriaceae family.

Not surprisingly, the non-avian vertebrate fauna is limited, represented only by a bat, the large forest eptesicus (*Eptesicus darlingtoni*), and two lizards — the Lord Howe Island skink (*Leilopisma lichenigera*) and a gecko (*Phyllodactylus guentheri*). Because of predation by rats the main habitat of the lizards is on Balls Pyramid and other offshore islands. On the main island

113

they survive only around areas of calcarenite where they are able to escape attack in holes in the rock.

Pride of place belongs to the birds, at least 130 species of which visit or live permanently on the islands. Twelve species of seabirds regularly breed in the group. It is the main breeding area in the world for the winter-nesting providence petrel (*Pterodroma solandri*) and possibly the largest breeding colony of the red-tailed tropicbird (*Phaethon rubricauda*). The group is one of the most southerly nesting sites of the sooty tern (*Sterna fuscata*). Seabirds form a constant background to holidays on Lord Howe Island and the breeding colonies in the Admiralty Group and Mutton Bird Point on the east side of the island are popular attractions with visitors.

The most famous of all the Lord Howe Island birds is undoubtedly the Lord Howe Island woodhen (*Tricholimnas sylvestris*). A brown bird about the size of a bantam, it is a symbol of the way a combination of rugged terrain and late conservation effort has enabled so much of value to survive on Lord Howe Island. At the same time its story is a reminder of the extreme vulnerability of the island's wildlife, which evolved without natural predators.

Writing in his journal about the incredible tameness of the birds, Arthur Bowes of the *Lady Penrhyn* (one of the ships of the First Fleet which called at Lord Howe Island in May 1788) recorded: 'We had nothing more to do than to stand still a minute or two and knock down as many as we pleased with a short stick. The pigeons also . . . would sit upon the branches of the trees till you might go and take them off with your hands . . .'

The most vulnerable were the ground birds, but all suffered a major worsening of conditions in 1918 when rats escaped from the ss *Makambo* aground off Neds Beach. Within a few years five species of native birds had been lost.

The woodhen, a flightless rail related to the New Zealand weka, was common when

*T*he Lord Howe Island woodhen (*Tricholimnas sylvestris*) only narrowly escaped extinction.

the area was first settled and for many years it provided easily caught food for the settlers and crews of passing vessels. By 1979 there were only two colonies left, probably numbering no more than thirty birds, on the remote Mt Gower and Mt Lidgbird. Elsewhere they had been eliminated by rats, dogs, cats and disturbance of the ground by wild pigs. A captive breeding program resulted in the rearing and release of about ninety woodhens in suitable depopulated areas. To complement this, an extensive rat poisoning and cat trapping program has been carried out and control of pigs and goats (introduced by early sea captains) is well underway. The problem is how to eliminate these introduced animals in the more inaccessible parts of the island.

The roll-call of destruction is bad. Nine out of Lord Howe Island's fifteen land birds (fourteen endemic forms) are extinct. Those that have gone include the white gallinule, another flightless bird (eliminated by 1840), a pigeon (extinct by 1870), a parakeet, a warbler, a thrush, a silvereye, a fantail and a starling. Among the survivors are the Lord Howe Island pied currawong (*Strepera graculina crissalis*), the Lord Howe Island silvereye (*Zosterops tephropleura*), and the Lord Howe Island golden whistler (*Pachycephala pectoralis contempta*).

Another victim of rats was the seven-centimetre-long endemic stick insect *Dryococelus australis* which some think may survive on Balls Pyramid. Rats, pigs and goats also greatly reduced the number of species of endemic land snails, particularly the large *Placostylus bivaricosus*. The whitened shells of these snails, sometimes with holes indicating rat attacks, are common on the forest floor.

The first recorded sighting of the Lord Howe Island Group was by Lieutenant Henry Lidgbird Ball in February 1788 on his way in HMS *Supply* to establish a settlement on Norfolk Island. Ball also made the first landing on his way back to Sydney. Several proposals to establish a penal colony on the island were rejected. The first few settlers arrived in 1834 and lived a subsistence life supplemented by bartering fish, fruit and meat with passing ships, chiefly whalers. Many of the early settlers were sailors who had seen the idyllic conditions at first hand.

In the 1880s, as the whaling industry declined, the islanders began to export fruit and vegetables to the Sydney market and established an industry based on the collection and export of palm seeds. In 1913 a board of control was set up to regulate the

*T*he remote forests of rugged Mt Gower are the home of the Lord Howe Island woodhen. The saving of this species was the result of late conservation action.

industry, which from then on took the form of a cooperative. This board, which still owns all the palms and controls the palm seed collecting, eventually became the body responsible for local government and all natural resources.

The island has no deep-water harbour and cargo has to be transported by lighters to Neds Beach or the lagoon from ships lying offshore. Nevertheless, Burns Philp commenced a steamer service to the island in 1893. This was the beginning of the island's tourist industry, which was boosted by the introduction of a regular tourist steamship run in 1932 and a flying boat service in 1947. In 1974 an airstrip was built for small twin-engined aircraft and there is now a frequent service between Lord Howe and Sydney, Brisbane, Port Macquarie and Norfolk Island.

The main changes on Lord Howe Island have been on the lowlands where the land has been cleared for farms, building, roads and, more recently, the runway. Together the settlement and rural areas cover eighty-three hectares — 6 per cent of the island. A wider area was cleared in the past and, while this has regrown so that the landscape of the settled area is now a pleasing mixture of farmland and bush, there are several exotics such as cherry guava, crofton weed, bitou bush, asparagus fern and tiger lily, which have the potential to invade the natural areas if not cleared.

The permanent population of the island, which was under 100 at the turn of the century, has grown to 257 people, who are largely dependent on two sources of income — tourism and the sale of palm seeds. Fruit and vegetable growing and the 200 cattle that roam the settled areas are mainly for consumption on the island.

Tracing the origins of conservation, which is now the dominant factor in the management of the island group, one can see that the government's nineteenth century decision to keep the island under the control of the crown was highly significant. Instead of agreeing to applications for title,

the government provided islanders with permissive occupancies which were later converted into perpetual leases for home and business purposes, permissive occupancies for farmland and special leases for other purposes. Preference was and is given to islanders. The remaining areas were left as vacant crown land.

The modern period of conservation began with concern over the fate of the endemic wildlife and the threat of too much tourist development. In the late 1960s, P. S. Green of the Royal Botanic Gardens at Kew urged that an environmental survey be conducted. He was particularly concerned about the adverse effect of the wild goats on the island flora. Kew's interest in the island dated back at least to the visit by the naturalists Milne and MacGillivray on HMS *Herald* in 1853. The environmental survey of Lord Howe Island, coordinated by Dr Harry Recher of the Australian Museum,

*A*n aerial view of the rainforest canopy showing palms mixed with flowering trees. The island has many endemic species.

Right
*T*he summit of the rarely climbed Mt Lidgbird (777 metres) from Rocky Run.

which began in 1970, confirmed the importance of the wildlife and provided the first full scientific assessment of the conservation status of its biota.

Publication of the survey report in 1974 provided convincing arguments for a conservation campaign led by New South Wales conservation groups and a few islanders, and by the Australian Conservation Foundation, which began to press for a national park and world heritage listing. The islanders generally were wary about the national park proposal, fearing that their future might be severely limited, and the Lord Howe Island Board suggested instead a reserve for the preservation of native flora and fauna.

After considerable debate a compromise solution was reached. The Lord Howe Island Amendment Act of 1981 provided for a permanent park preserve over the northern and southern forests and the offshore islands (75 per cent of the total area of the group). The New South Wales National Parks and Wildlife Service was required to prepare a management plan but responsibility for its implementation and for management remained in the hands of the board. A further plan for the marine zone is being prepared.

It was also clear that better planning of the settled areas was necessary to retain the integrity of the island as a whole. A year after Recher's report had been published, Nigel Ashton of the New South Wales State Planning Authority prepared a report on the future use and land management of Lord Howe Island. A planning scheme was adopted in 1976. With the island nominated for the world heritage list, the Lord Howe Island Amendment Act also provided for the adoption of a Regional Environment Plan. The plan was gazetted in December 1986, and incorporates the plan of management for the permanent park preserve.

When, in 1982, the group was inscribed on the world heritage list the settled areas were included as well as the permanent park preserve. No marine areas are included in the permanent park preserve but aquatic reserves have been proposed by the Fisheries Division for both the lagoon and Admiralty Islands.

The regional plan aims to ensure that development on the island does not destroy the natural environment and affect the lifestyle of the residents. It provides for six zone categories in addition to the permanent park preserve, one of which is a marine protection zone, and another set aside for 'special uses' to provide for utility installations in a manner sympathetic to world heritage values. The most productive agricultural land is also zoned to prevent its loss to subdivision. Some conservationists believe that no more land should be made available for subdivision but the plan identifies a further thirty lots. The minimum allotment size for each portion in an agricultural area is two hectares.

The threat of a burgeoning tourist industry is recognised and the number of tourist beds is restricted to four hundred. Accommodation is in one-storey guesthouses and lodges. The Lord Howe Island Board restricts the number of vehicles on the island to one per family.

Many problems remain. The amendments to the Lord Howe Island Act of 1981 gave the islanders majority control over the future of this international conservation area. Apart from giving the board responsibility for implementing both plans, it increased the islander representation on the board to three out of five. Currently the board does not have adequate funds to provide for management, maintain the wildlife and control plant introductions as well as dealing with disposal of waste and the maintenance of roads and other facilities. The wider Australian community must be ready to assist before what remains of the features that made Arthur Bowes think of a golden age can be considered safe.

GEOFF MOSLEY

Left
The Admiralty Islands, from Malabar Hill in the north of Lord Howe.

New South Wales Rainforests

New South Wales Rainforests

A hanging garden of ferns, mosses and orchids clothes a rainforest tree.

The world's eyes are on Australia as the only developed nation with rainforest within its borders . . . Australia has lost about three-quarters of its rainforest since European settlement. It must set an example in the conservation and preservation of this precious resource.

NEVILLE WRAN QC, February 1987

Previous pages
*M*orning mists hang over the subtropical rainforests of the Dorrigo escarpment.

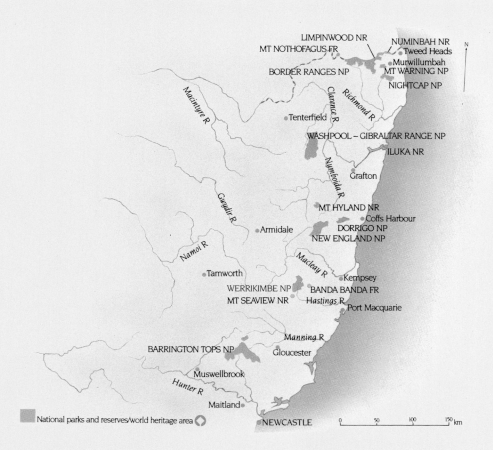

In the 1950s it took three punts to get to the fishing village of Iluka on the northern bank of the Clarence River where it meets the Pacific Ocean. The Clarence, one of the largest rivers of northern New South Wales, is called the 'big river' by locals. After winding across the coastal plain, through endless walls of sugarcane, the river spreads into a web of lakes, backwaters and channels, a gentle landscape of casuarina-lined banks, mangroves and sand flats, the resting points of black swans and pelicans.

The remote village, built on a neck between river and ocean, had no more than a few hundred inhabitants, mostly fishermen and their families. The fishermen lived in weatherboard shacks on stilts, built in sandy clearings hacked out of the dense banksia and eucalypt forest of the peninsula.

Our family spent the summer holidays there in a fibro shack. The ocean beaches were wild and beautiful in those days — a coastal wilderness unmolested by sandminers and developers. As a child I loved those long, empty beaches; it is here that a lifelong love of untamed and lonely places developed. However, the particular place that captured my imagination then and forever was tucked in the lee of the dunes — an extraordinary pocket of rainforest or, to my child's mind, 'jungle'.

It did not feel like just another part of the 'bush'. It had a roof; you entered it as you enter a building. It was cool and dark; there was no wind. Light penetrated only in dappled spots or a single, dramatic shaft. The pungent odours of tea tree and eucalypt were replaced by the moist smells of fungi and decaying logs. The atmosphere was both grand and mysterious. There were mighty trees, great radiating bird's nest ferns, hanging elkhorns and underfoot a thick layer of leaves.

When so many of the magic places of childhood have been destroyed, it is a particular pleasure that this small, special area of forest has not only survived, but has achieved world status as Iluka Nature Reserve, part of the New South Wales rainforests listing on the world heritage list.

The New South Wales rainforests became Australia's sixth formally declared world heritage site in 1986. The listing is an unusual one in that it is not a single geographical area but six separate centres of rainforest distribution. The six areas are mainly located along the Great Dividing Range between the New South Wales–Queensland border in the north and Newcastle in the south. They are the Tweed Volcano Group; the Washpool–Gibraltar Range Group; the Coastal Group; the New England Group; the Hastings Group and the Barrington Group. In all they cover sixteen national parks and reserves, an area of 203 088 hectares. Although the sites do not encompass all the remaining rainforest in New South Wales, they represent the major part of the high-quality, pristine forests.

The sites also include areas other than pure rainforest, particularly the extensive rainforest–sclerophyll forest overlap areas and other eucalypt forests that provide important buffer zones for the rainforest. They were chosen as examples of the four dominant rainforest types found in New South Wales and major variations of those types according to different locations and conditions. The listed sites include substantial wilderness areas and some fine stretches of wild and scenic rivers, particularly Washpool Creek.

The world importance of Australia's rainforests, not only those of New South Wales, is discussed in the chapter on the wet tropics. The New South Wales rainforests are particularly interesting because they include excellent examples of four major rainforest types: cool temperate, warm temperate, subtropical and the oddly named dry rainforest. In fact, most of the world's warm temperate rainforests are located in New South Wales.

The declared sites also meet the World Heritage Convention's criterion of 'exceptional natural beauty'. Rainforests are very beautiful places. Sometimes they are extravagant and luxurious, like the tropical and subtropical forests, sometimes subtle

*W*ashpool Creek, a wild and scenic river, flows through the Washpool wilderness.

*L*ooking east from the great escarpment over the magnificent wilderness
of the New England National Park.

and relatively simple like the warm temperate forests of mottled coachwoods or the mossy beech forests. On a grand scale there are the walls of the great escarpment, rising dramatically out of the coastal plain. The escarpment is a dominant landform feature of much of the east coast of the continent, but it is particularly impressive in northern New South Wales.

In the New England National Park the cliffs and steep slopes of the escarpment afford a view over a rugged wilderness of densely forested ridges and valleys. The Bellinger River, which rises here, is one of the major wild rivers of New South Wales. Probably the most spectacular scenery of the rainforest areas is the ancient volcano of Mt Warning on the New South Wales–Queensland border. The caldera, the great hollow that forms in the top of the volcano, is one of the largest in the world, while the central mountain mass of the volcano is a particularly dramatic sheer-sided plug.

Although the terms used to describe the New South Wales rainforests — subtropical, warm temperate, cool temperate and dry — are somewhat broad, they are widely used and understood. Scientists have criticised these classifications in that they infer that climate is the overriding determinant of rainforest type; other factors such as altitude, aspect, soil type and fire regimes are frequently as important, sometimes even more important.

Subtropical rainforests are second only to the tropical for richness of plant species. They are characterised by a profusion of plant forms: massive trees, strangler figs, buttressed trunks, great rope-like lianes, palms, ferns, orchids, mosses, every square centimetre of available surface, every niche in a tree smothered with living greenery.

Despite this richness in all forms of plantlife, subtropical rainforests are characterised by a number of species of large trees, including yellow carabeen (*Sloanea woollsii*), booyong species (*Argyrodendron* spp.), rosewood (*Dysoxylum fraserianum*),

Right
*L*uxuriant palms and tree ferns thrive in the moist
leaf litter of the forest floor.

white beech (*Gmelina leichhardtii*), pigeonberry (*Cryptocarya* spp.) and red cedar (*Toona australis*).

Of major scientific importance is the existence of plant forms that closely resemble ancient plantlife and known, for this reason, as primitive plants. Although the wet tropics have the richest concentration of these plants, there are many in New South Wales rainforests. Two genera, *Eupomatia* and *Tasmannia*, found in New South Wales are believed to resemble the earliest flowering plants. The conifers are even older than the angiosperms and are well represented in subtropical forests and their margins, particularly hoop and bunya pines (*Araucaria* spp.), she-pine (*Podocarpus elatus*) and scrub cypress (*Callitris macleayana*).

Subtropical forests prefer a combination of rich alluvial or basalt soil and high rainfall. Unfortunately this combination was also much sought after by settlers. As a result most of the accessible lowland subtropical rainforest has been destroyed, including the largest area in Australia, the so-called 'Big Scrub' near Lismore in northern New South Wales. Despite this history, remnants of subtropical rainforest do survive in the world heritage area, the

*R*ufous fantail (*Rhipidura rufifrons*).

*A*t left, rainforest and eucalypt species intermingle in a uniquely Australian forest type of great scientific interest. Among the most distinctive of all rainforest sights is the giant fig tree (*right*).

128

most extensive being in the Tweed Volcano Group of sites, especially the Border Ranges and Mt Warning national parks.

A particularly interesting area is Lever's Plateau in the Border Ranges National Park. It is the largest unlogged stand of booyong-dominated subtropical rainforest, with an overstorey of hoop pines (*Araucaria cunninghamii*). The plateau holds a special place in the folklore of conservation because John Lever, the sawmiller who had the rights to fell the forest, was so overwhelmed by its beauty that he vowed it would never be logged.

Dorrigo National Park, part of the New England Group, also contains some magnificent forests, due to the coincidence of basalt soil and high rainfall. Massive strangler figs (*Ficus watkinsiana*) are a memorable feature of the park. These trees literally strangle the host tree around which they wrap themselves. Another feature of Dorrigo is an understorey of palms, which creates a luxuriant atmosphere.

A distinct subtype of subtropical rainforest is littoral rainforest. The largest remaining stand of this forest type is the area previously described at Iluka. Despite its unlikely location behind the dunes, this is not depauperate rainforest: 187 plant species from seventy-three families have been located in this 136 hectare remnant. Smaller, more salt-tolerant species dominate the seaward side of the forest, sheltering a much taller forest behind.

The lushness of the subtropical forests is replaced by comparative simplicity in warm temperate rainforests, which are less complex in both structure and composition. The canopy is lower, between twenty-five and thirty metres, and trees are of a more uniform height. They are generally found on less fertile soils and more exposed sites than subtropical forests.

Only a few tree species, sometimes just one, dominate these forests. Frequently they are non-buttressed, smooth-barked species which do not attain great size.

The most common distinguishing tree is the lovely coachwood (*Ceratopetalum apetalum*). The grey bark of this slender tree is covered with a patchwork of lichens in shades of pink, orange, grey and white. Other species are the crabapple (*Schizomeria ovata*), sassafras (*Doryphora sassafras*), callicoma (*Callicoma serratifolia*), lillipilly (*Acmena smithii*) and corkwood (*Caldcluvia paniculosa*).

Warm temperate rainforests are particularly important to the world heritage status of the New South Wales rainforests as the major areas survive in this state. Willowie Scrub, covering 3000 hectares of the Washpool National Park, is the largest remaining area of coachwood in Australia and hence the world.

The third rainforest type, cool temperate rainforest, is characterised by a single tree species in the canopy and several species at lower levels. There are two distinct kinds of cool temperate rainforests in New South Wales: those in the south dominated by sassafras (*Doryphora sassafras*), and those principally further north where the Antarctic beech (*Nothofagus moorei*) dominates. Only the latter are represented in the declared world heritage areas. Although extensive cool temperate rainforest also exists in Tasmania, it is dominated by another *Nothofagus* species, the myrtle beech (*Nothofagus cunninghamii*). *Nothofagus moorei* forests are virtually restricted to New South Wales.

These forests are principally found at higher altitudes, above 800 metres, where cool humid conditions prevail. They are quite different in character from other rainforest types. Beeches are huge trees, sometimes growing in multistemmed coppice formations and sometimes as at Barrington Tops, tall and well formed. Persistent mists and rain provide an ideal habitat for the mosses, ferns, lichen and fungi that clothe the beech trunks and bases. The relatively uncluttered forest floor is covered in a deep carpet of gold and rust beech leaves.

Right

Mist and moss are natural companions to the Antarctic beech (*Nothofagus moorei*).

*T*he gnarled mossy bases of the Antarctic beech give the forest an enchanted quality.

Major areas of cool temperate rainforests are found in the Barrington Tops National Park, the Hastings Group, the New England National Park, Dorrigo National Park and parts of the Tweed Volcano Group, most notably the aptly named Mt Nothofagus Flora Reserve.

Barrington Tops is the southern limit for *Nothofagus moorei* and contains extensive stands. Here the beech is frequently overtopped by the tall *Eucalyptus*, especially *E. obliqua* and *E. fastigata*. More surprisingly, the beech forests open out at a certain height into subalpine woodland and meadows, making an ascent to the tops a varied and rewarding experience. One plant of particular interest is the epiphytic beech orchid (*Dendrobium falcorostrum*) which is confined to the upper branches of the beech trees. This lovely mauve and white orchid is highly fragrant and grows in dramatic spikes of up to twenty flowers.

The last rainforest type is the dry rainforest. This is characterised by a low to medium closed canopy with isolated taller emergents, including hoop pine, lace bark (*Brachychiton discolor*) and teak or crows ash (*Flindersia australis*). Some species of both layers of these forests may be deciduous or semideciduous. Generally these forests lack the palms, ferns, mosses and rich epiphytes of other forest types. They are usually located on rich soils, where the rainfall is markedly seasonal, or on rocky slopes.

The largest area of dry rainforest within the listed sites lies on the western side of the Border Ranges. The major emergent here is the spectacular hoop pine. A rare species now in these dry forests, but once common, is the onionwood (*Owenia cepiodora*). It was severely depleted because of the resemblance of its timber to the highly valued red cedar.

Mosaics of rainforest and eucalypt forests are a significant feature of the New South Wales world heritage forests. The interrelationship between the rainforest and these forests is unique to Australia and

*L*ichen-covered coachwood (*Ceratopetalum apetalum*).

therefore of scientific interest. Frequently tall eucalypts are found with a rainforest understorey. These transitional and overlap areas are particularly rich habitats for diverse wildlife.

While no species of mammal is totally restricted to rainforest, several appear to prefer rainforest and wet sclerophyll forests. The most commonly seen are the pademelons — the red-necked pademelon (*Thylogale thetis*) and the red-legged pademelon (*T. stigmatica*) — which can often be disturbed grazing in a rainforest clearing or hopping through the leaf litter searching for foliage and fruits.

Two other macropod species found in the forests are the parma wallaby (*Macropus parma*) and the now rare, black-striped wallaby (*Macropus dorsalis*). The mountain brushtail possum or bobuck (*Trichosurus caninus*) is common in the forests of the wet eastern slopes and often descends from the trees to forage for fruits, buds, fungi and lichen. The most common rodent is the

fawn-footed melomys (*Melomys cervinipes*). Scientists were excited by the rediscovery in the early 1980s in the upper Forbes Valley of another small rodent, the Hastings River mouse (*Pseudomys oralis*), which had previously been thought extinct.

The Washpool–Gibraltar Range Group is a rich habitat for mammal species, including the long-nosed potoroo (*Potorous tridactylus*) and rufous bettong (*Aepyprymnus rufescens*). The diversity of animals in this region is attributed to the absence of feral foxes and other feral animals. The Tweed Volcano Group is also an important habitat of thirty-two species of bats, a diversity exceeded only by the wet tropics.

Scientists believe that many of our common bird families evolved from rainforest species. Today rainforests are particularly important habitats for many birds, especially the fruit-eating species and those that forage in the insect-rich leaf litter.

*L*ong-nosed potoroo (*Potorous tridactylus*).

*T*he regent bowerbird (*Sericulus chrysocephalus*) is a fruit eater of the subtropical rainforests.

Among the fruit eaters are seven pigeon species, including the beautiful wompoo fruit-dove (*Ptilinopus magnificus*) and emerald-winged pigeon (*Chalcophaps indica*). Some of these pigeons are spectacularly coloured but are often difficult to see as they feast on the fruit in the canopy. Despite their often brilliant colours, one may become aware of them only by the soft rain of fruit fragments falling from the canopy to the forest floor. Among the other fruit eaters are the noisy but exquisite paradise riflebird (*Ptiloris paradiseus*), with its plumage of purple-black and iridescent green, the satin (*Ptilonorhynchus violaceus*) and regent bowerbirds (*Sericulus chrysocephalus*), and the brilliant emerald green catbird (*Ailuroedus crassirostris*).

A quiet visitor to the forest may become aware of a soft scratching noise and with caution can observe the handsome brush turkey (*Alectura lathami*), with its red bald head and frill of yellow wattles. The turkey rakes the ground litter with its powerful feet to uncover insects. Less frequently encountered is the shy but beautifully coloured noisy pitta (*Pitta versicolor*).

The far northeast of New South Wales is one of the richest bird habitats in Australia and is home to several rare species: the Coxen's fig parrot (*Psittaculirostris diophthalma* ssp. *coxeni*), the marbled

*T*he unspoiled rainforest remains a peaceful world of uncontrived beauty and harmony.

Grady's Creek flows through rich subtropical rainforest in the Border Ranges.

frogmouth (*Podargus ocellatus*) and the black-breasted button quail (*Turnix melanogaster*). The fig parrot is feared extinct mainly because of the disappearance of lowland rainforest.

The northeast also contains one of Australia's richest collections of frog species, including the extraordinary pouched frog (*Assa darlingtoni*). The male of this species carries the tadpoles in brooding pouches along its flanks. Snakes and lizards are well represented, although they are not as diverse as in arid regions.

The innumerable invertebrate species of the forest have a central role in the ecosystem, particularly in breaking down the leaf litter and wood to provide nutrients to be recycled into the forest. The New South Wales rainforests lay claim to some rather strange records, including the largest known earwig, the largest weevil and one of the largest of the world's land snails. Among the loveliest of the insects are the moths and butterflies. The brilliant black and green Richmond birdwing (*Ornithoptera priamus richmondus*), the largest butterfly in New South Wales, is confined to the Border Ranges and southern Queensland.

The archaeological importance of the New South Wales rainforests cannot be fully assessed because of lack of research. Limited evidence suggests that Aboriginal people certainly used the rainforest, although they may have preferred the fringes for camping. Reports of early explorers describe the capturing of rainforest-dwelling animals for food and the use of edible plants of the forest. More recent research has also located material objects such as dillybags, necklaces and clapping sticks made from rainforest plants. The many dramatic landscape features of the sites would certainly have been incorporated into the complex spiritual life of the people. Archaeological sites with surface deposits of stone artefacts have been discovered in Terania Creek and in the Washpool National Park.

*B*elow a towering canopy, epiphytes like the bird's nest fern thrive in the moist shaded atmosphere.

Unfortunately the great age and beauty of these forests had little impact on the white pioneers who rapaciously mined them for red cedar and other species. The timber fellers were succeeded by the agriculturalists who erroneously believed that such rich forests must grow on rich soil. They saw the forests as useless 'scrub', an obstacle to their endeavours. Vast areas were cleared and the lovely timbers piled up and burnt. The most tragic example is the famed 'Big Scrub' near Lismore, thought to have been one of the largest stands of subtropical rainforest in the world. Now all that remains of its 75 000 hectares is a minute 300 hectares of forest. However, in the postwar period, particularly after 1970, a growing body of scientists and conservationists argued that

Left
*T*he staunchly defended beauty of subtropical rainforest at the Circle Pool, Nightcap National Park.

the value of rainforest in its natural state far outweighed its value as timber or agricultural land.

Fortunately in 1982, after a decade of vigorous campaigning by the conservation movement, including the famous Terania Creek blockade, the New South Wales government adopted a comprehensive policy to protect much of the limited areas of rainforest by transferring them from the Forestry Commission to the National Parks and Wildlife Service. This decision came at the eleventh hour as an estimated three-quarters of the rainforest has disappeared in two hundred years of white settlement.

Despite the virtual wiping out of lowland subtropical rainforest, substantial high-quality sites do remain in the rugged areas of northeast New South Wales. Many of the warm temperate sites have been logged and will require many years to regain anything approaching pristine condition; some scientists believe they can never recover. The outstanding 3000 hectares of Willowie Scrub in Washpool National Park is still intact. The cool temperate forests are the least disturbed by humans, not because of foresight, but principally because beech is a poor timber. Although they have been adversely affected by logging of the coachwoods, overall they are well represented in protected areas and their future looks secure. Dry rainforests are poorly represented in reserves but the National Parks and Wildlife Service is actively seeking to enhance their conservation status. Conservationists stress that there are still some important rainforest remnants not within national parks and that the task of conserving these forests has yet to be completed.

Generally the future of New South Wales rainforests seems assured, although management will be required to prevent degradation from feral animals, weeds and fire. However, it must be stressed that while the 'rainforests' were 'saved', what in fact was saved were merely the last remnants of once great areas of forest.

PENELOPE FIGGIS

The Western Arid Region

The Western Arid Region

*U*luru, a place of great spiritual significance to western desert people.

*Space, light, chasms, gorges, and stupendous rocks —
these were my main impressions of the Centre. There was a bleached beauty
about it all that must surely make this one of the unique
landscapes of the world.*

LLOYD REES, *Each Man's Wilderness*, 1980

Previous pages
*K*ata Tjuta, 'place of many heads'. Its significance
has been recognised by world heritage listing.

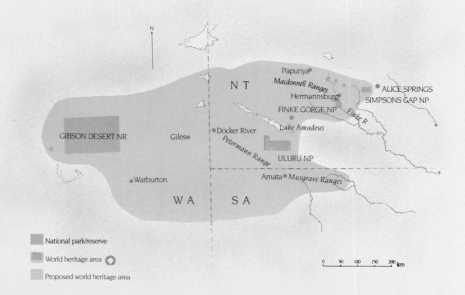

The western arid region covers most of the area more commonly referred to as central Australia, the heartland of outback Australia. It includes such well-known sites as the town of Alice Springs, the spectacular cleft of Standley Chasm, and Australia's most distinctive landscape symbol — Uluru (Ayers Rock). It is a vast area of magnificent scenery, remarkable landform features, and rich flora and fauna. To Aboriginal people, the region is of profound cultural significance; to non-Aboriginal Australians, it is a powerful symbol of their land.

Key elements of world heritage value within the region include the Macdonnell Ranges, one of the world's most ancient mountain ranges, the Finke River, claimed as the oldest rivercourse on earth, numerous endemic species, some of great evolutionary importance, and the richest reptile fauna in the world. Scientifically, the flora and fauna are of great interest for the often remarkable ways in which they cope with the arid climate. A small part of the region, the 132 566 hectare Uluru (Ayers Rock–Mt Olga) National Park, has been recognised for its world heritage values: it was inscribed on to the world heritage list in December 1987.

The environment of central Australia can be broadly divided into two major components: a series of often spectacular ranges and their surrounding slopes and floodouts, and the large areas of sandplains and dunes. Both ranges and plains are intersected by 'rivers', or more accurately predominantly dry rivercourses, some of which are buried underground.

The ranges of central Australia confound the image of the dead heart, of endless, flat, parched deserts. Although not particularly high, most of the ranges rise steeply from the surrounding sandplain. All have been chiselled and worn for millennia into often quite remarkable formations. Apart from their beauty and geological interest, the ranges also represent diverse habitats for plants and animals. The shady pools that lie in the deep gorges contain some of the few substantial resources of surface water in the centre. Many of the ancient plant species that vegetated central Australia when the climate was far wetter have survived here.

*M*orning mist obscures the great domes surrounding the central valley
of Kata Tjuta. The valley is reached by narrow gorges between the sheer walls.

The main ranges of the region are the Macdonnell Ranges, the Krichauff, James and George Gill ranges, and the Petermann, Musgrave and Mann ranges. The 300 kilometre Macdonnell Ranges, which run east and west of Alice Springs, are the longest of the central Australian ranges and, at an average of 600 metres, the highest. Mt Zeil is the highest point at 1511 metres. The series of parallel east–west ranges is cut by north–south aligned rivers. Foundation sedimentary and volcanic rock of the ranges goes back to Precambrian times, more than 2000 million years ago, making the ranges one of the oldest on earth. They were formed during a major mountain-building period around 350 million years ago when the existing rocks were steeply tilted and folded. The Macdonnells today are the worn-down bones of these original mountains. They are certainly an outstanding example of the earth's geological processes.

There is no element of biblical wasteland in these ranges, despite the arid climate. The Mereeni Valley, which lies between the main ranges of the western Macdonnells, the Chewings and Heavitree ranges, appears well vegetated, even lush, where stock have not depleted plants. Handsome river red gums (*Eucalyptus camaldulensis*) line the sand rivers that cleave the ranges, evidence of their underlying water resources. On the southern flank of the valley is a great row of hills, huge collapsed scallops that erosion has cut with unnatural regularity. Repetition of landscape features is a major characteristic of central Australia, particularly noticeable from the air. Near the end of the valley is beautiful Rutjubma (Mt Sonder), whose purple-blue bluffs have been immortalised by Aranda Aboriginal artist, Albert Namatjira.

The northern side of the valley features many narrow gorges which frequently contain permanent waterholes from either rain

Right

*T*he ancient weathered ridges of the Macdonnell Ranges,
a key heritage feature of the western arid region.

*H*aast Bluff soars steeply from the sandplain that encircles it.

collection or springs. The combination of water and spectacular rock formations is compelling and many of these gorges — Simpsons Gap, Standley Chasm, Serpentine Gorge, Ormiston Gorge and Ellery Big Hole — are key tourist attractions.

These shaded chasms where water can survive are vital habitats for rare plants and animals. The ranges are the major location of the rare and ancient cycad, *Macrozamia macdonnellii*. Their dark green appearance contrasts dramatically with the reds of the rock faces and the powdery white bark of the ghost gums (*Eucalyptus papuana*) whose contorted trunks cling to rocky clefts. The black-flanked rock wallaby (*Petrogale lateralis*), fat-tailed antechinus (*Pseudantechinus macdonnellensis*) and sandy inland mouse (*Pseudomys hermannsburgensis*) survive in this environment. The area may also contain the last surviving populations of the central rock rat (*Zyzomys pedunculatus*).

Inevitably, given the diversity of plants and animals and water resources, the Macdonnell Ranges were a centre for western desert Aboriginal people, principally Aranda. The region is rich in identifiable rock paintings and some carvings, but virtually every rock formation, every plant and animal has a place in the complex culture of the oldest continuing civilisation on earth. Aboriginal people still conduct ceremonies where they are not barred by pastoralists' hostility. A significant area of the Macdonnells, including Standley Chasm, is on land owned by the Iwupataka community, while most of the western end of the Macdonnells, including the impressive Mt Liebig area, is on land held by the Haast Bluff Aboriginal Land Trust.

South and mainly west of Alice Springs lie the Krichauff, James and George Gill ranges. These ranges, geologically younger than the Macdonnells, are mainly

Right

*T*he purple bluff of Mt Sonder is one of the most magnificent scenes of central Australia.

146

*S*tandley Chasm, worn by the erosion of a volcanic dyke. When the sun briefly illuminates its sheer quartzite walls, the rocks seem to catch fire.

*F*rom a boulder-strewn bed the coloured cliffs of Ormiston Gorge rise 300 metres. The gorge drains a huge natural amphitheatre.

*W*est of Alice Springs the Macdonnell Ranges rise from the valley in a
wave-like wall. The ridges are the remnants of an ancient mountain range.

sandstone–quartzite in composition. The water-absorbent sandstone is heavily dissected by gorges, creating a landscape of rugged beauty. The ranges are intersected by several rivers, including the Finke, Hugh and Palmer, as well as many minor creeks. The channels create great pathways of sand which occasionally become raging torrents after heavy falls of rain. It is a splendid part of arid Australia deserving, for both scientific and aesthetic reasons, a high degree of conservation. However the entire area has only two small parks: Finke Gorge National Park and the, as yet ungazetted, Kings Canyon National Park.

Right

*T*he complex geological history of the region is
revealed in the many-layered landscape
near Ellery Creek.

Finke Gorge National Park covers an area of 4610 square kilometres southwest of Alice Springs. It is the only conservation reserve within the James and Krichauff ranges. The park begins just south of Hermannsburg (Ntaria), probably the most important historical settlement in central Australia. In the 1870s Lutheran missionaries made an epic journey along the Finke to establish a mission among the Aranda people. As they tried to educate the 'savage' from his 'heathen' ways, some of the missionaries collected detailed anthropological research on the very culture that they sought to suppress. Because of the reliable refuges provided by permanent water, this area has always been comparatively heavily populated. Consequently the region is of immense continuing importance to the Aranda people.

The 'road' into the heart of the park is a bone-jolting four-wheel-drive track along the bed of the Finke River. The assault on the body is compensated for by the sweeping lines of Mt Hermannsburg and the highly coloured walls of the Finke Gorge. Large river red gums flank the wide sandy bed, their many hollows homes for a rich birdlife. Among the most common birds in the area are the rainbow bee-eater (*Merops ornatus*) and the superbly coloured Port Lincoln parrot (*Barnardius zonarius*).

About sixteen kilometres south of Hermannsburg a side stream, Palm Creek, enters the Finke from the west. The upper reaches, known as Palm Valley, are noted for their relict population of palms, *Livistona mariae*, remnants of the times when wetter forests clothed much of Australia. Palm Valley was Namatjira's special 'country', his dreaming place, and was often painted by the artist. The palms survive because of the constant seepage of water from the absorbent rocks. The valley has good populations of cycads and *Thryptomene wittweri*, also relict species. To date 460 plant species have been identified in the diverse habitats encompassed by the park. The Finke has been called the oldest river in the world because its general course, which flows through the park, has not greatly altered since it was cut in the late Palaeozoic period. As such it is of great geological interest.

*I*nitiation Rock in the Finke Gorge National Park.
This ritually important rock juts out into a wide cliff-walled valley.

Right
Palm Valley, a rainforest relict.

152

*T*he lush and sheltered gorge that perches above Kings Canyon has been called the Garden of Eden because of its permanent water and luxuriant cycads (*Macrozamia macdonnellii*).

Further south, approximately 350 kilometres from Alice Springs at the western end of the George Gill Range, is the Kings Canyon National Park. In its 720 square kilometres, the park features mountain range, waterhole and desert ecosystems. A biological survey conducted by the Conservation Commission of the Northern Territory in 1981 stated that the area is 'botanically the most important area in Central Australia'. The survey recorded 572 plant species, representing one-third of the flora of central Australia, and including seventeen relict species and forty-five that are rare or found elsewhere only at considerable distance. At least thirty different plant communities have been identified; most are in good condition due to the relatively small populations of cattle and feral animals and low degree of weed penetration.

Many of the rare and relict species grow in the sheltered gorges with permanent or near permanent water. Out on the sandplains superb stands of the slow-growing desert oak (*Allocasuarina decaisneana*) are found. The protected gorges support a good selection of central Australia's wildlife and the region generally is notable for reptiles and frogs.

The Watarrka area, as Aboriginal people call it, has international importance for its cultural and scenic qualities. Kings Canyon, the best known of the gorges, is over half a kilometre long, walled by towering cliffs in

Right

*T*his spectacular complex of weathered sandstone domes sits on the George Gill Range. Heavy tourist visitation could quickly degrade this outstanding site.

*L*ocated on Aboriginal land, the Petermann Ranges are rarely visited by
the Centre's many tourists. The ranges remain a vital cultural stronghold
of the western desert people.

some parts, pitted and cracked in others, smooth with streaks of vivid pinks, ochres and reds. On the floor of the canyon are huge boulders and blocks of sandstone interspersed with river red gums and cycads. At the head of the gorge is a shaded amphitheatre of rock enclosing a deep cold pool, above which is a rock cleft, a window to another higher gorge known as the 'Garden of Eden' because of its lush vegetation and strings of waterholes. On the plateau above the gorge is an extensive area of eroded, weathered domes locally known as the 'lost city'. These strange weathered sandstone formations are reminiscent of the Bungle Bungles in the Kimberley but on a smaller scale.

Left

*W*ind and water have carved the sheer walls of Kings Canyon, the Centre's deepest gorge. Here strong sunlight bleaches some of the fire from the sandstone's rich colours.

The area around Watarrka has always been important to Aboriginal people as a convergence point of several major dreaming tracks. There is outstanding potential for archaeological research, with many signs of past occupation including grinding stones, implements and a considerable number of cave paintings. Traditional owners have recently returned to live on small excisions within the park and have been closely involved with the development of a management plan.

The ranges that lie southwest of Uluru are much less well known to science and little known to the tourist. The Petermann, Mann and Musgrave ranges are all on long-standing Aboriginal lands. The Musgrave

157

*U*luru. This massive isolated rock standing at the centre of this oldest of
lands has become the primary landscape symbol of the nation.

Ranges are the most extensive and tallest of the ranges; Mt Woodruffe (1439 metres) is the highest peak in South Australia. The Musgrave and Mann ranges show well-developed talus fans, erosion slopes that fan out beneath vertical cliffs. The Everard Ranges share a characteristic of these southern ranges in having huge sheets of bare rock.

Like all the uplands of the centre, the southern ranges provide sheltered valleys and canyons where the harsh sun does not evaporate all the scarce water. These water-holes are of great cultural importance, the lifeblood of those who have survived in this region. Scientists believe that small mammals that are extinct or rare elsewhere may have found sanctuary here.

The major sandplain expanse in the western arid region is the area around Lake Amadeus extending beyond Kintore into Western Australia and the Gibson Desert. It includes a number of major salt lakes and several small ranges, as well as the sandplain and dune country that surrounds the great monoliths of Uluru (Ayers Rock) and Kata Tjuta (the Olgas).

The sandplains and dunes conform much more with the traditional concept of arid wilderness than the range country. Vast areas of central Australia are dominated by sharp-spiked, circular hummocks of spinifex. The harshness is frequently relieved by vibrant, if ephemeral, displays of wildflowers, flower-laden bushes such as grevilleas and thryptomenes, stands of desert oak and soft grey mulga (*Acacia aneura*). Only the shimmering expanses of the great salt lakes and the stony, apparently feature-less plains that cover large extents of the Gibson Desert provide starkly inhospitable images of a desert environment.

Right

*T*he immense pitted and pleated walls of Uluru
tower above the surrounding sandplain.

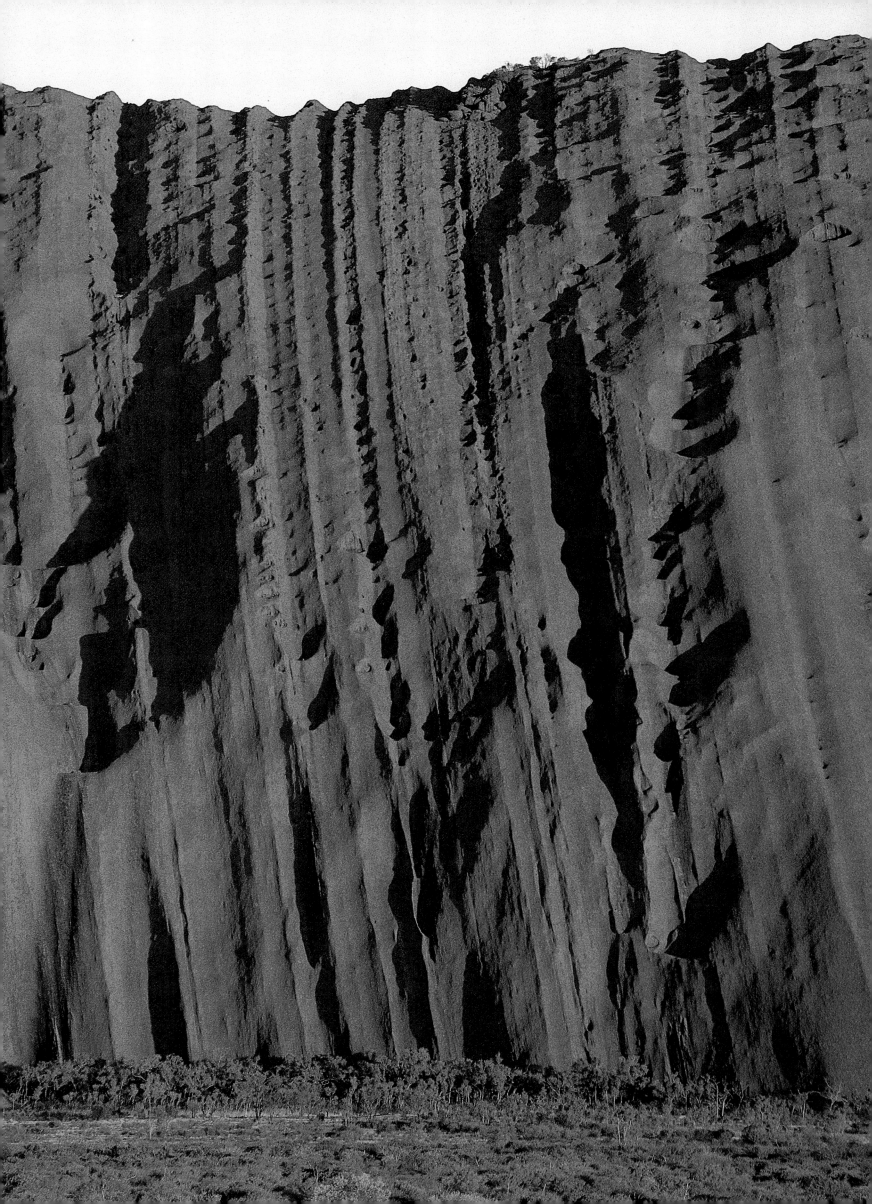

The wildlife of the sand country is often furtive, emerging in the cool of evening to find food. However, the signs of life are clearly written in the dunes. Among the bushes and flowers are sinuous grooves, paw prints, fine-toed scratches, among numerous tracks that reflect the remarkable variety of animals that can find a niche in this arid environment. Most of the sand graffiti is fine, for there are few large animals in these endless stretches of undulating sandridges. Of the large native mammals, only the dingo (*Canis familiaris dingo*), the red kangaroo (*Macropus rufus*) and common wallaroo (*Macropus robustus*) find an adequate habitat and survive on nutrient-poor vegetation. Of the feral animals, the camel, rabbit and cat manage to survive in the better areas, unfortunately to the detriment of native wildlife.

The main animals of these regions are small marsupials and native rodents, birds and reptiles. Most of the former are nocturnal, avoiding the extremes of day temperatures in burrows or shelters. Some of the more frequently encountered species are a charming little marsupial mouse, the mulgara (*Dasycercus cristicauda*), the stripe-faced dunnart (*Sminthopsis macroura*) and the spinifex hopping mouse (*Notomys alexis*). These small creatures find a protective environment in the spinifex mounds which are intimidating for many creatures as well as humans.

In the dense grey mulga thicket the exquisite turquoise wren (*Malurus splendens callainus*) and brilliant red-capped robin (*Petroica goodenovii*) can often be seen. Out in the open country the bustard or plains turkey (*Ardeotis australis*) stalks about, seemingly little concerned with its status as prime 'bush tucker'. These remote areas are strongholds for this bird, which has become extinct or rare over much of its once more widespread range.

Central Australia is unchallenged as the richest reptile habitat in the world, with many of the reptile species showing a close reliance on the spinifex clumps (*Triodia*

spp. and *Plectrachne* spp.) of the sandplains and dunes. The lizards range from the world's second largest, the magnificent perentie (*Varanus giganteus*), to the bizarre little thorny devil (*Moloch horridus*) and a tiny skink (*Menetia greyi*). Snakes are well represented and, more surprisingly, frogs, including the fascinating water-holding frogs (*Cyclorana* spp.).

One of the factors that may assist the survival of wildlife in the region is an underlying network of ancient river systems. Believed to be the remnants of once substantial tropical rivers that flowed across the land some 200 million years ago, these palaeodrainage systems are now strings of salt lakes often joined by channels through which underground water still moves slowly. Scientists believe that these channels slowly distribute water and nutrients along their paths, providing diverse habitats on which many species depend.

In pre-European times, Aborigines patch-burned areas to produce grasses and herbs that attracted wildlife for hunting, creating a mosaic of varied habitats. The lack of mosaic burning has allowed wildfires to devastate hundreds of square kilometres of land.

This dramatic change in fire regime, added to the devastating impact of the rabbit, has given central Australia another less proud superlative — the extinction capital of Australia, possibly the world. In less than 100 years of European settlement half of all the known mammals have become extinct. Although little research has been conducted, scientists believe that the remote salt lakes and dunefields of the western Northern Territory and the Gibson Desert region of Western Australia, which are often surrounded by pockets of rich vegetation, are vital habitats for many species that have elsewhere become rare.

It may seem strange in a discussion of central Australia to leave its most famous features, the mighty monoliths of Uluru and Kata Tjuta, until last. This is partly because they are unique, not typical features of the

Created about 130 million years ago when a comet plummeted to earth
with incredible force, Gosse's Bluff, the remnant of the original crater, lies
on the plain like a medieval walled city.

region, and partly because it is difficult to say anything adequate to their power, beauty and importance. Certainly their unique character has been recognised from their first sightings by humans who could write their response. In 1873 the explorer W. C. Gosse described what he called Ayer's Rock as 'the most wonderful natural feature I have seen', while Ernest Giles, who had named the Olgas the previous year, later wrote, 'I am sure this is one of the most extraordinary geological features on the face of the Earth'. The national and international significance of the two rock formations has been recognised in their uncontested acceptance for world heritage listing in 1987.

The region remains a central focus of religious, territorial, cultural and economic relationships among the western desert peoples. Despite substantial social prob-lems, the western desert remains a cultural stronghold where language and custom remain remarkably strong. Every feature of the two great rock formations, every cave, gorge, eroded pattern, tells some part of the Tjukurpa or creation story. The return of the park area to its traditional owners in October 1985 was a recognition of the vitality of the cultural affiliations.

When title was restored to Aboriginal people, they leased the park to the people of Australia to be run by the Common-wealth National Parks Service. All major policy decisions, however, are made by a board on which Aboriginal people have the majority. The 'Uluru model', as it is now called, is a world first for conservation on the land of indigenous people. It also points the way for the future. If Aboriginal owner-ship were acknowledged and Aboriginal people given a central role in decision mak-

161

*T*he Macdonnell Ranges, a key element of the world heritage value of the
region, remain inadequately protected in a string of small reserves.

ing, many of the areas discussed in this chapter might be brought under more active conservation management. Although the very large areas of Aboriginal land within the western arid region have been subject to relatively low impact, much could be done to enhance the conservation status of these lands. Measures might include the reintroduction of Aboriginal burning regimes, the breeding of locally extinct species such the brushtail possum (*Trichosurus vulpecula*), rufous hare-wallaby (*Lagorchestes hirsutus*) and bilby (*Macrotis lagotis*), and the control of feral animals.

At present central Australia is very poorly protected by national parks, despite its promotion nationally and internationally as a tourist destination. Less than 1 per cent of central Australia is within conservation reserves, while vast areas are under non-viable, destructive pastoral usage. This is most serious in the Macdonnell Ranges which, despite increasingly heavy tourist visitation, are inadequately protected in a string of tiny parks and reserves. This ancient landscape, so central to our self-image as a nation, so important to the cultural survival of its original inhabitants, must have its significance acknowledged by adequate conservation management.

PENELOPE FIGGIS

Left

*T*o the geologist, millions of years of weathering have produced Blanche's Tower. However, Aboriginal people know that it was created by ancestor beings in the Dreamtime.

The Wet Tropics

The Wet Tropics

A large Calophyllum overhangs the high tide mark, Cape Tribulation.

*T*he Greater Daintree region is the most beautiful of its kind in
Australia. Time will heal the scars inflicted upon this wilderness.
We are more than rich enough and secure enough to protect this land.
We have a moral duty not to harm. We have a duty
not to debase the world.

RUPERT RUSSELL, *Daintree: Where the Rainforest Meets the Reef*, 1985

Previous pages
*R*ainforest sweeps down Mt Donovan to Emmagen Creek, Daintree, north Queensland.

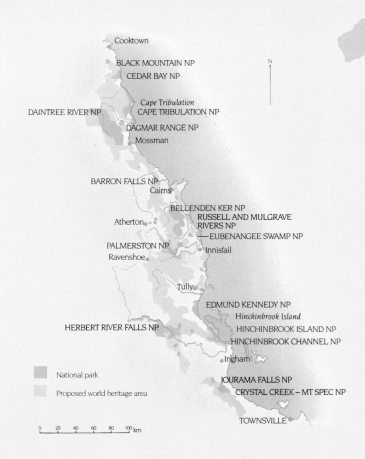

At Cape Tribulation in the Daintree region of north Queensland, the huge boughs of Calophyllum trees extend up to twenty metres over the beach. The rough scaly branches are a mass of epiphytes, orchids, ferns and mosses creating a hanging garden and a shaded retreat from the tropical heat. Streams emerge from the wall of forest to carve their way across the sand to the sea. They form intimate tunnels that allow access to the forest interior. The intricate forms of the forest are reflected in the many still pools that lie along the creek lines. From neat moss cushions to buttressed forest giants, every plant form appears in profusion. High in the closed canopy the mountain blue butterfly flashes in the unreliable sunshine.

Rising steeply from the coastal forest are mountain peaks which snag every passing cloud, drenching the forest so frequently that it eternally shimmers with light reflected from water droplets. From the peaks, the image of a paradise, a garden of Eden, is complete as fringing coral reefs in the turquoise waters of the Coral Sea trace the white beaches.

This is a unique environment. It is scientifically of immense importance, but it is also extraordinarily beautiful. These two qualities are the hallmarks of the wet tropics.

The wet tropics is a 500 kilometre strip of coastal mountains and lowlands lying between Cooktown in the north and Townsville in the south. At its broadest, it is approximately eighty kilometres wide. It covers an area of some 11 000 square kilometres and includes such distinctive features as the Daintree River catchment, the Cape Tribulation coastline, the Mt Windsor tableland, the Herberton and Atherton highlands, and the Bellenden Ker and Cardwell ranges. The description 'wet' is highly appropriate, as the region is one of the wettest on earth. However, some 60 per cent of the annual rainfall falls between December and March. Temperatures are more seasonably variable here than in the more northerly wet equatorial regions which support the most dense and luxuriant rainforests.

167

The principal characteristic that marks this area for world heritage listing is that it encompasses Australia's remaining wet tropical rainforests, which are regarded as of immense scientific value. Most of the rainforest occurs on the steep foothills and slopes of the major coastal ranges. The last bastion of virgin forest on land accessible to logging survives in the Mt Lewis–Carbine Tableland. The now rare coastal lowland rainforest occurs mainly in limited areas north of the Daintree River, with only remnants further south. In the Daintree Valley, the river wanders through the largest rainforest wilderness remaining in Australia.

Rainforests the world over are valuable and important as nature's richest storehouses of plant and animal species. However, the forests of northeast Queensland have special qualities which provide an overwhelming case for their inclusion in the world heritage list. The plants and animals of these forests have great intrinsic value. Their complexity is the result of tens of millions of years of evolution.

The wet tropical forests of modern Queensland are the relicts, the richest remaining fragments, of the ancient forests of Gondwana, a southern supercontinent that existed 100 million years ago. Over 90 million years ago it began to break up, eventually to become the separate continents of Africa, India, South America, Antarctica and Australia. The forests that clothed a great part of this huge ancient landmass were in some ways similar to tropical rainforests. Despite climatic fluctuations and the general drying out of the Australian continent, the northeastern ranges remained refuges for the rainforest. Although there were many losses and later acquisitions, the forests of north Queensland represent an extraordinary continuity of vegetation over perhaps 60 million years, from the late Gondwanan period.

North Queensland is among the world's richest habitats for primitive angiosperms or flowering plants. Of the nineteen known primitive families, twelve are found in the

*L*owland palm forests, dominated by the fan palm (*Licuala ramsayi*), are now rare.

168

*W*ind-pruned vegetation on the misty eastern slopes of Mt Sorrow.

wet tropics and two single-species families, Idiospermaceae and Austrobaileyaceae, are unique to this region. Australia's wet tropics, if allowed to survive, will be a living laboratory, the source of new scientific knowledge about the origin, evolution and migration of these plants.

Of particular interest is the fact that the familiar plants of the Australian bush — the eucalypts, banksias, grevilleas and hakeas — are also believed to have evolved from these ancient forests. These plants evolved as, 50 million years ago, the continent of Australia broke away from Antarctica and drifted north into hotter latitudes. Some of the ancestors of our well-known bush flora survive today in the tropical forests of north Queensland.

The region is unique in another way, too, for it holds the most complete remnants in the world from what scientists call the age of conifers and cycads, an earlier stage in

the evolution of plants. Among the beautiful palm-like cycads are the towering *Lepidozamia hopei*, one of the tallest cycads in the world, and the fern-like *Bowenia spectabilis*, one of the smallest.

However, the value of these forests is not limited to knowledge and aesthetic pleasure. They have the potential, like all tropical rainforests, to yield products of importance to humanity, in particular new crops and pharmaceuticals. Many of the world's staple foods — rice, taro, bananas — have originated in the genetic richness of the tropical forest. It has been estimated that one drug in four has come directly or indirectly from the world's rainforests.

Despite the overall identification of the region as 'wet tropical rainforest', thirteen major structural types have been identified and subdivided into twenty-seven broad communities of plants. The complexity of vegetation types reflects significant differences within the area of soil types, moisture, altitude, temperature, and the effects of wind and drainage. The rain-forests vary from the wind-stunted cloud forests on the peak of Bellenden Ker (altitude 1500 metres), to the spectacular, almost pure, fan palm (*Licuala ramsayi*) forests found in now rare patches on the coastal lowlands.

The forests contain a rich variety of epiphytic flora — the perching plants that clothe the trunks and branches of the trees and create so much of the luxuriant atmosphere. The many orchids of the region, both delicate and dramatic, vie with its exquisite butterflies for beauty honours. There are some ninety orchid species, including the lovely cerise Cooktown orchid (*Dendrobium bigibbum*). The moist warm environment also provides an ideal habitat for Australia's richest concentration of ferns and fern allies. About 92 per cent of the known fern genera in Australia are represented in the region.

The Bellenden Ker range contains some of the finest gorge scenery in Australia.

Cooktown orchid (*Dendrobium bigibbum*)

Overleaf

Outstanding lowland forests near Downey Creek have been largely destroyed by logging.

Near Cape Tribulation, tropical lowland rainforest with eucalypt
emergents lies directly behind a sea-edge buffer of dense mangroves.

Although the wet tropics qualifies for world heritage listing largely because of the values of its ancient rainforest, there are other important vegetation types within the region, including tall eucalypt forests, paperbark swamps and mangrove forests. The latter are particularly significant, for they contain a range of species as diverse as any in the world. An estimated thirty-five species of mangroves are found in north Queensland.

The much-maligned mangrove is now recognised as a resource of enormous economic importance because of its role as a breeding area for marine life. It has even been suggested that the world's mangroves may have originated in northern Australia. Whether this be proven or not, such a rich collection of species provides an excellent research resource into this ecosystem which is central to the world's fishing industries.

The world importance of the wet tropics is not confined to its vegetation. The persistence of these forests over millennia also means that they have provided refuge to many endemic species of fauna, at least some of which are relicts of the ancient wildlife of Gondwana. Despite representing a minute 0.1 per cent of the continent, the area is the richest animal habitat in Australia. The bare statistics are impressive: the wet tropics contains 30 per cent of all Australia's marsupials and frog species, 23 per cent of the reptiles and 18 per cent of the birds. Some fifty-four vertebrate species are unique to the wet tropics while another 160 are highly dependent on the region for their survival. Many of the species of the greatest

Left

The mangrove forests of the Hinchinbrook Channel are biologically an integral part of the wet tropics.

importance to science are confined to very small areas of specialised habitat. The endemic species are made up of nine mammals, thirteen birds, twenty frogs and sixteen reptiles.

Three great processes in the earth's formation can be illuminated by these animals. First, the wet tropics contains species that are believed to be relics of the ancient animals that inhabited the forests of Australia over 15 million years ago. Secondly, many of the species reflect the collision of the Australian and Asian continents about 15 million years ago. This, so to speak, reunited fauna which, while having a common ancestor, had been evolving separately for about 80 million years. Thirdly, some fauna reflect the effects of the Pleistocene glacial period, some 15 000 years ago, on a tropical area. It is believed that during this era the rainforest retreated into small areas, called refugia, which, like geographical arks, allowed the flora and fauna to survive until more clement times.

Among so many outstanding species, it is difficult to highlight only a few. However, some stand out as of particular interest. Scientists believe that the musky rat-kangaroo (*Hypsiprymnodon moschatus*) is a descendant of tree-living ancestors retaining several possum-like characteristics. A tiny animal, only twenty-five centimetres high, it is considered to be the most primitive of all macropods and is one of the many species that would be threatened by significant degradation of the rainforest habitat. Two species of the clumsy but appealing tree-kangaroo — Bennett's (*Dendrolagus bennettianus*) and Lumholtz's (*D. lumholtzi*) — survive only in this region.

*T*he musky rat-kangaroo (*Hypsiprymnodon moschatus*), a tiny primitive macropod.

Recently there has been considerable excitement over the photographic recording of the rare white lemuroid possum (*Hemibelideus lemuroides*). This lovely creature appears to be confined to the Mt Lewis–Carbine Tableland area. It is poorly adapted to survive in disturbed forests so the prevention of logging in its habitat may be crucial to its survival.

Many species have very restricted habitats. The Thornton Peak melomys (*Melomys hadrourus*), the largest of Australia's melomys, is found only in the uplands of the Thornton Peak massif. The rare Atherton antechinus (*Antechinus godmani*) has one of the smallest ranges of any Australian mammal. It lives in the dense mist-drenched forests above 1200 metres in the centre of the region. The antechinus is one of a primitive group of carnivorous marsupials called Dasyuroids which also includes quolls and dunnarts. Nine species inhabit the forests, giving this region yet another claim to the 'richest habitat' title.

As the dusk softens the light on the beaches of the Daintree, the solitude is pleasantly disturbed by flocks of rainbow bee-eaters (*Merops ornatus*) coast-hopping and congregating in noisy masses on mangroves or casuarinas. They wheel and tumble in a show of aerial gymnastics, displaying their elegant curved wings and fine extended tail feathers. These rainbow birds are not unique to the region but are one of the many pleasures provided in abundance for the ornithologist and bird enthusiast.

Predictably, the wet tropics is the most diverse bird habitat in Australia. Some 128 species have been listed. Thirteen species are endemic and a further thirteen, while not confined to Australia, are restricted to these forests within Australia. Most of the endemic species inhabit the higher altitudes. They include the beautiful golden bowerbird (*Prionodura newtoniana*), the chowchilla (*Orthonyx spaldingii*), the tooth-billed catbird (*Scenopogetes dentirostis*), the Atherton scrub wren (*Sericornis keri*), Bower's shrike-thrush (*Colluricincla boweri*),

*R*ainbow bee-eater (*Merops ornatus*).

the Australian fern wren (*Crateroscelis gutturalis*), the bridled honeyeater (*Lichenostomas frenatus*), the mountain thornbill (*Acanthiza katherina*) and the little tree-creeper (*Climacteris minor*). The four endemic species which also inhabit the lowlands are the pied monarch (*Arses kaupi*), Victoria's riflebird (*Ptiloris victoriae*), lesser sooty owl (*Tyto multipunctata*) and Macleay's honeyeater (*Xanthotis macleayana*).

Many other species, although not unique to Australia, are dependent on these forests. The huge southern cassowary (*Casuarius casuarius*), up to two metres high, belongs to one of the most primitive groups of birds on earth. Its great feet alone call up images of the age of dinosaurs. The magnificent buff-breasted paradise kingfisher (*Tanysiptera sylvia*) migrates yearly from New Guinea to the lowland rainforest. Its exquisite royal blue head and wings contrast dramatically with its trailing white central tail feathers.

The region is no less remarkable for its smaller denizens. Among the frogs that thrive in the warm moist forests are the rare *Litoria lorica*, which has been recorded only on Thornton Peak, and *Cophixalus neglectus*, which has been located only on the Bellenden Ker Range. A common but spectacular species is the giant tree frog (*Litoria infrafrenata*). One of Australia's largest frogs, it is a bright glossy green and looks like the model for every concrete frog.

Twenty-three per cent of Australia's reptiles — 160 species — are found between Cooktown and Townsville. Sixteen of these are restricted to the tropical rainforests. Some of the outstanding reptiles are the Boyd's forest dragon (*Gonocephalus boydii*), the elusive prickly forest skink (*Tropidophorus queenslandiae*) and the master of camouflage, the chameleon gecko (*Carphodactylus laevis*).

In this landscape dominated by shades of green, the butterflies provide a strikingly beautiful contrast. Many of Australia's loveliest butterflies grace the forest canopy.

A common sight is the mountain blue butterfly (*Papilio ulysses joesa*). Other spectacular species are the Cairns birdwing (*Ornithoptera priamus euphorion*), the red lacewing (*Cethosia chrysippe*) and Australia's, possibly the world's, largest moth, the atlas moth (*Coscinocera hercules*).

The rich butterfly fauna is also of great scientific interest, containing as it does many primitive and curious species and approximately 60 per cent of all Australia's species. Less beautiful, but no less interesting to the scientists, are the thousands of other insect types that throng the forest from the leaf litter to the canopy. Again, many are of highly restricted habitat and it is likely that new species await discovery.

These forests were once home to a distinctive group of Aboriginal people and still contain many culturally significant sites. Charcoal deposits on the Atherton Table-

*T*he atlas or hercules moth is a notable rainforest inhabitant. With a wingspan of twenty-five centimetres, it is among the largest moths in the world.

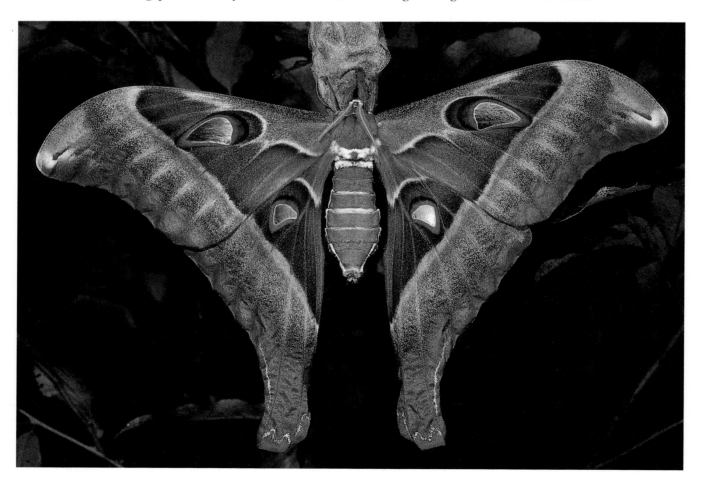

Right

*T*he magnificent rainforest wilderness of the Roaring Meg catchment, west of Mt Pieter Botte.

*W*ith its rich profusion and variety of plantlife, the rainforest is an aesthetic delight.

land suggest that their occupation may date back some 40-45 000 years. The limited evidence to date suggests that these Aborigines were small people with unique weapons and artefacts. They had learnt to process many of the toxic rainforest plants for food. Some of their descendants still live around the Bloomfield and Lockhart rivers, and are regarded as the last Aboriginal group on the east coast who still live, partly at least, in a traditional way.

Against the figures of some 40–45 000 years of Aboriginal occupation, the 120-odd years of white settlement seem barely significant. Yet in terms of impact on the region, the reverse is true. White settlement has altered this environment in a dramatic and largely devastating way.

With settlement in the 1860s, many accessible areas of forest were cleared for agriculture and dairying. The areas with good soils like the Atherton Tableland and the lowland rainforest were the most thoroughly destroyed. Most of the magnificent timber was simply piled and burned. Logging was rapacious and wasteful. All these activities reflected a belief — unfortunately still common — that nature is to be subdued, that the only worthwhile landscapes are those which produce tangible commodities for human use. The luxuriant tropical rainforests were simply problematic 'scrub' to be conquered.

The future protection of this heritage is at a crucial stage. Despite the strings of superlatives — 'the richest', 'the most diverse', 'the only' — just 14 per cent of the wet tropics is reasonably protected in national parks or reserves. Dr Aila Keto, an authority on the region, has identified five different rainforest types that are either poorly protected or totally unprotected.

The greatest threats to the area lie in logging, roads and clearing for 'tropical paradise' subdivisions. As the timber industry declines as a result of past overuse of an extremely slow-growing resource, its proponents have pressed for access to the more remote and rugged forests. Ironically, it seems to be the sites of most importance, the sites where most primitive endemic species have been located, that would be threatened if logging went ahead. The highly significant Mt Windsor Tableland and the beautiful Downey Creek forests have been largely destroyed by logging.

Right

*I*f left undisturbed, this buttressed fig may one day reach the mighty proportions of other rainforest giants.

*F*orest climbs the slopes of the mist-clad ranges, Hinchinbrook Island.

Other crucial sites which would be destined for the inevitable damage and degradation that logging causes include the Boonjie area, mounts Lewis and Spurgeon and the Lamb Range. If a bridge were ever constructed over the Daintree, logging could well threaten the wonderful hidden valley of the Roaring Meg catchment which lies behind the dramatic peaks of the Cape Tribulation coast.

Fortunately the steady destruction of this priceless area may be drawing to a close. In December 1987 the Commonwealth government nominated the wet tropics for world heritage listing. Most of the areas covered in this chapter are included, except for private lands. The World Heritage Committee will consider the nomination in 1988. Success should mean an end to many of the current destructive activities.

A great deal has been written about the notorious Cape Tribulation to Bloomfield road. Despite the highly questionable need

for such a road, the erodable soils and extremely steep slopes, the local council's bulldozers gouged through this last coastal rainforest wilderness in 1983 and 1984. Not only was immense damage wrought on the wilderness quality of the area and the forests, but the tonnes of run-off as torrential rain gathered up the exposed soils are likely to have damaged the fringing reefs. This road is not an unusual piece of vandalism; rather, it symbolises the ignorance and obstinacy that threaten Australia's natural heritage. A particular problem associated with the forcing of roads into undisturbed areas is the ease with which the cane toad, which is toxic to many wildlife species, can extend its habitat. With successful listing, this road could be closed and the area rehabilitated.

A third threat, which produces anger in most conservationists, is the subdivision of rainforest into residential development between the Daintree River and Cape

Right

*T*he oddly shaped granite peak of Mt Pieter Botte surveys a wilderness of forest, beach and reef.

The destructive subdivision of rare lowland rainforest will not be prevented by world heritage listing.

Only narrow rims of forest survive around the volcanic crater lakes of the Atherton Tableland.

Tribulation. Precious and irreplaceable remnants of tropical lowland rainforest are being carved up to produce quick profits for developers. Because of a decision to exclude privately owned land from the world heritage nomination, listing will not control this environmental vandalism.

The listing of the wet tropics for world heritage status has been one of the major priorities of the conservation movement during the 1980s. The Queensland government has remained adamant that these ancient world-significant forests are its concern alone, even worse, the concern of a few parochial local councillors. It is fervently to be hoped that not only will the 1987 Commonwealth moves to list the wet tropics on the world heritage list succeed, but that subsequent Australian governments will fulfil their international responsibility to manage this precious area to protect its values and restore as much of the damage as possible.

PENELOPE FIGGIS

Left
The Devils Thumb rises a spectacular 1300 metres above the narrow Mossman Gorge.

The Great
Sandy Region

The Great Sandy Region

A living fossil, the king fern (*Angiopteris evecta*) at Central Station.

Cooloola is blessed not only by magic and the uniqueness which it shares with Fraser Island. With Fraser Island, to which it was once joined, it forms an irreplaceable and valuable part of the world's natural heritage.

JOHN SINCLAIR, *Discovering Cooloola*, 1978

Previous pages
*S*wirling patterns of ocean and sand on Fraser Island.

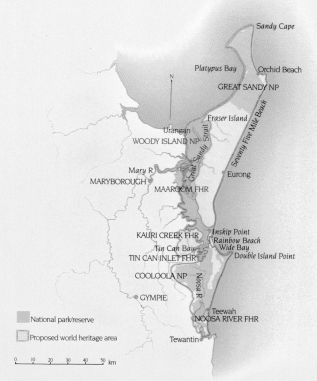

Sandy Cape

Platypus Bay · Orchid Beach

GREAT SANDY NP

Fraser Island

Urangan
WOODY ISLAND NP

Great Sandy Strait

Seventy Five Mile Beach

Eurong

Mary R.
MARYBOROUGH
MAAROOM FHR

KAURI CREEK FHR · Inskip Point
Tin Can Bay · Rainbow Beach
TIN CAN INLET FHR · Wide Bay
· Double Island Point

COOLOOLA NP

Noosa R.

· GYMPIE

Teewah
NOOSA RIVER FHR

· Tewantin

☐ National park/reserve
☐ Proposed world heritage area

0 10 20 30 40 50 km

The rainforest at Central Station on Fraser Island is magnificent. The towering, cylindrical columns of the kauri pines (*Agathis robusta*) and the great shaggy-barked satinays (*Syncarpia hillii*) soar to fifty-five metres. Their crowns create a vaulted ceiling under which a multitude of rainforest plants, piccabeen palms, fragrant carrol trees, ferns, mosses and lichens thrive. Arching over a beautiful creek gigantic ferns with individual fronds five metres long are living relics from the age of dinosaurs.

By any standards this is an outstanding forest. But it is much more than that; it is one of the wonders of the natural world. The creek reveals the miracle. Running through this lush, subtropical rainforest is a perfectly clear stream flowing over pure white sand. These mighty giants and the profuse life beneath are growing in pure sand — in fact, the largest sand island on earth.

Fraser Island, the Cooloola sand mass on the mainland, and the Great Sandy Strait between make up the Great Sandy region in southern Queensland. Fraser Island lies about 160 kilometres north of Brisbane; it is 120 kilometres long, varies from five to twenty-five kilometres wide and covers an area of 172 422 hectares. The Cooloola sand region is a long triangular piece of coastline of some 28 000 hectares with an additional inland area, the western catchment of the Noosa River, which covers 13 000 hectares. Together, Fraser Island and Cooloola create one of Australia's and the world's outstanding natural areas, an essentially wild and beautiful region of dunes, lakes, sea, swamp, heath and forests.

The Great Sandy deserves its place on the world heritage list principally because it is the greatest coastal sand mass in the world. Apart from a single dune, Mt Tempest on nearby Moreton Island, the dunes of the region are the highest and contain the oldest age sequence of any known dunes. These attributes alone make the region of great scientific interest; however, this great sand mass has many other outstanding features. Most surprising is the extensive system of lakes which perch in organically lined depressions, often high in the dunes.

Consolidated sand cliffs, coloured by minerals and eroded into fantastic shapes, are a feature of both Cooloola and Fraser Island.

Perhaps the other most remarkable feature of the region is the wide range of vegetation types — from coastal heath and mangrove communities to well-developed, subtropical rainforest — that the sand masses are able to sustain. The rainforest on Fraser Island is the only rainforest community in the world growing on high coastal dunes. Beyond its obvious scientific value the area is one of exceptional natural beauty, as well as geological, biological and cultural values of international stature.

Fraser Island can be divided roughly into two major regions: the 'top end', which includes most of the Great Sandy National Park; and the southern 'lakes district', which incorporates almost all of the tall forests and perched lakes.

The 'top end', a wild and lonely area that has retained its wilderness quality, is the least known part of the island. It extends from the northern tip of the island where the historic Sandy Cape lighthouse (built in 1870) is situated to near Lake Bowarrady where the tall forests begin. Ironically, this area which, being within the Great Sandy National Park, is the best protected by law, contains few of the island's outstanding elements. Its major features are Lake Wanhai, the largest lake on the island; Indian Head and Waddy Point, the two rocky headlands that punctuate this sand mass; and the spectacular coloured cliffs known as the 'Cathedrals'. The most colourful cliffs lie between Akuna Creek and the national park headquarters at Dundubara.

Both fine rainforest and stately black-butts flourish in the southern zone. High quality forests are found in the upper catchment of Eli Creek, the largest creek on the island and one of the few that flow to the east. It rises in a spectacular small gorge of pristine rainforest and develops into a fast-flowing stream of exquisitely clear green-tinged water. Nearer the beach it flows through pandanus-lined banks and finally empties five million litres of water per hour into the ocean.

Other outstanding forested areas in the centre and south of the island are Yidney Scrub with its giant kauri pines, and Bowarrady Scrub with its distinctive hoop pine overstorey. Central Station is much visited for its superb rainforests.

Fraser Island's astonishing and beautiful perched lakes are in the southern area. Lake McKenzie, one of the most enchanting, has perfectly clear water that is unstained by organic material. This 'white' water over pure white sand produces a shade of aqua-marine that is reminiscent of the Barrier Reef. The lake's beauty is enhanced by a fringe of large gnarled paperbarks.

Apart from the perched lakes the island has several barrage lakes. These are formed when sand blows dam a watercourse. Lake Wabby, the deepest of them, is believed to

Right
The luxuriant rainforests of the Great Sandy region thrive on a foundation of pure sand.

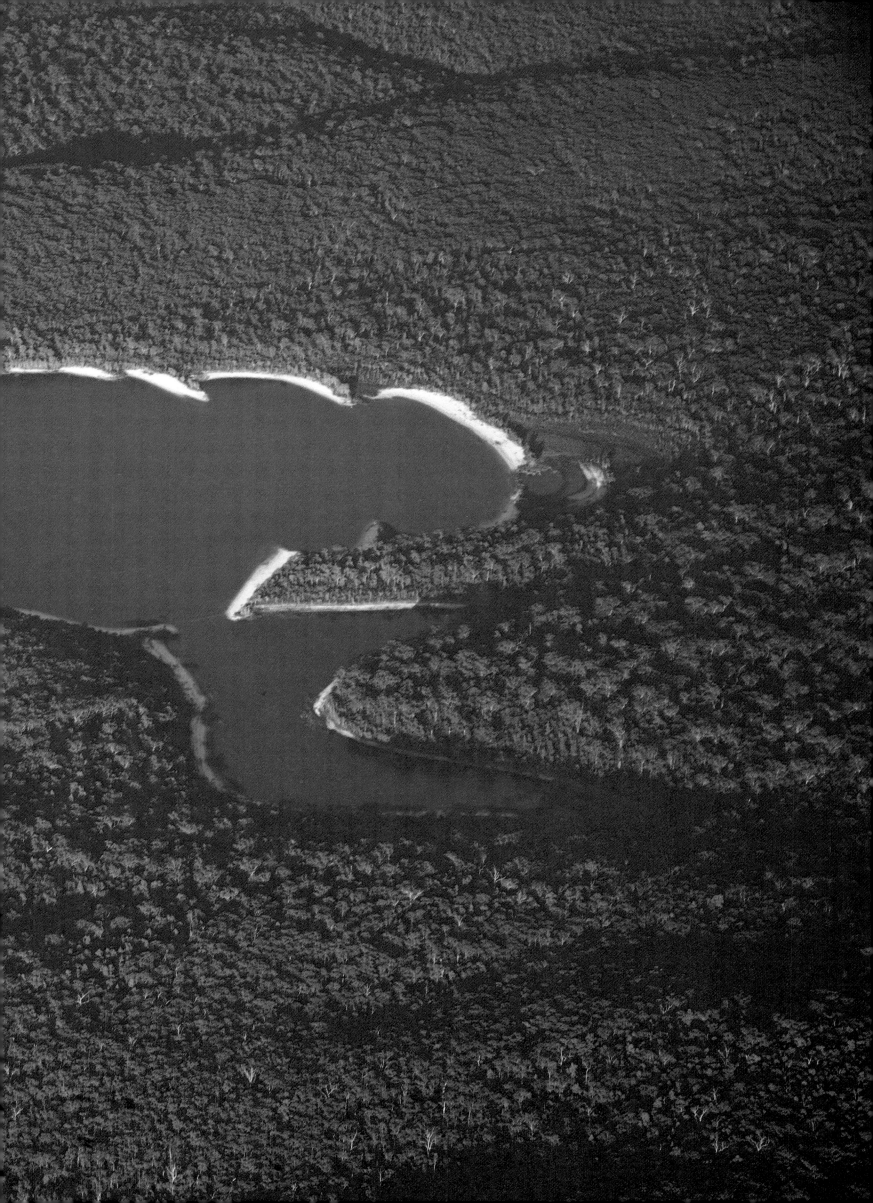

have been sacred and a ceremonial centre to Aboriginal people. It is gradually being engulfed by the same sand blow that created it.

The marine areas of the Great Sandy are the Great Sandy Strait and Tin Can Bay, both tranquil, largely unpolluted estuaries of tidal wetland and extensive mangrove flats. Tin Can Bay is regarded as one of the most pristine natural estuaries in Australia.

Although less famous than the much disputed Fraser Island, Cooloola has its own special qualities. Two long 'zeta curve' (reverse J) beaches are separated by the twenty hectare knob of rocky Double Island Point; both are distinguished by spectacular coloured cliffs. Teewah Beach is a magnificent straight stretch of sixty-four kilometres, starting at Double Island Point and curving to an end at the popular resort of Noosa Heads. North of Double Island Point another long, northwesterly-curving beach terminates at Inskip Point. Both Fraser Island and Cooloola feature sand blow areas where the stabilising vegetation has lost the battle and the relentless winds force the sand inland. The two major sand blows of Cooloola — Carlo Blow (thirty hectares) and Cooloola Sand Patch (120 hectares) — are particularly striking. From a distance the glaring white-massed sand strongly resembles a snowfield.

The Cooloola sand mass, one of Australia's most accessible coastal wildernesses. Behind the steep coloured cliffs that edge the long beaches, sand and stabilising vegetation battle for dominance.

Previous pages
*H*igh in the dunes, the waters of Lake McKenzie are contained by a lining of peat and sand.

*I*n its middle reaches the Noosa River meanders through a tranquil
landscape of *Melaleuca* woodlands.

While the coast gives a feeling of drama, of processes still shaping the land, the landscapes of the Noosa River and its lakes communicate tranquillity. The river rises on the Como escarpment. It meanders through waterlogged treeless heaths in the centre of the park, then passes through a series of shallow lakes, often rimmed with large paperbarks, before joining the sea at Noosa. There are five lakes on the Noosa River: Como, Cooroibah, Doonella, Weyba and the large Lake Cootharaba which covers several thousand hectares.

The Great Sandy region has been created by the accumulation of vast quantities of sand over perhaps 500 000 years. This sand, formed by the grinding down of the ancient mountains of the Great Dividing Range, was tumbled and smashed into ever smaller particles by the fast-flowing rivers of northern New South Wales and southern Queensland. The fine sands were then swept north by the prevailing southeasterly winds until, snagged by rocky outcrops, they piled up into a series of great sand masses stretching some 350 kilometres along the southern Queensland coast. These masses include the Moreton Bay islands — Stradbroke, Bribie and Moreton — which have not to date been included in world heritage proposals. Moreton in particular may have potential as an addition because of its essentially unspoilt wilderness quality and as the location of Mt Tempest (285 metres), the world's highest sandhill.

The principal geomorphic features of the region are the dune systems and the perched lakes. Behind the long ocean beaches that characterise both Cooloola and the east coast of Fraser Island are foredunes, many of which feature richly coloured sands in dramatic eroded shapes. Behind the foredunes lies a great series of dunes. Many of those on Fraser Island are huge U-shapes, or parabolas, their steep sides stabilised by vegetation. The highest dunes on Fraser Island reach 240 metres

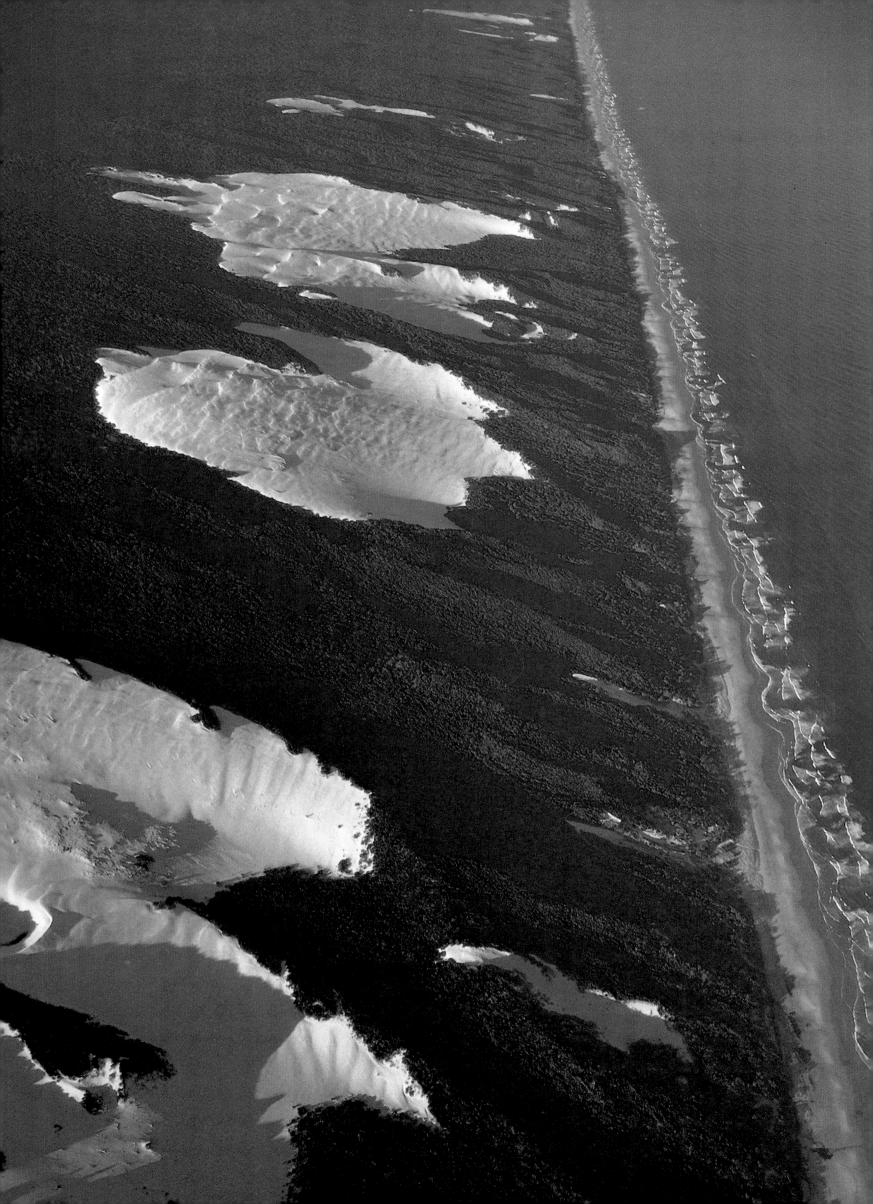

above sea level, while those in Cooloola rise some 280 metres above the ocean beach.

Scientific interest in the dunes arises from their great age. Scientists believe that the sands have been accumulating for hundreds of thousands of years. The dunes certainly contain the most complete representation of dune systems yet recorded in the world. While the oldest verified date is 140 000 years, researchers believe the dunes are probably considerably older. As such, they can tell scientists much about the geomorphology of island sand masses under varying conditions.

The dynamic nature of the region is illustrated by the numerous sand blows — areas where, through storm, cyclone, erosion or disturbance, the sand has broken the protection of the vegetated foredune and is being pushed inland by the prevailing winds. Such blows, which often cover hundreds of hectares, have been likened to glaciers in reverse, their remorseless progress swamping everything in their path.

Fraser Island has forty perched dune lakes; Cooloola has five major lakes. They are formed when organic matter — leaves, bark, dead plants — gradually builds up and hardens in wind-created depressions to create impervious 'saucers' which can hold reserves of water.

Among Fraser Island's lakes are the highest perched lakes in the world, the Boomerang Lakes at 130 metres above sea level, and the largest perched dune lake, Lake Boomanjin, which covers over 200 hectares. Due to the filtration of water through sand, the waters of these lakes are deemed among the purest in the world. Despite their apparently similar origins the lakes differ markedly in character; some nestle among tall forests while others are

Lake Wabby is the deepest of Fraser Island's lakes and contains the most species of fish. It was formed by the damming of a watercourse by a large encroaching sand blow.

Left
The Great Sandy is characterised by long straight beaches and vegetated dunes with large sand patches.

surrounded by open heath and woodland. They also differ in colour: some are absolutely clear; others are reddish, tea-coloured, green, blue, even milky white.

Surprisingly, the sand mass is also a giant water storage, holding up to 30 per cent of its volume as water. This water takes decades to emerge from the sand. It seeps out slowly in tiny rivulets or gushes out in the numerous freshwater creeks — Fraser Island alone has more than fifty creeks. On Teewah Beach the fresh water seeping through the beach sand meets an impervious layer and bubbles up over the beach to create a phenomenon called 'the bubbler'. Smaller bubblers occur elsewhere.

The Great Sandy region supports four main plant communities: rainforest, tall sclerophyll forest, low sclerophyll forest, and grassy woodland and heath. Scientifically the rainforests are classified as simple evergreen notophyll vine forest and mixed notophyll evergreen forest. The principal location for rainforest in both Cooloola and Fraser Island is well-protected corridors between the dunes. The major large trees of the rainforest are satinay (*Syncarpia hillii*), brush box (*Lophostemon confertus*), kauri pine (*Agathis robusta*), piccabeen palm (*Archontophoenix cunninghamiana*) and hoop pine (*Araucaria cunninghamii*). Carrol (*Backhousia myrtifolia*) is common in the understorey. Satinay, with its handsome deeply furrowed reddish bark, has been likened to a smaller Californian redwood. The species is largely confined to the Great Sandy region. Unfortunately for the conservation of these internationally unique forests, most of these species are highly prized for timber and many of the region's forests have been severely degraded by logging, which continues despite a growing international recognition of their importance.

On the forest floor, among the tangle of tree ferns, climbing pandanus, wild passion flowers, orchids and mosses, the most notable plant is the living fossil king fern (*Angiopteris evecta*).

The tall sclerophyll forests of the Great Sandy region are usually located on high dune areas adjoining the rainforested areas. Some of these forests are dominated by the single species blackbutt (*Eucalyptus pilularis*) while others are a mixture of blackbutt with tallowwood (*E. microcorys*), red bloodwood (*E. intermedia*), brush box (*Lophostemon confertus*), scribbly gum (*E. signata*) and forest oak (*Allocasuarina torulosa*).

The low sclerophyll forests are dominated by scribbly gum (*Eucalyptus signata*), bloodwood (*E. intermedia*) and the pink-barked *Angophora costata*. The banksia family, especially *Banksia aemula*, *B. serrata* and *B. integrifolia*, are common elements in these attractive open forests. This forest type occupies the upper catchment of the Noosa River, the Wide Bay training area and substantial areas on the western and eastern margins of the Fraser Island high dunes and in the northern section of the Great Sandy. These low open forests are known as 'wallum', after the Aboriginal name for the banksias which are a major feature of the forests. This plant community

*K*auri and hoop pines are among the most characteristic trees of the Great Sandy's rainforests.

Right
*P*icabeen palms (*Archontophoenix cunninghamiana*) line Woongoolbyer Creek on Fraser Island.

is now poorly represented in protected areas outside the Great Sandy region.

Apart from the four major vegetation divisions there are various important sub-groups including paperbark forest, cypress forest, tall dry heath, coastal pioneer associations, estuarine fringe associations and riverine fringe associations. The Great Sandy region is renowned for spectacular wild-flower displays on the heathlands of the Noosa Plain and Fraser Island. Cooloola has more flowering plants than any other part of coastal Queensland.

Despite the rich mosaic of habitats provided by the flora of the sand masses, the fauna of the region is comparatively sparse. The number of mammal species is low but the region is a significant habitat for the false water rat (*Xeromys myoides*) and the yellow-bellied glider (*Petaurus australis*). There are only two macropodids, the swamp wallaby (*Wallabia bicolor*) and the eastern grey kangaroo (*Macropus giganteus*). The rodents and bats are better represented with seven species of rodent and at least four bats, including the smallest of the nectar-eating bats, the Queensland blossom bat (*Syconycteris australis*), which clings to the banksia with hooked claws to extract its nectar.

Queensland blossom bat (*Syconycteris australis*).

*B*anksias (*Banksia aemula*), grass trees (*Xanthorrhoea* sp.) and paperbarks (*Melaleuca quinquenervia*).

200

Between 200 and 300 dingoes live on Fraser Island; they are regarded as the purest strain of dingo remaining in eastern Australia. A picturesque element of the Fraser Island fauna is the feral horse or brumby. Galloping at full stretch along the beach, these wild horses make an appealing sight, but they trample the foreshores and undoubtedly cause considerable damage.

In contrast to the lack of mammals, the birdlife of the region is abundant, and more than 230 species have been recorded. Among the rare species are the turquoise parrot (*Neophema pulchella*), glossy black cockatoo (*Calyptorhynchus lathami*), bronze-wing pigeon (*Phaps elegans*), powerful owl (*Ninox strenua*), grass owl (*Tyto longimembris*), plumed frogmouth (*Podargus ocellatus plumiferus*) and peregrine falcon (*Falco peregrinus*). Cooloola's low heathland provides one of the last strongholds for the en-

dangered ground parrot (*Pezoporus wallicus*).

The region is an important resting point on the flight paths of migratory wading birds, many of which breed in Siberia. The resident seabirds and waders are probably the most conspicuous wildlife of the Great Sandy region. The handsome Brahminy kite (*Haliastur indus*), with its white head and deep chestnut body, and the white-bellied sea eagle (*Haliaeetus leucogaster*) are frequently seen soaring over the beaches. One of the most common beach residents is the comic pied oystercatcher (*Haematopus ostralegus*) with its formal black and white suit offset by red beak, eyes and legs. It busily probes the sand at the ocean edge, hardly stirring at the passing four-wheel-drive traffic.

The highly acid waters of the perched lakes and swamplands are the habitat for rare varieties of 'acid frogs': Freycinet's

*F*raser Island's dingoes are regarded as the purest strain in Australia.

*B*rahminy kite (*Haliastur indus*).

frog (*Litoria freycineti*), Cooloola tree frog (*L. cooloolensis*), white-striped tree frog (*L. olongburensis*) and wallum froglet (*Ranidella tinnula*).

The marine fauna of the region is rich and diverse. The ocean beaches have always been known to amateur and professional fishermen as havens for many species. A lot of these fish will have bred in the shallow, nutrient-rich mangroves and seagrass meadows of the Great Sandy Strait and Tin Can Bay. These areas are nurseries for numerous fish species and support large populations of prawns and mud crabs. The sheltered estuaries also provide habitats for the endangered dugong (*Dugong dugon*) as well as for dolphins and turtles.

The abundant seafood was part of the diet of the three main Aboriginal groups that occupied this territory: Ngulgbara, Badjala and Dulingbara, subgroups of the Kabi people. Carbon dating of shell middens has established that Aborigines were resident in the region around 300 AD. However, archaeological research has been very

limited and evidence of earlier settlement may still be found. Dr Peter Lauer, curator of the Anthropological Museum, University of Queensland, has identified the area as one of great potential importance, possibly as significant as Willandra Lakes. Two hundred and thirty midden sites have been identified on Fraser Island and more than a hundred in Cooloola.

The demise of the Aborigines began with the arrival of the timber getters in 1862 and the use of the island by merchant seamen who brought disease, alcohol and opium. Numbers rapidly declined and survivors were scattered, far from the tranquil waters full of fish and turtle and the gentle moaning of the she-oaks, for which Cooloola is the Aboriginal name.

The timber industry has been in the region since 1863, attracted principally by the magnificent kauris, hoop pines, satinays

*P*eregrine falcon (*Falco peregrinus*) with fledglings.

*T*he dugong (*Dugong dugon*), a herbivorous mammal.

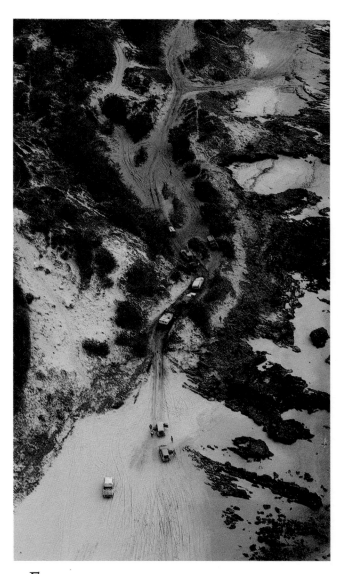

*F*raser Island is heavily used by four-wheel-drive vehicles. Inadequate management policies threaten the fragile ecosystem.

and blackbutts. The era of the bullock teams and steam trains that pulled the great logs to loading jetties finished with the Second World War. Since the war the timber getting on Fraser Island has been far less selective and, aided by technology, far more destructive.

Until the 1960s the region remained the province of the timbermen and the more adventurous fishing enthusiast. Then tourist interest and facilities began to increase. In 1963 the sandminers arrived. The essentially successful battles that followed to safeguard the unique environments of Cooloola and Fraser Island are major chapters in the history of conservation in Australia. They

Left
*T*he Great Sandy Strait between Fraser Island and the mainland is an important marine habitat.

are remarkable stories of remarkable individuals, many of whom dedicated their lives to preserve these places of importance for all Australians.

Despite their efforts and some outstanding victories for conservation, both areas remain vulnerable to damage from many sources. The potential threats to the region cover seven pages of the draft world heritage nomination. Apart from logging, the greatest dangers probably come from the high numbers of people who wish to enjoy these fragile regions. The beaches have become busy highways for four-wheel-drive vehicles which disturb the littoral fauna and violate the wilderness feeling of the area.

Heavy utilisation means the proliferation of tracks and campsites with related erosion and damage to vegetation. This is particularly serious on the fragile foredune vegetation which fights back the shifting sand. Littering, bushfires, denudation for firewood, and sewage pollution of the pure lake and stream waters are just some of the problems associated with an area being 'loved to death'.

The booming tourist town of Noosa to the south of Cooloola has already degraded the estuarine environment at the mouth of the Noosa River with dredging, canal estates and pollution. Developers still look with hungry eyes at the 'potential' of the undeveloped north side of the Noosa River. Tragically, the tall forests of Fraser Island and the Cooloola sand mass continue to be logged. The damage from soil disturbance, tracks and roads is creating conditions conducive to the introduction of dieback.

This outstanding area is at the crossroads. Full acknowledgment could be made of its beauty and importance, and sympathetic management put in place to ensure its high quality is maintained. On the other hand, political wrangling and poor decisions in favour of non-conservation land use could severely degrade this region which, according to mythology, the Aborigines called *K'gari* or 'paradise'.

PENELOPE FIGGIS

Cape York Peninsula

Cape York Peninsula

Termite mounds stand like sentinels in the Lakefield National Park.

*The dominant impression is of a wide open country free of most
restrictions: for some an opportunity to liberate the spirit; for others,
unfortunately, an opportunity for unrestrained plunder and destruction
of wildlife, beauty and Aboriginal heritage.*

PETER STANTON, Botanist and National Parks Investigator

Previous pages
A wild, dark river symbolises the tropical wilderness character of the peninsula.

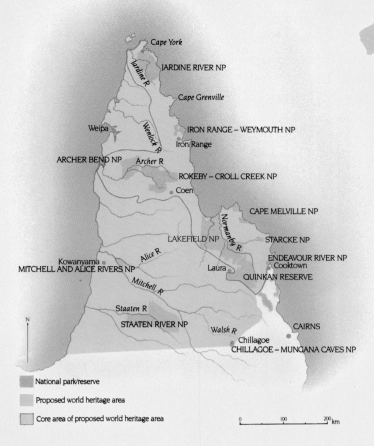

Cape York Peninsula is a big region even by Australian standards. Only by flying over this huge area can one begin to understand its immensity, isolation and diversity. Ideally the observer takes off from Cairns at first light, heading for Cape York by way of the east coast. After Cooktown the traveller leaves behind the tight huddle of rainforest-cloaked coastal mountains and enters a more expansive land. The rainforest is now in patches, a series of islands of darker colour stretching towards the Cape, often in a complex mosaic with eucalypts and grasses. At the Lockhart and Nesbit rivers the rainforest seems to spill down from the ranges, along the rivercourses on to the plains, creating an intricate braided pattern.

Signs of human existence are few. Occasionally there is the merest impression of a road or homestead, but otherwise the boundaries are those of nature. The Olive River is dark and mysterious and then, dramatically, the landscape brightens as the plane flies low over thousands of hectares of sandhills with countless lakes the colour of rich amber.

Another fifty kilometres on and the aviator crosses the 'wet desert' near the Jardine River. The plane loops over Cape York and refuels at Horn Island, before beginning the return down the western side of the peninsula. Now the plane passes over the curling estuaries of major rivers, and then the vast red open cuts of the bauxite mines at Weipa. At the Archer Bend National Park it turns southeast to fly over one of the least known parts of the peninsula — a vast plain of eucalypts and open scrub, with hundreds of lakes and lagoons punctuated by the course of westward-flowing rivers.

A suitable southern boundary for the Cape York Peninsula is a line from Cairns to a point on the Gulf of Carpentaria a few kilometres north of Karumba but excluding the wet tropics area between Cairns and Cooktown. From north to south the region measures about 750 kilometres; at the base it is about 400 kilometres. England and Wales would fit comfortably into its area of 15 million hectares.

The Normanby River flows through the Lakefield National Park into Princess Charlotte Bay.

This is one of the most remote parts of Australia, the tropical counterpart of the wilderness of western Tasmania. Wilderness is a resource for the nurture of the spirit but it is also the best protector of natural scenery and wildlife. The peninsula is among the most important areas in Australia for the protection of threatened species and, like the wet tropics to the south, has the added advantage for conservation of being adjacent to the already listed Great Barrier Reef.

Cape York Peninsula is the nearest part of Australia to New Guinea and over millions of years there has been considerable interchange of fauna and flora: the northeast ranges have rhododendrons and New Guinea has several species of eucalypts. The more humid climate of New Guinea provided a refuge for Australian species during dry periods. The last land connection was between 80 000 and 6500 years ago and, although the peninsula shares many plants and animals with the Trans-Fly area of New Guinea, the biota remains essentially Australian. Elements found also in New Guinea are particularly important in the northern part of the peninsula because the Laura Basin forms a barrier to plant and animal migration.

Rainfall is the main factor in the classification of the region, and the major division is between the wetter east and north and the drier centre and west,

*T*he rainforests of the east coast reflect the wetter climate.

although some writers have recognised the distinctive Laura Basin as a separate subregion. Open forests with patches of rainforest predominate in the east; more open woodlands and shrubs characterise the southwest.

The region's climate is strongly divided into wet and dry seasons, the Wet being associated with the northwest monsoon which lasts from late December until April. For the remainder of the year most of the region experiences drought, the exception being the east coast where the ranges intercept the southeast trade winds, producing cloudiness and showers to create a subequatorial climate with few extremes of temperature. The Iron Range area receives an annual average rainfall of 1980 millimetres, which is typical of the eastern uplands. Most of the tip of the peninsula north of Cape Grenville has over 1600 millimetres annually.

Geologically the area is dominated by two sedimentary basins — the Laura Basin and the Carpentaria Basin — separated by a north–south axis of sedimentary and metamorphic rocks. The axis, which from the Palmer to the Olive River coincides with the Great Dividing Range, is comprised mainly of granite, visible in the beautiful gorges on the eastern side of the McIlwraith Range, but ancient Precambrian shield rocks outcrop on its western fringe. The sedimentaries of the two basins are generally of Quaternary and Recent age. East and south of the Laura Basin harder

Palaeozoic rocks have created higher-lying landscapes. Cretaceous sandstones occur around Laura and between Iron Range and Cape York. A belt of laterite forty kilometres wide is the basis of bauxite mining near Weipa.

The ranges of the eastern axis reach a height of 600 to 800 metres and, with the exception of streams in the Laura Basin, most of the major rivers rise near the east coast and flow westward to the Gulf. In the wet season rivers like the Mitchell and Gilbert have heavy flows which form many channels in the delta areas near the southwest Gulf coast. At the end of the Wet the rivers fade away, but not so the Jardine River in the wetter north which, although it has only a relatively small catchment, has the second greatest flow in Queensland.

The Jardine is a big perennial river, a long-time obstacle to travel, and now an invaluable wilderness national park.

Right
On the southwest Gulf coast, the rivers end in an intricate web of branching channels.

Cape York Peninsula has a number of unique landscapes based on geological conditions. At the southern end of the peninsula, 130 kilometres west of Cairns, is the Chillagoe limestone deposit (Chillagoe–Mungana National Park), heavily eroded by rainwater into fluted columns of stone and limestone caves of great beauty.

Even more spectacular are the series of dunefields at Cape Flattery, Cape Grenville and Orford Ness. The Cape Grenville field between Olive River and Shelburne Bay is the most dramatic, its dunes reaching over 100 metres at White Point. Scores of dunes are moving northwest through the field, with window lakes following inside their trailing arms. Some of the lakes may be

*F*luted columns and shawl-like stalactites are among the many beautiful cave formations at Chillagoe. Grey swiftlets and bats inhabit the extensive cave system.

Previous pages

*T*he Chillagoe limestone is a geological and biological treasurehouse, both above and below the ground.

Right

A balancing rock in the Chillagoe karst.

Mobile dunes, Cape Grenville–Shelburne Bay area.

Patterns form where sand meets water.

perched on impervious rock layers. The angle of the coastline and the topography suggest that these areas are another product of the southeast trade winds.

The greater part of the peninsula is affected by the seasonal nature of the climate, and the vegetation is open eucalypt woodland or savannah. *Eucalyptus tetrodonta*, *E. polycarpa* and *Erythrophleum chlorostachys* are the main species. Areas of heath in the far northeast are the result of the sandstone soils. Open communities are dominated over large areas by very few species, some of which have adapted to a wide range of conditions. *Melaleuca* species, for instance, occur in such widely contrasting situations as vine forest, mangrove swamp and windswept heath. The tall gallery forests on the levee banks of major rivers are often dominated by different *Melaleuca* species — *M. argentea* prevails along the Archer and Wenlock rivers and *M. leucadendron* on the Jardine. Other common *Melaleuca* species include *viridiflora*, *quinquenervia* and *arcana*.

Previous pages

High dunes, dense forest and diverse lakes characterise the peninsula's dunefield landscape.

Right

Surprisingly thick forest thrives on the poor sandy soils of the peninsula's northeast coast.

Saltflats and marine plains occupy the most recently formed land in the deltas of the southwest coast and the northern edge of the Laura Basin. In the latter area the plains are dotted by groves of the attractive palm *Corypha elata*, which flowers once in its lifetime and then dies. Mangroves are common in this zone, the tall mangrove forests fringing Kennedy Inlet near Cape York being the most extensive area of mangroves in Australia.

Conservation interest focuses on the chain of monsoon rainforest areas along the eastern ranges and coasts, and on the gallery forests that follow the corridors of the peninsula rivers. The nature of the rainforest depends to a considerable extent upon the underlying rock and soil types. In the McIlwraith and Iron Range areas the tallest semideciduous mesophyll vine forests are developed on igneous and metamorphic materials and alluvium. Hoop pine

*S*altflats, Lakefield National Park.

Below
*R*ainforest-vaulted creek, Lockhart River district.

*S*ubequatorial rainforest blankets the Iron Range.

Below

*A*n unusual waterfall in the tropical wilderness.

(*Araucaria cunninghamii*) occurs in the forests of this type in the Olive River and southern McIlwraith Ranges areas. On coastal sand country they occur as a lower vine forest with a high sclerophyll content, particularly *Melaleuca* and *Leptospermum* species, and very few semideciduous plants. The largest rainforest area on the peninsula, the Lockerbie Scrub covering about 12 000 hectares near Bamaga, is basically of this type.

One of the most interesting aspects of the rainforest is its occurrence as a vine forest thicket or vine woodland on the coastal foredune where the substratum is sand. As the deciduous or semideciduous species lose their leaves in the dry season, these rainforests have a quite different appearance from those of the wet tropics. Deciduous species in the woodlands include *Bombax ceiba* and *Gyrocarpus americanus*.

It is not easy to determine the role of such factors as soil, climate, hydrology and fire in the complex interrelationships between the sclerophyll and rainforest communities. The early explorers reported on the Aborigines' extensive use of fire throughout the dry season. Signs that the area of rainforest is currently extending in a number of places may be the result of the end of large-scale Aboriginal burning. Another theory suggests that the rainforests may be reconstituting because of more favourable climatic conditions, allowing the gradual accumulation of a limited variety of plant species.

Among the specialised plants of the peninsula is the pitcher plant (*Nepenthes mirabilis*), the largest Australian plant of its kind. It traps and digests insects in its elaborate teacup-sized pitcher to make up for deficiencies in the soil of its swampy home. Another interesting group characteristic of the paperbark forests is the epiphytic ant plants (*Myrmecodia* sp.). Their tuber-like stems function as water storage chambers for the dry season and also serve as homes for colonies of small ants.

The fauna of the region, like much of the flora, awaits detailed investigation. It is at its richest in the mid-peninsula monsoon rainforests of the McIlwraith and Iron ranges. Many of the species shared with New Guinea appear exotic to Australian eyes. The mammals include the spotted cuscus (*Phalanger maculatus*) and the grey cuscus (*Phalanger orientalis*) which, as they have relatively bare faces and sometimes hang upside down from their tails, are often mistaken for monkeys. The cuscuses, the spiny bandicoot (*Echymipera rufescens*), and the bare-backed fruit bat (*Dobsonia moluccensis*) are found only in the monsoon rainforests north of Coen.

Also restricted to these forests are two of Australia's four fruit-eating birds of paradise, the magnificent riflebird (*Ptiloris magnificus*) and the trumpet manucode (*Manucodia keraudrenii*), the strong-beaked palm cockatoo (*Probosciger aterrimus*), the noisy eclectus or red-sided parrot (*Eclectus roratus*), the marbled frogmouth (*Podargus ocellatus*) and a possible local race (*yorki*) of

*E*clectus parrot (*Eclectus roratus*), Cape York.

the helmeted friarbird (*Philemon buceroides*). Similarly, the green-backed honeyeater (*Glycichaera fallax*) reveals its northern affinities by being the only Australian representative of its genus.

The rainforests, with their rich food sources and shelter, are of critical importance for wildlife even though they may cover small areas. Zoologist John Winter found an isolated fifty hectare patch to be 'bursting with bandicoots, pademelons, melomys and scrub fowl'. Pigeons such as the Torres Strait pigeon (*Ducula spilorrhoa*) use the rainforests as they move down the peninsula; they are also the habitat of many species of parrots including the rare double-eyed fig parrot (*Psittaculirostris diophthalma coxeni*) and the red-cheeked parrot (*Geoffroyus geoffroyi*).

The swamps and lagoons of the plains fringing Princess Charlotte Bay in Lakefield National Park provide invaluable dry season refuges for northern waterfowl such as magpie geese (*Anseranas semipalmata*), white pygmy geese (*Nettapus coromandelianus*) and brolgas (*Grus rubicundus*).

Right

*P*alms form an understorey in the dense Iron Range rainforest. Its fauna awaits detailed study.

The Quinkan Reserve contains a wealth of Aboriginal rock art.

Cape York Peninsula has two endemic bird species. The white-streaked honeyeater (*Trichodere cockerelli*) occurs in swamps, while the golden-shouldered parrot (*Psephotus chrysopterygius*) is restricted to termite hill plains in open savannah country. It builds its nests in actively funct-ioning conical-shaped termite mounds.

Saltwater crocodiles still find a secure home in the peninsula rivers, particularly in the major estuaries such as Port Musgrave on the northwest coastline. The green python (*Chondropython viridis*) is an attract-ive resident of the rainforest. There are sev-eral endemic skinks, including *Anomalopus pluto*, known from a single individual near Bamaga, and two endemic species of frogs.

The long-nosed tree frog (*Litoria longirostris*) also occurs in southern New Guinea.

The size of the Aboriginal population of Cape York Peninsula at European contact has been estimated at 10 000, which is about the present total population of the region, including the large mining settle-ment at Weipa. Aboriginal lifestyles varied enormously, with so many different types of country in the region and some influences from outside, including the interchange of materials, ideas and customs with Melanesians to the north.

While Aboriginal physical life has been shattered by the European invasion, the critical aspects of their culture have been retained. The sandstone country south of

Below

Depictions of humans and animals overlap on a Quinkan cave wall.

Laura contains a remarkable record of Aboriginal life extending over thousands of years. In 1960 road builders discovered a major group of Aboriginal art galleries in rock shelters at Split Rock about thirteen kilometres south of Laura. Since then hundreds of galleries have been found; there are probably thousands.

A minimum date of 13 200 years has been determined for the earliest artform, an engraved pecking style. Later works involve the use of many colours in elaborate figurative art. The figures portray plants and animals, aspects of daily life such as hunting, and ancestral beings and spirits. They record innovations in technology and the effect of climatic change on food

227

sources. The area was named Quinkan, after the most important of the supernatural spirits, by Percy Tresize, one of the main discoverers of the galleries. In 1970 Aborigines and Europeans purchased part of Crocodile cattle station to provide better protection for these treasures.

Aboriginal people put up a spirited defence against the European invasion of their land. Dutchman Willem Jansz, whose instructions included the capturing of slaves, lost nine men on the west coast in 1606. In 1770 Captain James Cook claimed the east coast of Australia for King George III on Possession Island rather than risk a ceremony on the mainland.

Land exploration began in the mid-nineteenth century. In 1848 most of Edmund Kennedy's party perished on a journey up the eastern side of the peninsula. In 1864 the Jardine brothers traversed the drier, more open country further west while taking cattle to the newly established port of Somerset. Both parties found that the greatest obstacles were the swamps and rivers of the 'wet desert' around the Jardine River and Kennedy Inlet.

The discovery of gold on the Palmer River in 1872 and then at other locations dealt the Aborigines a further blow. A considerable number of people were killed as miners entered the area and others died as diseases such as influenza, smallpox and syphilis took their toll.

In the last three decades of the nineteenth century the peninsula was divided into cattle stations and the problem of Aboriginal resistance was 'solved' by moving the Aborigines into missions and reserves on infertile coastal sand country. When evaluation of resources in these reserves changed, the Aborigines were quickly pushed aside. A silica sand mining industry was established at Cape Flattery and whole communities were moved to make way for bauxite mining at Weipa. In 1978 the reserves were replaced by shires.

Over the last two decades Aboriginal people have developed an interest in returning to the lands from which they were separated and gaining real title to them. They have been strongly opposed by the government of Queensland, which has favoured more European-style ventures for the Aborigines such as clearing the rainforest near Bamaga and cultivating palm oil plantations at Lockhart River.

Attempts have been made to improve pastures in the Laura Basin and at Heathlands, south of the Jardine catchment, but stocking rates for most of the peninsula are very low. The infertility of the soil, seasonal drought and the great distances from markets have provided a springboard for conservation in the region.

Before 1973 there was only one small park on the peninsula, near Cooktown. Then the state government began to assist leaseholders to extricate themselves from their financial difficulties by creating a series of national parks. Early in 1978 the premier of Queensland announced a long-term program to turn the whole of Cape York Peninsula into a wilderness and wildlife reserve. In the same year the 537 000 hectare Lakefield National Park was purchased. It provides a means for attempting to stop the poaching of young golden-shouldered parrots and other rare birds. Other former cattle stations which became national parks included Staaten River (470 000 hectares), Mitchell and Alice Rivers (37 100 hectares) and Rokeby–Croll Creek (291 000 hectares).

Other national parks which have been established in the peninsula over the last fifteen years include Cape Melville (36 000 hectares), Archer Bend (166 000 hectares), Jardine River (235 000 hectares) and Iron Range–Weymouth (52 150 hectares). Altogether the parks comprise 1 631 000 hectares, approximately 11 per cent of the area of the peninsula.

The promise of a continuous park from Cairns to Cape York is far from being fulfilled, the difficulty being illustrated by the situation at the site of the proposed Olive River–Cape Grenville National Park.

*S*inclair Creek curves through a landscape typical of the Gulf coast.

Here the Queensland government has issued mining leases in the dunefield area and only the intervention of the Commonwealth government in 1987 prevented the development of open-cut silica sand mining for the Japanese glass industry, like that already established at Cape Flattery. Similarly, the government has decided not to proceed with the proposed McIlwraith Range National Park in the richest part of the peninsula rainforest.

The area with the highest wilderness and scientific conservation values is undoubtedly the eastern coastal region from the north shore of the Endeavour River to the tip of Cape York. The Australian Conservation Foundation has proposed that at the latitude of Aurukun the park extend westward across the peninsula from coast to coast. Already the two national parks — Rokeby–Croll Creek and Archer Bend — protect much of the catchment of the Archer River, although the McIlwraith Range decision leaves a big gap.

The establishment of this unified park and its nomination for world heritage list-ing, along with isolated parks in other parts of the region, would greatly improve the position of the Aboriginal people. Consideration would have to be given to granting of title followed by a leasing arrangement similar to those already operating at Kakadu and Uluru.

There are many problems to overcome. Apart from the sand mining proposals there are plans for new bauxite mines, for agricultural developments at Silver Plains, and for logging on the west side of the McIlwraith Range. A proposal to reroute the main peninsula road eastward within the Jardine River catchment would intrude on the peninsula's finest primitive area. Wider land use problems vital to successful conservation include preventing the spread of exotic and feral animals. The region as a whole retains its back country character: roads are still unsealed and are impassable in the Wet. A proposed space centre near Weipa could bring all this to an end and must be assessed in relation to the world heritage values of the region.

GEOFF MOSLEY

The Kimberley

The Kimberley

The boab (*Adansonia gregorii*) is the most distinctive of the Kimberley's trees.

*The peak we had ascended afforded us a very beautiful view: to the
north lay Prince Regent's River . . . to the south and south-westward
ran the Glenelg, meandering through as verdant and fertile a district
as the eye of man ever rested on.*

George Grey, *North-West and Western Australia, 1837–39*

Previous pages
The majestic sandstone ramparts of the Bungle Bungles in the eastern Kimberley.

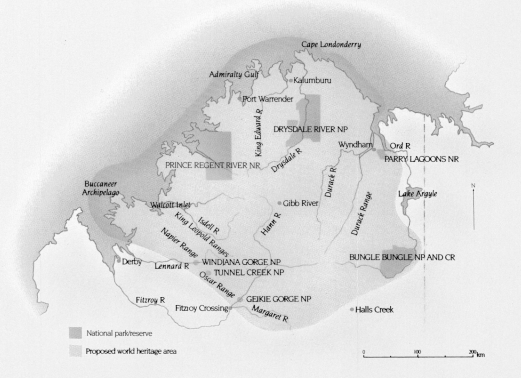

Cape Londonderry

Admiralty Gulf · Kalumburu

Port Warrender

DRYSDALE RIVER NP

Wyndham · Ord R

PARRY LAGOONS NR

PRINCE REGENT RIVER NR

Buccaneer
Archipelago

Lake Argyle

Walcott Inlet · Gibb River

King Edward R
Drysdale R
Durack R
Durack Range

Isdell R
King Leopold Ranges
Hann R

Napier Range

BUNGLE BUNGLE NP AND CR

Derby · WINDJANA GORGE NP
Lennard R · TUNNEL CREEK NP
Oscar Range

Fitzroy R · GEIKIE GORGE NP
Fitzroy Crossing · Margaret R · Halls Creek

National park/reserve

Proposed world heritage area

0   100   200 km

N

ear Port Warrender in the Admiralty Gulf on the northwest Kimberley coast of Western Australia, turquoise seas surge through wide expanses of dense mangroves backed by mudflats. Barramundi and crocodiles frequent these waters, which ebb and flow with the big tides and turn brown with silt during the Wet. High sandstone and basalt cliffs provide a spectacular backdrop to the Timor Sea. Patches of tropical rainforest, thick with foliage and teeming with wildlife, grow under cliffs and stretch up the slopes on to the escarpment and plateau beyond. On the Mitchell Plateau nearby, the eucalypt forest reaches up to thirty metres in height. On the red laterite surface of the higher ground, the understorey is dominated by attractive eight-metre-high Mitchell fan-palms.

This, the wettest part of Western Australia, is also its most biologically diverse. It contains many rare and little studied species of vegetation and wildlife. Rivers like the Mitchell and Lawley flow throughout the year between banks fringed with dense vegetation and thronged with birds. To the west of the plateau, the sandstone country is open but broken, festooned with hummocks of prickly spinifex and dotted with trees. Here the Mitchell Falls drop over ancient rocks into a narrow gorge many kilometres long. Here also are magnificent Aboriginal rock paintings which depict the people and wildlife that once inhabited this land, and the supernatural spirits, the Wandjinas, who created it in the time of the Dreaming.

This is only one small part of the vast, remote, almost pristine northwest Kimberley wilderness. It is a land of contrasts: rugged, beautiful, sparsely populated, truly one of the world's great wilderness areas. It is spectacular country, among Australia's finest, and scientifically extremely important. It is in Australia but belongs to the world. Without any doubt it should be protected as a world heritage area.

The area referred to here as the Kimberley is the northern, wetter and higher half of the state's Kimberley Region. It lies within the tropics and covers some 180 000 square kilometres — an area four-fifths the size of Victoria. At its widest it is about 600 kilometres across. An arc with a radius of 480 kilometres drawn from Cape Londonderry roughly defines the area's southern boundary. Its major subregions are the subhumid coastal region, the tropical semiarid inland region, and the hundreds of islands off the northwest coast.

The north Kimberley has hot wet summers and warm dry winters. The Wet, with temperatures often above 35° Celsius and high humidity, can be most uncomfortable. Not surprisingly, the main tourist season is during the winter Dry when the climate is usually very pleasant. Annual rainfall, which is fairly dependable, varies from about 500 millimetres in the south of the semiarid region to about 1600 millimetres on the Mitchell Plateau in the northwest. Most of the rain is monsoonal; occasional tropical cyclones bring very heavy rain and can cause serious flooding. About 70 per cent of all Western Australia's rain falls in the area. It is drained by some of Australia's largest rivers, including the mighty Fitzroy, the Ord and the Drysdale.

The north Kimberley meets most, if not all, of the criteria required for world heritage listing. It has outstanding biological and geological diversity and richness; extensive areas of wilderness; a spectacular rocky coastline; large areas of mangroves and many patches of rainforest; hundreds of tropical islands, important as wildlife refuges; beautiful gorges and spectacular ranges; and a rich and ancient history of Aboriginal use.

The area contains superlative natural phenomena. Beautiful coral reefs fringe many of the offshore islands. The coast's outstanding features include high cliffs, peaks such as Mt Trafalgar, the spectacular King George, Mitchell and Morgan falls, the giant tides and whirlpools of George

*T*he estuary of the King George River is marked by an eighty-metre drop from rugged sandstone cliffs.

*T*he Drysdale River. The national park that bears its name was
proclaimed in 1973 to protect the area's ranges, rivers and savannah woodland.

Water and Walcott Inlet, the seafall at Talbot Bay, the sheer escarpments overlooking Prince Frederick Harbour and the long, straight run of the Prince Regent River. The inland region includes the fossil-rich Geikie, Napier and Oscar ranges, the Bungle Bungle massif, the beautiful Brooking, Geikie and Manning River gorges, and the dramatic King Leopold, Durack and Carr Boyd ranges.

Within this diverse region there are numerous habitats which support populations of rare plants and wildlife. Many more are still to be identified as most of the area is unstudied or little known to science. Few of the area's extensive forests and woodlands have been cleared. Pastoralism in the inland region has caused substantial soil erosion and water quality problems, but the coastal region has been little disturbed

and remains much as it was before European settlement.

The Western Australian government has considered nominating the Bungle Bungle and Devonian Reef national parks (Geikie Gorge, Tunnel Creek and Windjana Gorge) for world heritage listing. They undoubtedly merit such recognition. Indeed, the Kimberley as a whole merits listing, particularly its wetter northwestern half which includes the Mitchell Plateau, the Prince Regent River Nature Reserve and the Drysdale River National Park. The deeply incised coast extends for some 770 kilometres. Rugged and majestic, swept by huge tides, it is Australia's longest continuous rocky coast and features magnificent harbours, inlets and high cliffs, which sometimes rise precipitously to over 200 metres, as at Mt Trafalgar.

Right

*M*t Trafalgar rises from the surrounding ranges.
Weathering has contributed to the region's
dramatic landscape.

The hundreds of islands on the broad continental shelf off the northwest Kimberley coast formed part of the mainland as recently as 10 000 years ago, before they were isolated by rapidly rising seas. The Buccaneer and Bonaparte archipelagos are the main groups of offshore islands. The islands and coastal region, and most of the inland area, form part of the Kimberley Basin, which consists of ancient sedimentary and volcanic rocks, mostly Proterozoic sandstones. These have been heavily eroded to produce rugged plateaus with deep gorges and impressive escarpments. During the Devonian period, some 360

*W*olf Creek crater, the remains of a meteoritic impact, is the second largest in the world.

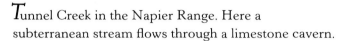

*T*unnel Creek in the Napier Range. Here a subterranean stream flows through a limestone cavern.

Previous pages

*T*he rugged cliffs of Geikie Gorge, cut through an ancient limestone reef by the Fitzroy River.

Right

*H*ardy vegetation clings to the clefts between the jagged battlements of Windjana Gorge.

million years ago, geological processes in the south of the area created two spectacular formations — the Bungle Bungle massif in the southeast and the Devonian Reef limestone ranges in the southwest.

The Bungle Bungle massif is Australia's finest example of sandstone towers, which rise to nearly 300 metres above the surrounding sandplain. Unique depositional processes and weathering have given them their spectacular black and orange banded appearance. A large meteoritic impact crater in the centre of the massif has added to its geological interest. The Devonian Reef ranges stretch over many kilometres and rise to a hundred metres above the surrounding plains. They are a relic from the time when most of the area was mainland fringed by a tropical sea. Some of the limestones are rich in fossils, mainly algae and corals. Strange armoured fish (placoderms) were dominant in these ancient seas. Their fossils can be seen in concretions scattered over the plains that were once reef lagoons.

The Kimberley is in Western Australia's North Botanical Province, with the Great Sandy Desert to the south marking the change to the dry Eremaean Botanical Province. Vegetation in the area has closer links with that to the north and east than to the south. Due to continental drift, at some time millions of years in the past, elements of Indo–Malesian vegetation and wildlife invaded Australia. These links with Southeast Asia are most noticeable in the mangroves and rainforests along the coast.

For millions of years, the forces of wind, rain and storm have weathered the rocks of the Kimberley, shaping them into strikingly beautiful patterns and textures.

Right
The northwestern area of the Bungle Bungles is less well-known than other parts of the sandstone massif.

*T*he thickly vegetated Mitchell River in the north Kimberley meanders through the Mitchell Plateau and drains into the Admiralty Gulf.

A significant number of Kimberley species are not found elsewhere in Australia or extend eastward for a relatively short distance into the Top End of the Northern Territory. The most interesting of these is undoubtedly the boab (*Adansonia gregorii*), an extremely important plant to the Aborigines. Massive and gnarled, this long-lived tree grows on sandy plains, stony ridges and in creekbeds throughout the area. It is one of ten species in the genus *Adansonia* which probably share a common·ancestry in the ancient southern supercontinent of Gondwana. Eight are endemic to Madagascar and the other, the baobab, is widespread on the African mainland.

The Kimberley has five main vegetation types: mangroves, dense rainforest, riverine vegetation, savannah woodlands (mainly on sandstone but some on basalt) and hum-mock grasslands. The subhumid coastal region, and to a lesser extent the islands, have all of these types. However, the semi-arid inland region has no saltwater mangroves, few rainforests, little riverine vegetation and more open woodlands, which become increasingly sparse away from the coast as the land becomes drier.

Mangroves occur along the whole of the Kimberley coast and are most extensive in gulfs and inlets which offer some protection from wave action. There are large stands at George Water, Secure Bay, Port Warrender and St George Basin. Seventeen species have been recorded in Western Australia and all occur in the area. The holly-leaved mangrove (*Acanthus ebracteatus*) has been found only along the King River near Wyndham while the yamstick mangrove (*Scyphiphora hydrophyllacea*) is restricted to

Previous pages
*T*he scalloped towers of the Bungle Bungles rise nearly 300 metres from the sandplain.

Right
*T*o the Aborigines, the boab was a special tree, a source of shelter, food, ornaments and even water.

A fig (*Ficus* sp.) clings to a rocky outcrop.

the coast near Cape Londonderry, the state's northernmost point. However, both species are found elsewhere in the tropics.

Some 500 patches of rainforest, the largest covering about 100 hectares, have been recorded in the area. Because they are isolated remnants, they have a high conservation value. More than 300 plant species have been found in these forests, four-fifths of which are unique to this habitat. Most are of Indo–Malesian origin, evergreen or semideciduous, and in appearance have little in common with the hard-leaved eucalypts and acacias typical of Australia. They include trees up to thirty metres high, vines, shrubs and ferns.

The riverine vegetation fringing rivers, creeks, perennial waterholes and swamps is dominated by cadjeput trees, including *Melaleuca leucadendron* and *M. argentea*. Screw pines such as *Pandanus aquaticus*, gums such as the river red gum (*Eucalyptus camaldulensis*), figs and ferns are some of the many species found. The freshwater mangrove (*Barringtonia acutangula*), a small tree

*F*igs, screw pines, eucalypts and native tropical grasses are nourished by this Kimberley billabong.

*F*reshwater mangrove (*Barringtonia acutangula*).

with pendulous sprays of red flowers, the striking Kimberley Christmas tree (*Grevillea pteridifolia*), and the tropical *Banksia dentata*, which has attractive golden flowers, all favour seasonally wet sites.

Eucalypts and, to a lesser extent, acacias dominate the savannah woodlands. The trees are often fairly stunted. Gums which favour sandstone include the widely distributed silverleaf bloodwood (*E. collina*) and woollybutt (*E. miniata*). The tropical red box (*E. brachyandra*), Kimberley gum (*E. confluens*) and Kimberley yellowjacket (*E. lirata*) are more restricted. Two acacias, *A. delibrata* and elephants-ear wattle (*A. dunnei*), and the kapok bush (*Cochlospermum fraseri*) are common on sandstone areas, while the cycad (*Cycas basaltica*) favours basalts. The Drysdale fan-palm (*Livistona loriphylla*) grows on sandstone while the Mitchell fan-palm (*L. eastonii*) is usually found on laterite. Grasses in the savannah include spinifexes, particularly the curly spinifex (*Plectrachne pungens*) and *Triodia* species, and canes (*Sorghum* spp). The open hummock grasslands include a wide range of grasses. Shrubs found in this habitat include *Hakea arborescens* and the native bauhinia (*Lysiphyllum cunninghamii*).

Sixty-two species of native mammals are known from the area, some fifty of which live in the Mitchell Plateau region. Many have a restricted distribution. These mammals include the warabi (*Petrogale burbidgei*), golden bandicoot (*Isoodon auratus*), scaly-tailed possum (*Wyulda squamicaudata*), rock ringtail (*Pseudocheirus dahli*), little northern native-cat (*Dasyurus hallucatus*), little rock wallaby (*Peradorcas concinna*), golden-backed tree-rat (*Mesembriomys macrurus*), a native mouse (*Pseudomys laborifex*), the tree-dwelling black flying fox (*Pteropus alecto*) and ghost bat (*Macroderma gigas*).

The Kimberley's extensive mangroves and rainforests have an abundance of fruit, flowers and leaves, and teem with insects. They support a wide range of wildlife. The mangroves contain the richest mangrove bird fauna in the world. They include the Kimberley flycatcher (*Microeca tormenti*), dusky gerygone (*Gerygone tenebrosa*) and collared kingfisher (*Halcyon chloris*).

The birds of the Kimberley rainforest include the rose-crowned pigeon (*Ptilinopus regina ewengii*), rufous owl (*Ninox rufa*), orange-footed scrub fowl (*Megapodius reinwardti*), and rainbow pitta (*Pitta iris*). The elaborate display bowers of the greater bowerbird (*Ptilonorhynchus nuchalis*) are often found. The rare rough-scaled python (*Morelia carinata*) lives in this habitat but is seen very infrequently. The rainforests also contain at least seventy species of land snail, many restricted to this habitat.

The riverine vegetation, too, supports a large number of birds. Two riverine species are the purple-crowned fairy wren (*Malurus coronatus*) and the partridge pigeon (*Geophaps smithii blaauwi*), the latter favouring riverine flats. Birds which favour sandstone outcrops in the savannah woodlands include the black grasswren (*Amytornis housei*), the white-lined honeyeater (*Meliphaga albilineata*) and the white-quilled rock pigeon (*Petrophassa albipennis*).

Most reptiles restricted to the Kimberley are found in the subhumid coastal region. They include the superb dragon (*Diporiphora superba*), the bearded dragon (*Amphibolurus microlepidotus*), the elapid snake *Demansia simplex*, the geckos *Gehyra xenopus* and *G. occidentalis*, the skinks *Ctenotus burbidgei* and *Lerista walkeri*, and two undescribed species of burrowing frogs. The skinks *Egrenia douglasi* and *Lerista apoda* are found in the south and east Kimberley.

The islands are important breeding sites for seabirds and turtles, including flatback turtles (*Chelonia depressa*), believed to nest only on Australian coasts. Most of the area's rare native animals are found on one or more of the islands, which are thus important refuges. Noteworthy fish include the barramundi (*Lates calcarifer*), Leichhardt's sawfish (*Pristiopsis leichhardti*) and coachwhip stingray (*Himantura uarnak*).

*L*ittle corellas (*Cacatua sanguinea*).

*B*arnett River Gorge, north of Derby.

*W*andjina figures, Mitchell Plateau.

Aborigines have lived in the area for at least 40 000 years and possibly much longer. Traditionally, they lived in distinct communities and centred their lives on the river valleys and waterholes, which helped support quite large populations and harboured plant and animal resources. The valleys also provided pathways through country which is often extremely rugged. The boab was their special tree; it provided shelter, camp sites, seeds for food and ornaments, gum, bark for twine, and sometimes even water.

The tribes exchanged rare and prized materials such as ochre and flints along trade routes that stretched far beyond their own lands. Although their rock paintings are widespread, the most outstanding are found in the sandstone region of the northwest, in Wororan country. The Wororan tribes produced Western Australia's most dramatic paintings — the spirits called Wandjinas and the Bradshaw 'stick' figures.

European occupation, starting in the 1870s and preceded by smallpox and other foreign diseases, devastated these people. Their waterholes and sacred sites were invaded and vast tracts of tribal lands were taken for cattle stations. Gold discoveries inland and the pearling fleets along the coast added to the disruption. Those who resisted were often hunted down and killed, occasionally in large numbers. Some found refuge in remote places such as the ranges and Bungle Bungle massif. One legendary

*T*he Mitchell Plateau has attracted recent scientific interest as a region of rich and unique flora and fauna.

Cockatoo Island is one of hundreds of islands off the northwest Kimberley coast.

leader, Jundumurra, led the fight against European settlement in the west Kimberley for three years before being killed in 1897.

The disruption continued well into the twentieth century. Aboriginal children were taken from their parents and subjected to a European education. Different tribes were forced together at feeding stations, on missions and settlements outside towns. They were taken away from the bush and firmly repressed. Tribal lands were depopulated to the extent that the lush and once well-populated land between the Prince Regent and Glenelg rivers, which George Grey explored in 1838, is now uninhabited.

Some 2600 Aborigines live in the north Kimberley today, making up about 30 per cent of the sparse population of the area. Although much of their traditional tribal knowledge has been lost, families and groups are now returning to their ancestral lands and living, in part, off the bush. The homelands settlement movement is gaining strength and the younger generation is showing renewed interest in the past. Aborigines are being appointed as rangers and

the Purnululu Aboriginal community, traditional owners of the Bungle Bungle, is having a voice in its management.

The Kimberley also has an interesting non-Aboriginal history. Fishermen from the north, now Indonesia, have visited the coast and offshore islands for many centuries to collect bêche de mer, trepang, clams and other shellfish. Dutch navigator Abel Tasman sailed close to the coast in 1644. He was followed by the English adventurer, William Dampier, in 1687 and the French explorer, Nicolas Baudin, in 1801 and 1803. Philip Parker King, an Australian, charted the Kimberley coast from 1818 to 1822; George Grey explored a small part of the northwest in 1838. Alexander Forrest discovered the extensive grasslands of the Fitzroy and Ord river valleys in 1879. His glowing reports fuelled the scramble for pastoral lands in the 1880s, led by the Duracks, Emanuels and other 'overlanders' from Queensland. It was not until 1901, however, that the remote coastal region was properly explored, by Frederick Brockman.

The greatest threats to the north Kimberley lie in the lack of protection for its many fine areas. They need to be protected in at least eight ways — through legislation; through proper assessment; against the spread of exotic species, particularly feral animals; against wanton destruction of wildlife and vegetation; through community education; through the employment of many more people as managers; and against the powerful forces of mining and pastoralism.

Over half the north Kimberley, including the wilderness covering about 90 per cent of the coastal region, merits reservation for conservation. However, only 8 per cent, in ten localities covering 14 400 square kilometres, has been reserved. All but 500 square kilometres of this are within the three largest reserves — Prince Regent River, Drysdale River and Bungle Bungle. The Department of Conservation and Land Management has recommended that another 5200 square kilometres (2.9 per cent), including some Aboriginal lands, should also be reserved. The Walcott Inlet, Carr Boyd Range, Cape Londonderry, part of the Oscar and Napier ranges and the offshore islands are the largest of these. Another 3230 square kilometres of Crown land at Rust Range may also be included after study.

The above localities total nearly 13 per cent of the area. However, there is a good case for at least half the area to be included in conservation reserves. The laterite-rich Mitchell Plateau, coveted by miners, the Gibb River Road gorges and escarpments, the King Leopold and Durack ranges, the full extent of the Oscar–Napier–Geikie ranges from the Gibb River Road to National Highway 1 and the Chamberlain River country are some of the outstanding localities which merit conservation status.

The number of visitors attracted to the area is increasing rapidly but is not being matched by funds for management. Research funding is meagre. There is no ranger or fisheries officer at the Prince Regent and Drysdale rivers, the two largest conservation reserves in the Kimberley.

*I*n the Dry, the remote Mitchell Falls are a thin stream; in the Wet they become a raging torrent.

The third largest, Bungle Bungle National Park, is under increasing pressure from tourists but there are not enough rangers and facilities are almost non-existent.

Due to the shortage of rangers, some of the area's outstanding wildlife and vegetation is being stolen or destroyed, including beautiful finches and spectacular tree orchids. Aboriginal sites are being vandalised. Modern exploration is mainly for minerals and conservation reserves are not off-limits, the Drysdale River National Park being a particular target. The state government's latest move — to allow mineral exploration in conservation reserves subject to parliamentary approval — indicates that it is unlikely to nominate any part of the area for world heritage listing. Hopefully, a future government will reverse this policy. When that is done, much of the spectacular wilderness country of the north Kimberley may be given the protection it deserves in a world heritage area.

DAVID DALE

Shark Bay

Shark Bay

*T*he ancient algal stromatolites of Shark Bay are the finest in the world.

Shark Bay is a natural area of international value. It was once, and may in the future become, a major area of concentration of great whales. It is home for rare marsupials . . . splendid populations of ospreys, eagles and seabirds . . . and sea turtles . . . It is a place of uncommon wildness, beauty and freedom, whether in storm or peaceful sunset.

PROFESSOR PAUL ANDERSON, letter to the Dolphin Welfare Foundation, Shark Bay, 1983

Previous pages
*D*isappointment Reach. Sand and seagrass are features of the Shark Bay landscape.

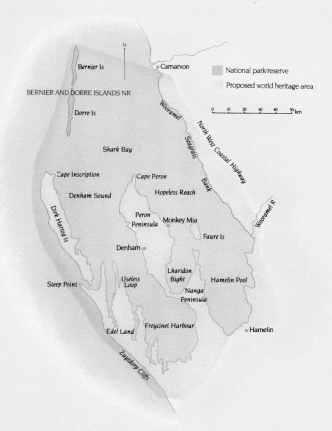

Shark Bay is the best natural harbour on the west coast of Australia, and its warm and sheltered waters are home for an abundance of creatures. The world's finest algal stromatolites accumulate in the blue hypersaline waters of Hamelin Pool, whose shores are built of countless tiny white coquina shells. Further north, along the eastern arm of Shark Bay, the world's only wild dolphins accustomed to a human presence frolic among tourists who flock to share the waters with them at Monkey Mia. Out in the bay several hundred dugong, one of the world's largest populations, forage on extensive seagrass meadows which also provide food and shelter for countless other marine fauna. The bay teems with many species, including sharks, manta rays, turtles, seasnakes, occasional humpback whales, and large schools of fish and shellfish. Magnificent limestone seacliffs, some over 100 metres high, flank the west of the bay for over 160 kilometres.

The Shark Bay area is about 250 kilometres long and 130 kilometres wide. It covers some 35 000 square kilometres, about 60 per cent of which is sea. Among its distinctive marine features are Hamelin Pool, the Faure Sill and the Wooramel seagrass bank. Dirk Hartog, Bernier and Dorre islands, the Edel Land, Peron and Nanga peninsulas, and Steep Point are noteworthy land features of the region.

The area is semiarid, the western part being wetter than the east. The average annual rainfall is below 300 millimetres and the annual evaporation rate seven times higher. The climate is warm Mediterranean with hot, dry summers and mild winters. Most of the little rain falls during winter but rain-bearing cyclones occasionally blow through from the north in summer. Strong southerly winds are common during the summer, when the area experiences about thirty days of high heat discomfort. The area forms part of the Carnarvon Basin, a thick sequence of sedimentary rocks mainly deposited in the Cretaceous and Tertiary eras. The younger deposits form the peninsulas that enclose Shark Bay. They generally consist of sandstone on the Peron and Nanga peninsulas and limestone on the west coast.

259

These rocks are extensively overlain by much younger sands, of quartz and limestone, which were shaped by ancient winds to form series of longitudinal dunes. These now well-vegetated dunes vary in colour and have ridges up to fifty metres high. This striking landform is very noticeable on the Peron and Edel Land peninsulas.

The algal stromatolites of Hamelin Pool are the outstanding natural feature of the area. They are accumulated extremely slowly from sediments trapped by blue-green algae which thrive in the hypersaline waters. They form a variety of weird shapes, including 'toadstools'. Stromatolites represent the oldest form of life on earth, first forming some 3500 million years ago. Hamelin Pool is the only place in the world with a range of stromatolite forms comparable to fossils in ancient rocks.

The Faure Sill, a large, shallow sand and seagrass bank stretching across the eastern arm of the bay, greatly restricts tidal flushing into Hamelin Pool and Lharidon Bight. This, together with the low rainfall and high evaporation rate, has created waters up to twice as salty as 'normal' seawater.

Among the unusual phenomena produced in this unique marine environment are the ooid shoals and coquinas. Ooid shoals are limestone sands caused by precipitation of calcium carbonate from hypersaline waters. They are common in ancient geological sequences but rarely found in modern seas. Coquinas are sedimentary rocks made of the shells of marine organisms. At Shark Bay they have accumulated from populations of a small bivalve, *Fragum hamelini*. Spectacular white beaches, such as Shell Beach on Lharidon Bight, and beach ridges show where they are forming today. These light, white rocks are easily sawn and blocks have been quarried at Hamelin Pool for use in local buildings.

*S*hell Beach is made up of millions of bivalve shells. Coquinas, the rocks formed from these organisms, have been used as a unique local building material.

Right

*V*egetated dunes on Dirk Hartog Island. The island has potential as a valuable nature reserve.

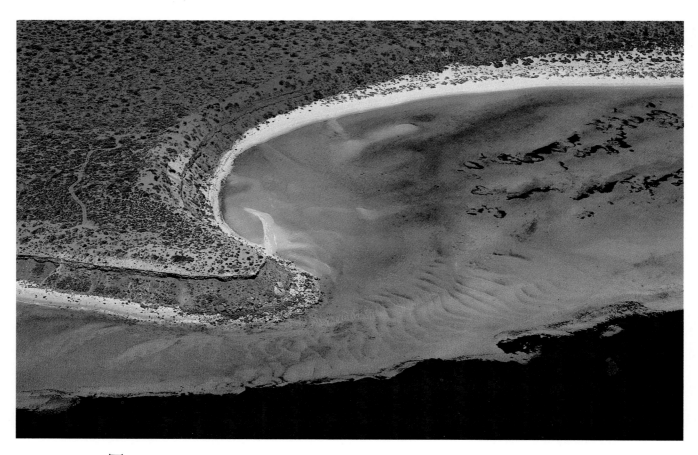

*T*he wilderness coastline of Peron Peninsula: on the east (*above*) and west (*below*).

The seacliffs and claypans are other out-standing geological features of the area. Magnificent light brown limestone cliffs stretch almost continuously for over 300 kilometres from Kalbarri, well to the south, to historic Cape Inscription on the north of Dirk Hartog Island. They include the spectacular Zuytdorp cliffs and Steep Point, the most westerly point on the Australian mainland. They reach their highest on Dirk Hartog Island. High and spectacular cliffs also occur elsewhere at Shark Bay, especially on the Peron Peninsula. There the greyish cliffs at Eagle Bluff, near Denham on the west coast, provide a vivid contrast with the burnt orange-red cliffs that stretch between Monkey Mia and Herald Bluff on the opposite coast.

Claypans, sometimes referred to as 'birridas', are common in interdunal depressions on the Peron and Nanga peninsulas. Rich in gypsum, they usually swell to form a central raised platform, surrounded by a 'moat' which is normally dry.

Right
*T*he imposing but treacherous Zuytdorp cliffs bear the scars of their battering by the Indian Ocean.

A view from the continent's western edge across South Passage to Dirk Hartog Island.

*S*altpans stretch across the coastal flats.

Big Lagoon, an attractive, biologically important feature north of Denham, is probably a series of claypans in the making.

Shark Bay, by virtue of its position on the west coast, was a key destination for European navigators visiting New Holland in the seventeenth and eighteenth centuries. Antonie Caen visited the bay in 1636 and was the first European to record sighting the black swan, state emblem of Western Australia. William Dampier explored Shark Bay in the spring of 1699 and saw many strange plants and animals. He was the first European to describe kangaroos (presumably the banded hare-wallaby), the wedge-tailed eagle and shingleback. He named the bay after the abundance of sharks and found the remains of a dugong, which he thought was a hippopotamus!

In 1801 Nicolas Baudin was impressed by green turtles and great numbers of large whales in the bay. His scientists spent about fifteen days on Bernier Island, where they collected ten species of birds and seventy plant specimens, then mostly unknown to science, as well as new species of fish, shellfish, reptiles and insects.

*T*he dugong, one of Shark Bay's treasures.

Bernier and Dorre islands are now important nature reserves which provide island refuges for at least eight species of rare native fauna.

The vegetation, both in the sea and on land, is of world importance. Shark Bay is at the meeting point of Western Australia's three main climatic regions. It is also at the transition of two of the three botanical provinces in the state and thus contains a mixture of two biotas. The bay's dominant organism is seagrass, which grows prolifically in the shallow, protected waters where light intensities are high. Seagrass covers about 4000 square kilometres, including most of the southern waters other than hypersaline Hamelin Pool and Lharidon Bight. It is most abundant in the eastern waters. There the Wooramel seagrass bank covers an area of some 1030 square kilometres, extending for over 130 kilometres with an average width of eight kilometres and to a depth of about eight metres. The seagrass bank is the largest structure of its type in the world and is a vital part of the Shark Bay ecosystem.

The seagrass beds provide the only food source for the many dugongs in Shark Bay. They are also nursery areas for some fish, prawns and other shellfish, and feeding areas for turtles, seasnakes and cormorants. There are fifteen species of seagrass in the bay, of which *Amphibolis antarctica* is the most common. It occurs at the northern

*T*he Faure Sill partially encloses Hamelin Pool, creating a uniquely hypersaline marine environment.

*E*xtensive saline flats and seagrass banks mark the Wooramel River delta.

limit of its range and contrasts with *Halodule uninervis*, a tropical species. A large bed of the latter, off the Wooramel River delta near Gladstone on the east coast, provides a crucial summer food supply and refuge for the dugong herd.

The transition between the two genera, *Eucalyptus* and *Acacia*, which dominate Australia's vegetation is highlighted at Shark Bay. The *Eucalyptus*-rich South West Botanical Province is at its northern limit on the white sandplain country in the southwest. The drier Peron Peninsula and east coast have reddish soils and form part of the Eremaean Botanical Province, dominated by *Acacia*. The transition from one province to the other lies close to the main road running up the Nanga Peninsula. There is a mix of species from the two provinces along Edel Land and on Dirk Hartog, Bernier and Dorre islands.

The western coastal dunes are covered with the coarse *Spinifex longifolius* and shrubs such as *Olearia axillaris* and *Myoporum insulare*. The southwestern vegetation occurs as dense heath — trees, shrubs and herbs, with a wide variety of species. These include eucalypts, hakeas, melaleucas and other members of the myrtle family, and acacias. The York gum (*E. loxophleba*) is at its northern limit but *E. roycei* and *E. beardiana* occur only in this area. Other outstanding species found only at Shark Bay are *Beaufortia dampieri*, an *Eremaea* species, *Grevillea rogersoniana* and false paperbark (*Lamarchea hakeifolia*). Their attractive blossoms add to the glorious wildflower displays which appear in the area every July and August. *Newcastelia chrysophylla*, *Stipa crinita*, *Acanthocarpus robustus* and *Macarthuria intricata* are also only found locally.

*A*n extensive stand of white mangroves (*below*) grows at Guichenault Point, Peron Peninsula (*above*).

In contrast with the southwestern vegetation, the arid Eremaean vegetation is much more open. Belts of acacia scrub and spinifex grassland, typical of Western Australia's desert flora, predominate. The principal species at Shark Bay are Bowgada scrub (*Acacia ramulosa*) and two hummock grasses, *Triodia plurinervata* and a soft spinifex, *Plectrachne schinzii*. *Acacia drepanophylla* and *A. galeata* are restricted to the region. The state's southernmost extensive mangroves, a stand of white mangrove (*Avicennia marina*), occurs at Guichenault Point on the Peron Peninsula.

Dampier explored Dirk Hartog Island in August 1699, at the height of the flowering season. He was impressed by some very small blue flowers. These were the species *Dampiera incana*, one of fifty species in Western Australia of a genus that now bears his name. The everlasting daisies in

*D*enham Sound separates the eastern coast of Dirk Hartog Island from the mainland.

the area are magnificent in spring. *Cephalipterum drummondii*, in whites and yellow, and pink *Schoenia cassiniana* are particularly common species.

With such diverse vegetation it is no surprise that the area also harbours a rich selection of wildlife. A significant number of species are rare or endangered. Bernier and Dorre islands are key refuges since they contain the only known populations of three species of native mammals which were once more widespread: the banded hare-wallaby (*Lagostrophus fasciatus*), the barred bandicoot (*Perameles bougainville*) and the Shark Bay mouse (*Pseudomys praeconis*). The rufous hare-wallaby (*Lagorchestes hirsutus*) is found only here and in a small area of the Tanami Desert. The boodie (*Bettongia lesueur*) is found only on Bernier and Dorre and two other islands, about 600 kilometres further north, while the variegated fairy-wren (*Malurus lamberti bernier*) is restricted to Bernier Island.

Dirk Hartog Island once had populations of the same marsupial species as Bernier and Dorre islands. It has the only known populations of the white-winged fairy-wren (*Malurus leucopterus leucopterus*), a subspecies of the blue and white fairy-wren, common on the nearby mainland.

The many islands and the mainland of Shark Bay support other important bird populations, including the white-bellied sea-eagle (*Haliaeetus leucogaster*), the pied cormorant (*Phalacrocorax varius*) and the wedge-tailed eagle (*Aquila audax*). The thick-billed grasswren (*Amytornis textilis textilis*), an endemic bird species, is restricted to thick acacia scrub mainly near Big Lagoon on Peron Peninsula.

Shark Bay is on the edge of the western desert and has become a refuge area for a diverse reptilian fauna. It supports thirteen reptile families and nearly 100 species, the distribution of which is largely determined by the soil types. Many of the reptiles are

272

known only from a few specimens and much remains to be discovered about their biology and habitat requirements.

There are thirty-two species and subspecies of skinks in the area, the shingleback (*Trachydosaurus rugosus*) being very common. *Lerista connivens*, *L. humphriesi* and *L. petersoni* are three sand-swimming skinks found only at Shark Bay. Geckos, including *Diplodactylus michaelseni*, snakes such as the blind-snake (*Typhlina leptosoma*) and dragon lizard species are also found. Ten of the thirty dragon lizard species found in Australia occur in the vicinity of Shark Bay.

The large islands and peninsulas of Shark Bay provide a refuge for seven endemic reptile species. They include the recently discovered sandhill frog (*Arenophryne rotunda*), a new genus which seems to have no need for surface water, the legless lizard (*Aprasia haroldi*) and the skinks *Ctenotus youngsoni* and *Menetia amaura*. Further studies in the area will no doubt lead to the discovery of new reptile and insect species.

Shark Bay is justly renowned for its marine mammals and other marine fauna. The Shark Bay population of dugong (*Dugong dugon*), which is at its southern limit in the bay, is scientifically among the most important in the world. The bay's bottle-nose dolphins (*Tursiops truncatus*) are becoming increasingly well known. Tourists flock to the Peron Peninsula to marvel at, feed and interact with them in the waters off the beach at Monkey Mia. Such acclimatisation to humans is found nowhere else in the world. Another mammal, the huge humpback whale (*Megaptera novaeangliae*), uses the bay's sheltered waters as a wintering area. Plentiful at Shark Bay until the early 1800s, these mighty creatures are returning in slowly increasing numbers after having been hunted almost to the point of extinction.

Green (*Chelonia mydas*) and leatherback (*Caretta caretta*) turtles occur in the bay near their southern limits. They nest in significant numbers on the northern beaches

*L*eatherback turtle (*Caretta caretta*).

of Dirk Hartog Island and the Peron Peninsula. The waters also harbour a sub-species of seasnake (*Aipysurus laevis pooleorum*), found nowhere else, and the black-lipped pearl shell (*Pinctada margaritifera*), first reported by Dampier. Among the other marine wildlife of the bay are whaler sharks (*Carcharhinus* sp.) and manta rays (*Manta birostris*). Snapper fish (*Chrysophrys unicolor*), which appear to show speciation in the bay, and western king prawns (*Penaeus latisulcatus*) are caught in large numbers in the region.

The Aborigines, who occupied most of the area, made good use of the bay's plentiful fish and shellfish. Little of their prehistory is known, but they must have lived in the area for many thousands of years before European occupation. Although they left little rock art, a considerable number of kitchen midden sites have been found, particularly on Peron Peninsula and Dirk Hartog Island. Their small numbers, estimated at about two hundred, were dictated by the limited availability of water in the near-desert environment.

The first recorded European contacts were made by the 1803 French scientific expedition led by Nicolas Baudin. He observed Aborigines living near Big Lagoon to be very tall, strong and vigorous. Their 'village' consisted of twelve to fifteen huts, equipped with fireplaces and rubbing

*B*ellefin Prong is one of several distinctive peninsulas jutting into Shark Bay.

stones. Three closely allied tribal groups lived in or moved seasonally through the area. They dug wells and traded in valuable items, such as flints and stone grinders, up and down the coast.

The next stage of occupation, based on pearling and guano mining, began in the early 1850s. The newcomers included Europeans, Chinese, Malays and Pacific Islanders, almost all men. The need for fresh water made it necessary for the early settlers and Aborigines to live near each other close to the limited sources, such as at Freshwater Camp, now Denham. Needless to say, that supply, carefully conserved by the Aborigines, was eventually polluted by the settlers. The expansion of pearling and whaling, and then the establishment of pastoral stations, induced rapid changes. Traditional Aboriginal society quickly broke down and much of their tribal knowledge and culture was lost.

Later, for a few years in the early 1900s, came the miserable 'lock hospitals'. Aborigines suffering from leprosy and venereal diseases introduced from overseas were brought to Shark Bay from distant parts of the state. They were taken to the remote islands — men to Bernier and women to Dorre Island. Although the area does not have a distinct Aboriginal community today, Carnarvon, to the northeast, has a significant Aboriginal population.

The area has a rich European cultural heritage, mainly associated with early landings and explorations. Dirk Hartog, the first recorded European to land in Western Australia, in 1616 visited the island since named after him. He left a pewter plate which was found by de Vlaming in 1697 and taken back to Holland. Two years later Dampier made his explorations of the bay. In 1712 the ship *Zuytdorp*, owned by the Dutch East India Company and sailing for Batavia (now Djakarta), was wrecked off the towering cliffs which now bear its name.

In 1772 St Allouarn landed near Cape Inscription and claimed Western Australia for the French king. French scientific surveys followed in 1801, 1803 and 1818 and added a great deal to European scientific knowledge of Australia. Many of those French explorers, including Hamelin, Peron, Bernier and Dorre, have left their names and those of their ships on maps of the west coast, particularly at Shark Bay.

The greatest threats to the area are lack of legislative protection for most of its outstanding features, inadequate funding for management at a time when tourism is growing rapidly, and continued pastoralism on land with high conservation values.

Although nearly all the land in the area belongs to the crown, most is tied up in pastoral leases and very little has been reserved for conservation. The conservation reserves comprise isolated Bernier and Dorre islands and a few small island and land reserves. Virtually all the waters are unprotected, despite Cabinet endorsement, in 1976, of the Environmental Protection Authority's recommendations that most of the land and waters should be included in national parks and nature reserves. Implementation of those recommendations would have resulted in the pastoral stations on Dirk Hartog and Faure islands and on the Edel Land, Nanga and Peron peninsulas being acquired for conservation reserves. With the elimination of feral predators and the reintroduction of rare native wildlife, Dirk Hartog Island has the potential to become Australia's finest island nature reserve. Unfortunately, successive state governments have failed during the past twelve years to buy back any of this crown land, partly because of opposition from the pastoral lobby.

Conservationists were outraged by the state government's Shark Bay Region Plan, released in March 1988, and the decision not to seek world heritage listing. The plan is based on a 1987 draft plan, prepared by two government departments with little public consultation, which was strongly condemned by the Environmental Protection Authority and many conservation groups. Dirk Hartog Island is not to become a nature reserve and the designated national parks are restricted to the Steep Point locality on Edel Land Peninsula and the northern part of Peron Peninsula. Furthermore, important dugong habitats near Gladstone Landing, north of Hamelin Pool, and around the north Peron Peninsula have been excluded from proposed marine protection zones.

The other major threats lie in rapidly growing tourism in the area and inadequate funding for management of its outstanding natural environment. Shark Bay is sparsely

*D*olphin and human, an extraordinary interaction.

populated and has been relatively unaffected by change, apart from degradation caused by pastoralism, four-wheel-drive vehicles and overfishing. However, the completion in 1985 of a sealed road into the area, coupled with media attention on the dolphins of Monkey Mia, triggered a sharp growth in tourism.

This growth has not been matched on the management front. One fisheries officer, based at Denham, has responsibility for some 18 000 square kilometres of water and the adjacent coast. On land, rangers are restricted to Monkey Mia and the north of Edel Peninsula. There is no ranger presence on about 90 per cent of the land. Meanwhile, the largely uncontrolled tourism in Shark Bay's fragile coastal and bay environments is causing serious problems. Furthermore, the Environmental Protection Authority has highlighted the environmental problems and low economic returns from pastoralism in the area and has called for the progressive destocking of lands with high conservation value.

The area has a very long coastline where the elements of land and sea blend closely. The creation of Australia's first land and sea regional park as a world heritage area at Shark Bay would help resolve current management problems and provide a fitting showcase for its heritage values.

DAVID DALE

275

The Eastern
Arid Region

The Eastern Arid Region

*H*eavy rains will stimulate new plantlife in the arid Simpson Desert.

*The extraordinary topography and rainfall controls have made the
Lake Eyre region the outstanding example of what has been called
Australia's whimsical changefulness.*

SIR GRENFELL PRICE, *Lake Eyre, South Australia*, 1955

Previous pages
*I*n flood, the Diamantina creates a filigree of interlacing channels.

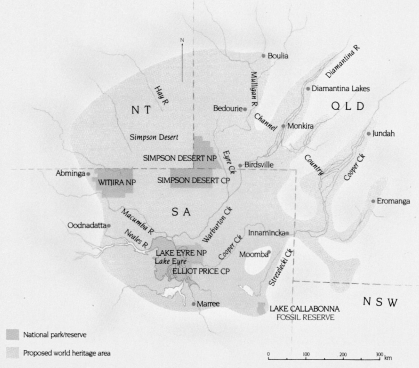

National park/reserve

Proposed world heritage area

0   100   200   300 km

The eastern arid region of central Australia is a sprawling 400 000 square kilometre area of irregular outline straddling the corners of three adjoining states — South Australia, the Northern Territory and Queensland. It comprises Lake Eyre, some southern mound springs of the Great Artesian Basin, the Tirari Desert, Sturt's Stony Desert, tongues following the lower courses of the Cooper, Diamantina and Georgina rivers and, to the north of all this, the Simpson Desert. Its relief is generally low, the land surface ranging from fifteen metres below sea level in the southern bays of Lake Eyre to little more than 200 metres above sea level in the northwest Simpson Desert.

Many attributes of this region combine to give it world heritage quality. Exemplifying *natural property*, there is its geological and geomorphological evolutionary history — the sagging earth's crust, the formation of the Great Artesian Basin, the development over millions of years of the great fresh–saltwater lake and the adjoining sandridge and stony deserts. Then there is the unique hydrological behaviour of the rare cyclonic storms and the resulting floods traversing the extraordinary 'channel country', the extreme range of fluctuation between water and aridity in Lake Eyre itself, and the unique mound springs.

There is the explosion of wildlife following the filling of Lake Eyre and the biological diversity exhibited in the Coongie desert lakes. There are the unique flora associations and wildlife populations moulded by adaptation to the demanding desert environment. In particular there are the rare and endangered species: trees, plants, birds, mammals and reptiles. Mammalian fossil sites in the Tirari Desert record palaeontological history from the Tertiary and Quaternary eras.

Exemplifying *cultural property*, there is the history of the former way of life of the Aborigines as they came to terms with the desert environment, their survival on sparse food resources and the water of carefully tended native wells. This history includes the mapping of ancient trade routes where Aborigines transported and bartered a range of goods and materials.

279

*A*fter rain, wading birds, such as these brolgas (*Grus rubicundus*), converge
on temporary waterholes where they find a plentiful supply of insects.

There is also a rich modern history of the European explorers — of Edward John Eyre, who discovered Lake Eyre and had his advance to the interior blocked by it; of Charles Sturt, the first to cross the region during his epic attempt to reach the centre of the continent, and the first to see and describe Cooper's Creek, Sturt's Stony Desert and the Simpson Desert; of Burke and Wills, whose ill-fated, mismanaged expedition, ending in death on Cooper's Creek, left them more famous than other more successful explorers; and of John McDouall Stuart, whose success in crossing the continent from south to north rested largely on his part in the discovery of the string of mound springs curving round the southwest flank of Lake Eyre. There is subsequent history in the ruins of old telegraph stations built around 1870, and later history again in the central Australian railway line and its famous Ghan train, now also dismantled and abandoned.

The Conservation Council of South Australia and the Australian Conservation Foundation have prepared a tentative world heritage area proposal for an 'Eastern Aridlands', conforming in many respects to the region defined in this chapter.

The geological story effectively began with the Mesozoic Era, 225 million years ago. The crust began to sag and sediments progressively infilled the basin during the Triassic. In the Jurassic, freshwater sands were deposited to form the aquifer of the subsequent Great Artesian Basin, but invasion by the sea in the Cretaceous laid down impervious marine sediments, sealing in those sands. So, 70 million years ago, the Great Artesian Basin was complete.

Lake Dieri, the ancestral Lake Eyre, came into existence about that time. Under high rainfall it was a freshwater lake surrounded by swamps and dense vegetation through which sluggish streams meandered. There was later an arid phase, but by

Right

*I*rregular rains dramatically alter the appearance of
the normally arid Simpson Desert.

the Pliocene it was warm and wet again, and the Tirari Desert fauna (now fossil) flourished at its end. Aridity developed again in the Pleistocene, and the lake was reduced to the *playa*-cum-*salina* of today.

The present land surface consists of the comparatively thin sand and gravels deposited during the Tertiary and Quaternary eras (the past 70 million years), with sometimes the older Cretaceous showing through. Parts of this have weathered on the surface over millions of years to a silicified 'duricrust' (silcrete) which forms the 'breakaways' and gibber deserts of today. Winds have swept and marshalled fluviatile sands into the dune assemblages of the present sandy deserts.

Topographically and geologically the region lies over the lower concavity of four superimposed basins, two of which extend far beyond its limits. The lowermost is the Great Artesian Basin whose strata lie deep beneath the land surface and which encompasses 1 400 000 square kilometres (nearly one-fifth of the area of Australia); above it the Lake Eyre catchment or drainage basin is nearly as extensive, with an area of 1 300 000 square kilometres. Next in the series of concentric basins is the Lake Eyre Depression which is the inner part of the catchment and includes some 20 000 square kilometres below sea level. Finally there is the 9300 square kilometre Lake Eyre itself. The underlying Great Artesian Basin is one of the most extensive geological formations in the world. The water of its underlying aquifer is its most significant resource, but also contained within the basin are the oil and gas reserves of the Cooper sub-basin.

*L*ake Eyre is part of a huge drainage basin. Normally a vast expanse of salt-encrusted mud, it fills, on rare occasions, as a result of waters that drain into it from rivers in southwest Queensland.

Lake Eyre is the driest — as well as the lowest — part of the continent. The median mean rainfall here is under 100 millimetres per annum, but its seasonal incidence is highly irregular. Within the region the median mean rainfall increases northward and eastward, reaching 200 millimetres per annum at the northern limits of the Simpson Desert and 200–300 per annum where the tongues terminate along the Cooper and Diamantina. With its low rainfall, low humidity and high temperature range, the region fits Köppen's accepted 'hot climate' classification.

The whole region is dry and harsh. The Simpson is Australia's harshest desert, albeit lacking the extremes of aridity of some other world deserts such as the Sahara. But while aridity is the keynote, it is the occasional — and often overwhelming

— incursion of water that contributes variety and interest to the region.

Huge cyclonic downpours occasionally drench northeast Australia, causing great floods to course down the river channels, and then gush into, and even fill, Lake Eyre. Smaller, more or less annual, floods from lesser, seasonal rains flow down the Cooper to a preliminary terminus in the Coongie Lakes — a nearly permanent wetland supporting a wildlife population of world significance — while the similar annual floods down the Diamantina regularly reach Goyder Lagoon and may spill into Lake Eyre.

Lake Eyre, whose bed covers 9300 square kilometres, is rarely completely filled, although it is partly flooded from time to time. Briefly, 90 per cent of the lakebed is dry for 90 per cent of the time. The greatest known volume of water in the filled lake is 32.5 million megalitres, and it permanently contains some 500 million tonnes of soluble salts, mainly sodium chloride. If a 'minor flooding' is when there is sufficient water in the lake to submerge less than half its bed, a 'major flooding' when more than half is submerged and a 'filling' when the bed is completely submerged to its well-defined shoreline, then it can be said that a minor flooding occurs approximately every three years, a major flooding perhaps every ten years and a filling two to four times a century.

Such a vast expanse of water in the desert as the filled Lake Eyre is a remarkable phenomenon and a striking sight. Although shallow, with a mean depth of three metres, this 'inland sea' can generate sizeable waves which crash upon and erode the friable shores. Fascinating in quite a different way is the subtle beauty of the dry lakebed.

*T*he waters of Cooper's Creek snaking towards Lake Eyre will contribute to one of its very rare fillings.

Right
*T*he crust of salt covering the bed of Lake Eyre, its harshness softened by the morning sun.

*M*ound spring, Purni Bore.

*D*alhousie Springs, northwest of Lake Eyre.

The wonderful mound springs have been formed by water leaking upward from the Great Artesian Basin at certain places where its underground aquifer is tapering and curving towards the surface. They tend to be located along geological faults. Although mound springs are also found in Queensland and New South Wales, the most numerous and significant are those of South Australia lying in an arc southwest, west and northwest of Lake Eyre.

The underground waters here are heavily mineralised with carbonates, chlorides and sulphates. Over many thousands of years, evaporation at the springs has resulted in precipitation of the solutes — mainly calcium carbonate — as well as the deposition of colloidal material, to form characteristic mounds. Some are conical, with an elevated water cup one to four metres above the plain. Smaller springs are sedge-ringed pools flush with the ground surface.

Spring flow was greater in the Pleistocene, and today some huge, extinct mounds, up to forty-three metres high, represent former springs. At Dalhousie, 200 kilometres northwest of Lake Eyre, are particularly active springs, one flowing at 14.3 megalitres per day. The veritable oasis here has prompted the creation of a national park in the area.

*P*ools like this one, downstream from the borehead at Purni Bore, create a rich habitat for birdlife.

*T*he thermal spring at Blanche Cup, a superb example of a mound spring.

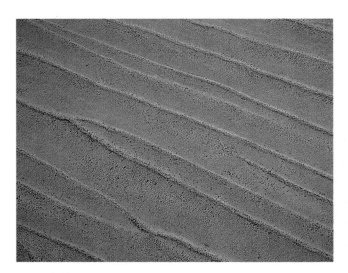

*W*indblown sandridges, Simpson Desert.

By far the largest component of the eastern arid region — nearly half of it — is the Simpson Desert north of Lake Eyre. This shield-shaped desert stretches some 300–500 kilometres across and has an area of 170 000 square kilometres, making it about as large as England and Wales combined. It is a great grid of parallel ridges of sand with an alignment approximately from north-northwest to south-southeast. There are about 1100 ridges across an east–west section, on average 400 metres apart and ten to thirty metres high. Most ridges continue for long distances before petering out and sometimes they form Y-junctions. The sand is often deep red,, particularly in the north. The interdune valleys, or swales, and sand slopes are sparsely vegetated, but the dune crests are usually windblown and bare. Formed by winds blowing from the southeast and southwest, the sandridges are asymmetrical, the east side being steeper than the west.

The channels of some rivers and streams draining the Macdonnell Ranges enter the northern desert and continue partway into it between the dune chains. Only in very wet seasons do large flows reach the desert, to flood out and soon be lost. In the south, groups of parallel swales are occupied by elongate *playas* or, more correctly, *salinas*. They are not river-fed, and receive their water from rare, heavy local rains.

*H*ardy tussock and other stunted vegetation clings to the water that settles in the interdune depressions.

288

The Tirari Desert, a 12 000 square kilometre sandridge desert against the east side of Lake Eyre, is really a southward extension of the Simpson Desert, separated from it only by the Warburton (Diamantina) River. It is, however, bisected by Cooper's Creek. What makes the Tirari Desert really significant is the presence of fossil vertebrate fauna from the Miocene to Pleistocene in a string of four *salinas* just east of Lake Eyre — lakes Palankarinna, Ngapakaldi, Kanunka and Pitikanta. Perhaps the most interesting discoveries are the fossil mammals, including species of *Perikoala*, *Dasyurus* and *Diprotodon*.

East of the Simpson and Tirari deserts, lying between the Warburton (Diamantina) and the Cooper, is the ill-defined but important 30 000 square kilometre area of Sturt's Stony Desert. It consists of residual plateaus of weathered 'duricrust' or silcrete with a surface of wind-polished stones known as gibbers. Some isolated sand dunes occur there, but essentially it is an area from which the sand has been swept by the wind. The gibbers are coated with 'desert varnish', a silica- and iron-rich skin containing a trace of manganese.

In 1845 Charles Sturt came upon the stony desert in his attempt to reach the interior. 'These plains', he wrote, 'are so thickly covered with fragments of indurated quartz as to exclude vegetation . . . In some places their debris is fine and looks glassy in the sun . . . In others the stones are larger like the mixed stones on a sea beach . . .'

*T*he exposed, wind-polished gibbers of Sturt's Stony Desert.

Right

*W*ind has blown the sand from the surface of this desert, creating a barren and forbidding landscape.

Cooper's Creek flows across the Simpson Desert,
a network of channels radiating from its main course.

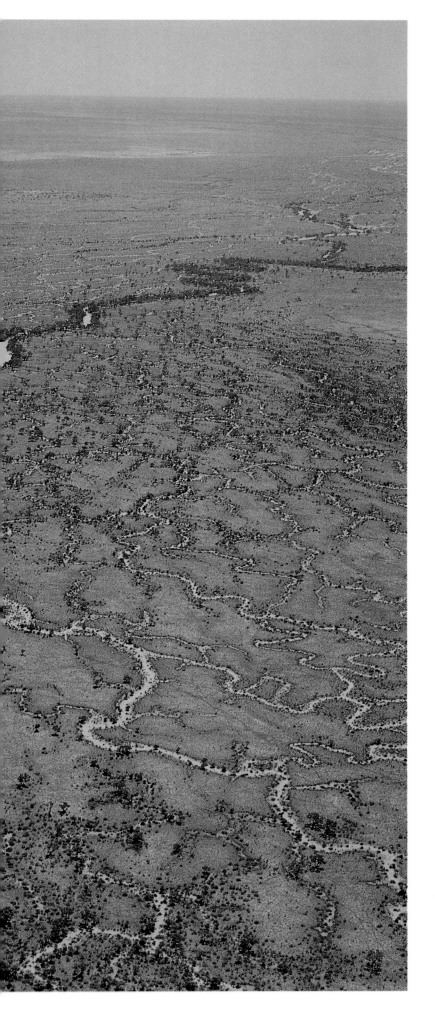

Among the Lake Eyre rivers the Cooper best exemplifies the peculiar channel country floodplain behaviour, particularly where it opens out below Windorah in southwest Queensland. In the periodic, sudden floods, the river level rises and water spreads out over an immense plain more than thirty kilometres wide. It moves through a maze of small channels, surrounding and isolating areas of slightly higher ground. Countless streams then reach out and slowly invade the isolated areas, and the extraordinary pattern develops. Meanwhile other streams gradually lose themselves by separating into progressively smaller ones until they disappear into the cracked soil. As the ground becomes saturated the pattern moves onward, and further dry islands are invaded. Paradoxically, the stream pattern is the reverse of the usual; distributaries flow outward from the main channel instead of tributaries flowing into it.

The floodplain of the Diamantina is less than ten kilometres wide until the Durrie Plain below Monkira, and it does not develop the full Cooper distributary pattern until Goyder Lagoon in South Australia. The flow of the Cooper, even in high flood, is greatly slowed in the channel country, and it sometimes takes months to reach Lake Eyre. The Diamantina, in contrast, moves faster, accomplishing the same journey in weeks.

The Cooper in South Australia has a different sort of floodplain, an important feature of which is the Coongie Lakes which form the seasonal terminus of the northwest branch below Innamincka. This desert wetland is remarkably rich in flora and fauna.

The extent and diversity of the eastern arid region — sand desert and stony desert, salt lake, river channel and floodplain — is reflected in the variety of its flora and fauna.

Sandhill cane-grass (*Zygochloa paradoxa*) grows on desert sandridges, with sandhill wattle (*Acacia ligulata*), elegant wattle (*A. victoriae*), parrot bush (*Crotalaria cunning-*

hamii), native senna (*Cassia pleurocarpa*) and needlebush (*Hakea leucoptera*) on the slopes. Buckbush (*Salsola kali*) and groundsel (*Senecio cunninghamii*) may appear after rain. Spinifex (*Triodia basedowii*) covers the lower slopes and swales, and saltbush (*Atriplex spongiosa*), bindy-eye (*Sclerolaena limbata* and *S. intricata*) and samphire (*Halosarcia halocnemoides*) grow in claypans.

The stony plains are often bare but occasionally support saltbush (*Atriplex nummularia*), bluebush (*Maireana aphylla*) and related *Atriplex* and *Maireana* species. Elegant wattle, dead finish (*Acacia tetragonophylla*), mulga (*A. aneura*) and willow wattle (*A. salicina*) can be found growing in the gullies of the gibber plains.

Low open woodland is characteristic of the river channels and permanent lakes. Among the most common species are the coolibah (*Eucalyptus microtheca*), river red gum (*E. camaldulensis*) and gidgee (*Acacia cambagei*). Lignum (*Muehlenbeckia cunninghamii*) and swamp cane-grass (*Eragrostris australasica*) may cover the flats.

The shores of Lake Eyre are characterised by hummocks of nitre-bush (*Nitraria billardieri*) and samphire (*Halosarcia halocnemoides*), with occasional shrubs like needlebush (*Hakea leucoptera*) and native willow (*Pittosporum phylliraeoides*). Among the rare and endangered plants are the elegant waddy wood (*Acacia peuce*), an acacia in two patches at opposite ends of the Simpson Desert, and the rare aquatic plant *Eriocaulon carsonii*, recently discovered in a mound spring at Hermit Hill, beside Lake Eyre South.

The gibber bird (*Ashbyia lovensis*) and cinnamon quail-thrush (*Cinclosoma cinnamomeum*) inhabit stony and sand plains, and the Eyrean grasswren (*Amytornis goyderi*) occurs throughout the Simpson Desert, while uncommon elsewhere in the region. The very rare night parrot (*Geopsittacus occidentalis*) may be found on the Cooper floodplain. The eastern grass owl (*Tyto longimembris*) and grey grasswren (*Amytornis barbatus*) frequent lignum swamps, while

the blue bonnet (*Northiella haematogaster*) and the red-rumped parrot (*Psephotus haematonotus*) occupy riverine woodlands. The wideranging but endangered Australian bustard (*Ardeotis australis*) is also known in the region.

Notable among the mammals of the region are the fawn hopping mouse (*Notomys cervinus*), dusky hopping mouse (*N. fuscus*), kowari (*Dasyuroides byrnei*), narrow-nosed planigale (*Planigale tenuirostris*) and the greater bilby (*Macrotis lagotis*), which is now extremely rare. The reptiles include Bynoe's gecko (*Heteronotia binoei*), Grey's skink (*Menetia greyii*) and the specialised white Lake Eyre dragon (*Amphibolurus maculosus*) that subsists on ants at the lake's edge.

When Lake Eyre fills there is an explosion of fauna. Birds migrate there to feed on the large numbers of fish that temporarily live in the lake. Among the most numerous fish are bony bream (*Nematolosa erebi*) and Lake Eyre hardyhead (*Craterocephalus eyresii*). The common feeding birds are pelicans (*Pelecanus conspicillatus*), black cormorants (*Phalacrocorax carbo*) and whiskered terns (*Chlidonias hybrida*). As the lake evaporates, the fish are killed and the birds depart or die. Endemic to the mound springs is the Dalhousie hardyhead (*Craterocephalus dalhousiensis*), a native fish well adapted to high temperature and salinity.

The Coongie Lakes deserve particular mention because of their biological richness. Over 180 species of birds — a third of which are waterbirds — are known and many breed there, and large numbers of migratory waders and shorebirds visit the area. The density of breeding birds of prey is one of the highest in the world. Also recorded are twenty-five mammals, forty-seven reptiles, eight frogs and sixteen fishes.

The presettlement Aborigines who lived on semipermanent river waterholes had some security; those who lived in the desert occupied a hard, demanding environment. Their primary need was water: knowledge of its whereabouts was all-important, and they were adept at excavating and main-

Coongie Lakes, an oasis for desert wildlife.

taining the scattered desert wells. They were organised into several tribes, like the Wongkamala, Wongkanguru, Jeljendi and Dieri, and spoke the same group language or related individual languages. Before European settlement, the region's population numbered over 2000; today it numbers only 200, including Europeans.

Aborigines over a wide area of Australia traded in commodities like red ochre and grinding stones from the Flinders Ranges and the narcotic pituri plant and ground-edge axes from Queensland. The main north–south route passed through the region, crossing the Cooper at Kopperamanna (a trading centre), while a branch curved round Lake Eyre along the mound springs. The trade routes had a religious significance, following 'dreaming trails' — the paths of mythological ancestors. The mound springs were more than just on a dreaming trail — they were primary, named sites of important dreaming events.

Those parts of the region having statutory conservation protection are the Simpson Desert Conservation Park in South Australia (6927 square kilometres), the Simpson Desert National Park in Queensland (5050 square kilometres), the Witjira National Park, including Dalhousie Springs (7769 square kilometres) and the Lake Eyre National Park (12 280 square kilometres). If the 190 square kilometre Coongie Lakes Conservation Zone in the proposed 14 000 square kilometre Innamincka Regional Reserve is added to this, some 32 216 square kilometres, or 8 per cent, of the eastern arid region is protected.

Much of the area is subject to prospecting for oil and gas, including those parks where licences predated their creation. Damage to the Simpson Desert has been caused by the driving of grids of seismic exploration lines, some of which have been turned into permanent tracks by an increasing number of visitors in four-wheel-drive vehicles. However, proliferation of the latter usage is being controlled in the parks, and the petroleum companies are adopting an increasing respect for the environment.

The mound springs have suffered much from trampling stock and careless visitors, but some are now being fenced, with financial help from the South Australian government, World Wildlife Fund and the mining companies. A greater threat in the form of diminution in flow arises from proposed heavy artesian water withdrawals for the giant Roxby Downs (Olympic Dam) mining operation.

C. WARREN BONYTHON

Southwest Western Australia

Southwest Western Australia

Grass trees (*Xanthorrhoea preissii*) and wildflowers in low woodland.

The noteworthy divergences of Australian flora have always excited the attention of botanists, but that interest has been most specifically centred on the plants of the South West, for this area is the oldest part of the Australian land mass, and, in a broad sense, the cradle of Australian plant life.

C. A. GARDNER, *Wildflowers of Western Australia*, 1975

Previous pages
*F*rom Bluff Knoll, the ragged peaks of the Stirling Range stretch to the horizon.

Visitors to southern Western Australia often have a preconceived image of the land as essentially flat and somewhat featureless. An exploration of the semiarid mallee heathlands northwest of Esperance confirms this impression. For kilometre after kilometre the dirt track keeps a dead straight path through the white-skinned mallees with their understorey of brilliant wildflowers. Barely a hill comes into view. Some eighty kilometres northwest of the old whaling town of Albany the first sight of the Stirling Range is therefore surprising. The range erupts suddenly, rearing steeply out of the surrounding plain into a profile of imposing bluffs and ragged peaks. Although the highest peak, Bluff Knoll, is only 1073 metres, the impact of this isolated upland is truly dramatic.

The peaks attract high rainfall, frequent mists and even occasional winter snow. The moisture persists in pockets, creating a diverse habitat that supports a remarkable variety of plants. A walk or climb up one of the trails in spring is a magnificent experience as the flowering plants reach their climax. A profusion of banksia, grevillea, melaleuca and pea species attract throngs of nectar-feeding honeyeaters. The birds are also attracted to the lovely mountain bells (*Darwinia* spp.) for which the Stirlings are famous, eight species being confined to the range.

Although topographically unusual, the Stirling Range is to some extent a microcosm of the southwest corner of Western Australia. It shares with the rest of the region great scenic beauty and an outstandingly rich flora, including an unusually high number of restricted endemics. Of the nearly 1000 species of plants recorded in the park, over fifty are confined to the range. The national park typifies many of the problems of the southwest in that it is an island, a limited area of natural vegetation surrounded by profoundly altered agricultural land. It therefore suffers the pressures that impinge upon the southwest corner of Western Australia where conservation has had to battle constantly against competing claims for land use and, with a few exceptions, has often only succeeded in achieving small and vulnerable reserves.

Southwest Western Australia covers almost 310 000 square kilometres and encompasses a wealth of environments: high forest, woodlands, heathland, shrublands and a wild, wind-buffeted coastline of great beauty. Despite this diversity, the area is accepted as a biogeographical entity united principally by climate and vegetation. The boundaries adopted in this chapter are based on a widely accepted botanical region called the South West Botanical Province, acknowledged throughout the world as a botanical treasurehouse rich in unique species.

The province encompasses three climatic zones, all of which are variations of Mediterranean climates with rain falling principally in winter. The far southwest is designated moderate Mediterranean; it has up to 1400 millimetres of winter rain, and three to four dry months. Further inland a broad band of dry Mediterranean zone with rainfall rates between 600 and 350 millimetres extends from Jurien in the north to Israelite Bay in the west. The extra dry zone stretches from Shark Bay to the curve of the Great Australian Bight. Rainfall in this zone can be as low as 300 millimetres per annum.

Contrary to popular belief, it is not the broad species richness which makes the botanical heritage of southwest Western Australia so outstanding. On a world scale the region is moderately rich, with nearly 4000 species of plants recorded. It is also notable for high local species richness within small land units and highly variable species composition from unit to unit. But the chief characteristic that gives the area world standing is the very high number of endemic species. Some 83 per cent of species in the South West Botanical Province are considered endemic. They include every kind of plant, from the mighty karri trees to diminutive shrubs and herbs of the dry heathland.

A further feature of importance is the high number of species in a particular genus. There are, for example, 300 species

*T*he prevailing southwesterly winds batter the wild seascapes of Leeuwin–Naturaliste National Park.

*P*eaceful karri-lined river valley in the Warren National Park.

of acacia, 170 of eucalyptus, 160 of melaleuca, 120 of grevillea and eighty of hakea. The two features of high endemicity and high species-to-genus ratio are outstanding on a continental landmass.

The high rate of endemism is related to the palaeohistory of the region. The South West Botanical Province sits on one of the earth's oldest land surfaces, the Yilgarn block of the Western Shield, the underlying rocks of which date back 2900–2500 million years to the Archaean age. The region has remained essentially stable over the last 570 million years, except for a period of lateritisation which began about 35 million years ago.

Lateritisation broke the ancient crystalline rocks down into infertile sands and clays with a hard gravelly crust. Over subsequent millennia the laterite mantle which covered most of the southwest was dissected by relatively young rivers to form a complex soil mosaic of subtly different, nutrient-poor soils.

Before the lateritisation process, most of the southwest, like much of the continent, was covered in closed rainforest. Most of the antecedents of the present wildflower genera were seemingly present as understorey in forests of giant beeches, podocarp conifers and ferns. As the Australian continent drifted north to its present position,

302

increasing general aridity, combined with lengthy periods of little or no rain, wiped out the rainforest flora and encouraged the survival of those plants with the greatest ability to tolerate dry conditions and low levels of fertility.

By the early Pliocene period (5 million years ago) rainforest species had largely been replaced by many of the major sclerophyllous families — the Proteaceae, Myrtaceae and Leguminosae — which dominate Australian flora today. Around this time Western Australia became isolated from eastern Australia through the severe aridity and hostile limestone soils of the Nullarbor Plain. Over the following 5 million years the now isolated flora and fauna of the southwest were subject to at least twenty major fluctuations in climate.

Scientists believe these climatic stresses were the major force behind the evolution of so many endemic plants. During wet cool periods species radiated out, opportunistically colonising the diverse array of habitats as they became suitable. As the climate turned more adverse they contracted to refugia, often moisture-catching uplands like the Stirling Range. During these periods of expansion and retreat, populations would have been split, cut off, intermingled with different species, exposed to different soil types and generally subject to variable influences, the result being the development along different evolutionary paths. Climatic stress is most pronounced in the transitional rainfall zone (600 millimetres–250 millimetres) which significantly is also the areas's richest zone of plant speciation.

Southwest Western Australia is justly famous for its magnificent wildflowers. They are a major tourist attraction and provide the basis for an expanding industry in seed and cut flowers. The richest areas for wildflowers are the sandplains or sandheaths known to botanists by the Aboriginal name Kwongan. Patches of this vegetation type occur throughout the province with major areas in the Stirling Range and

Fitzgerald River, but perhaps the best known area is the northern sandplain between Perth and Geraldton. Kwongan covers a range of vegetation communities from heaths to open shrubland with small trees, but low shrubs, less than a metre tall, are characteristic.

In spring and early summer the plains are ablaze with colour, both strident and subtle, as the numerous shrubs and smaller plants reach their peak flowering period. There is a wealth of variety in form, even within the same genus. Great sheets of brilliant colour are created by the many feather flowers (*Verticordia* spp.), especially the brilliant yellow *Verticordia nitens*. The

*R*ed lechenaultia (*Lechenaultia formosa*).

low-growing lechenaultias add small mounds of exquisitely pure blue or crimson. Banksias, dryandras, grevilleas, wattles, myrtles, numerous forms of the pea family, hakeas, hibbertias all flower as if in competition as to which can provide the most attractive display. In fact, competition for scarce pollination agents may be the scientific explanation for the splendid colours of the plains flora.

An area of importance within the northern sandplains is the Mt Lesueur Nature Reserve northwest of Jurien. Mt Lesueur is a near-circular mesa, 313 metres high, formed by dissection and erosion of ancient sedimentary rocks. It is regarded as one of the refugial areas referred to earlier where plants have been able to persist during adverse climatic periods. The area is exceptionally rich in species, including a high number of restricted endemic plants such as the Lesueur hakea (*Hakea megalosperma*), pine banksia (*Banksia tricuspis*) and Gairdner Range starbush (*Urocarpus phebalioides*).

Other features of interest north of Perth are the towering coloured cliffs of the Murchison Gorge in the Kalbarri National Park, the cave systems at Yanchep and Drover's Cave national parks and the strange forest of limestone pinnacles in the sand dunes of Nambung National Park.

Early botanists were astonished that towering forest should grow on soils where little more than heath would normally be expected. The major forest types of the southwest are the jarrah and karri forests; small areas of tuart and tingle forest also survive. All the forest trees are endemic. The main occurrence of jarrah (*Eucalyptus marginata*) is now restricted to approximately 1.4 million hectares, lying in a band thirty to fifty kilometres wide running from the Darling Range east of Perth southward some 300 kilometres to near Manjimup. Jarrah grows best on the deep laterite soils which are also rich in aluminium oxide or bauxite, the raw material of aluminium.

Jarrah is a stringybarked tree of between ten and thirty-five metres in height. It usually grows in mixed forests, often with marri (*E. calophylla*) and blackbutt (*E. patens*). The dense understorey of dry-tolerant shrubs and herbaceous plants which characterises most jarrah forests is particularly attractive in spring when it becomes a natural garden of pink boronia, blue lechenaultia, purple hardenbergia, scarlet banksias, primrose orchids and a myriad other flowers. A sculptural element is added by the common grass tree (*Xanthorrhoea preissii*) and low palm-like cycad (*Macrozamia riedlei*).

Due to the strength, durability and attractive appearance of jarrah timber, the

*L*imestone pillars, Nambung National Park.

304

forests have been extensively harvested since early settlement. Many or most of the larger trees have gone and have been replaced by smaller immature trees. Conservation of the jarrah forests has been the focus of public concern over the past fifteen years. They have been, and remain, subject to a number of threats. Salinity caused by the rising of the water table after clearing for bauxite mining and agriculture threatens not only the forests but also the water quality of 90 per cent of the population of Western Australia. Other threats include plagues of insects and proposed open-cut gold mining.

Probably the most serious long-term threat is the spread of a root fungus called *Phytophthora cinnamomi*, more commonly known as 'dieback' because of the gradual death of an infected tree. Jarrah, its understorey flora and many Kwongan species are highly susceptible. Dieback has been called the worst plant epidemic in recorded history, with 13 per cent of jarrah forests affected to date. The fungus is spread by disturbance and is therefore exacerbated by mining and logging and their associated road systems.

Despite these problems, negotiations between the government, Alcoa, the main bauxite mining company, and conservationists have led to the creation of several secure jarrah reserves including the 54 000 hectare Lane Poole Jarrah Reserve centred on the Murray River Valley and Darling escarpment close to Perth. Nevertheless, conservationists feel that many more areas must be set aside and managed before the future of these forests is secure.

Noted Australian naturalist Vincent Serventy has said: 'Surely there can be no greater cathedral than forests such as those of the karri' (*Karri at the Crossroads*, 1982). The great white columns of virgin karri (*Eucalyptus diversicolor*) soaring seventy to ninety metres inspire such metaphors. The karri is among the largest of all living things.

*S*unrise over the jarrah forests of the Darling Ranges.

Previous pages
*T*he uplands of the Stirling Range are the habitat of an outstanding variety of plants and animals.

Sadly, the over-romanticised pioneers and their modern equivalents have seen only timber footage where others have seen majesty. This magnificent forest of international importance has been relentlessly logged and then subjected to some of the most barbaric forestry practices in Australia. Comparatively huge areas have been clearfelled for export woodchips and then burned, ostensibly to stimulate regeneration. The clear streams that once bubbled through the forest have been turned into drains choked with logging debris.

In 1988 the licence to continue turning this outstanding part of the world's natural heritage into paper products will be reconsidered. Despite the tragic past and the uncertain future a few gains have been made: after a decade of campaigning a major national park, the Shannon Basin National Park, was created in 1987. It covers approximately 60 000 hectares of which 20 000 is karri. However, this area can be little more than a 'tree museum' unless the woodchip industry is halted.

Mature karri forest supports large populations of birds although no species appears to be entirely restricted to the forest. Seventy-six species have been recorded including the lovely red-capped parrots (*Purpureicephalus spurius*), white-breasted robins (*Eopsaltria georgiana*) and the rare red-eared firetails (*Emblema oculata*). Interesting mammals which favour the forest as habitat are the brush-tailed phascogale (*Phascogale tapoatafa*), brushtail possums (*Trichosurus vulpecula*) and tiny mardos or yellow-footed antechinus (*Antechinus flavipes leucogaster*).

Pockets of karri, in pure stands and mixed forest, survive in the beautiful coastal areas between Cape Naturaliste and Walpole–Nornalup National Park. In particular the area southwest of Point D'Entrecasteaux, sometimes called the 'karri coast', has fine pockets of karri throughout. Its conservation status has been recently improved with substantial additions to D'Entrecasteaux National Park.

D'Entrecasteaux National Park contains extensive dunes backed by heathland and woodland.

The coast has areas of high wilderness value, long deserted beaches and the scenic splendour of the Southern Ocean crashing on to the continent with often fearsome force. Behind the windswept beaches and dunes lie knee-high wildflower heaths and lovely lakes with evocative names like Jasper and Crystal where large populations of waterfowl and migratory birds peacefully feed and breed.

The waterbirds also find tranquil sanctuary in the many inlets and estuaries along the coast. Some of the major estuaries are the Blackwood sheltered by Cape Leeuwin, the Broke Inlet at the mouth of the Shannon River and the Nornalup Inlet near Walpole. Peel Harvey near Mandurah and Vasse Wonnerup near Busselton are both estuarine wetlands of international importance. All support large flocks of Western Australia's major wildlife symbol, the black swan (*Cygnus atratus*).

310

Coastal wilderness, D'Entrecasteaux National Park.

Nature's artwork at the high tide line.

Above: Broke Inlet at the mouth of the Shannon River.
Below: Basalt columns soar above the surf, Cape Beaufort.

Right

Coastal limestone has been eroded into towering cliffs, D'Entrecasteaux National Park.

The 400 kilometres of coastline between Albany and Cape Arid is scenically superb. It is a region of snug coves, curved bays, craggy headlands, sheer cliffs and beaches where the clean, cold water of the Southern Ocean breaks on to pristine white sand. More or less midway along this stretch of coast, between Bremer Bay and Hopetoun, is the Fitzgerald River National Park. Although not well known to the general public, conservationists and scientists regard this coastal region as one of Australia's most valuable areas.

The 270 000 hectare park was granted international status in 1978 as a Biosphere Reserve under a UNESCO program to preserve pristine areas as benchmarks. The chief characteristics that mark the area as of particular significance in such a generally outstanding region are its scenic grandeur,

wilderness quality and exceptional botanical richness including many endemics. Much of the drama of the park is created by a coastal mountain range called the Barrens. Not only are they true mountain shapes, but they rise out of the ocean.

The mountains are composed of metamorphosed sea sediments which were tilted in the distant past. About 40–43 million years ago the sea levels rose, leaving the Barrens as islands in an extensive shallow sea. During this period billions of sponge skeletons were laid down with clay and silt to form a soft rock called spongolite. Over millennia wind and water have eroded the rock into magnificent multicoloured cliffs flanking valleys up to ten kilometres across. Two of the loveliest valleys have been carved by the two major rivers, the Fitzgerald and Hamersley, which

*S*pongolite cliffs rise above the plains, Fitzgerald River National Park. The park has received international recognition as a UNESCO Biosphere Reserve.

Left
*W*illiam Bay National Park is noted for its rich flora and fauna, and unspoilt coastal scenery.

*T*he brackish Fitzgerald River winds sluggishly to the sea.

flow intermittently through the park. The northern section of the Fitzgerald is an upland plateau separated from the marine plain by a fifty-metre-high escarpment. The rocks here are ancient Precambrian granites, polished and worn over the ages. The view from this plateau across the wide coastal plain with its coloured cliffs to the distant Barrens is one of the great wilderness views of Australia.

Despite early recognition of the Fitzgerald's unique flora, the region is still being explored and new species found. The latest lists record over 1760 species and varieties (105 introduced), with approximately sixty species either totally or largely confined to the Fitzgerald.

The factors discussed earlier to explain high endemicity in the province are accentuated in the Fitzgerald by its geological and geomorphic complexity which has created a patchwork of distinct habitats in which plants have taken hold and evolved. The ebbing, flowing and intermingling of species over time have been, and continue to be, dynamic. Climatic stresses also play a major role in this region. It is a comparatively dry area, a rainshadow wedged between the wetter south coast regions near Albany in the west and Esperance in the east. Again, this creates the stresses so strongly associated with endemicity.

Among the wealth of wildflowers are the spectacular royal hakea (*Hakea victoria*) with its stiff layers of intensely coloured leaves, the Qualup bell (*Pimelea physodes*) and the deep crimson Barrens regelia (*Regelia velutina*). Two gazetted rare and endangered species are the tiny but fiery orange-yellow *Lechenaultia superba* which grows on the quartzite of the Barrens and the scarlet *Eremophila denticulata*, one of the dry-country plants which find a niche in the Fitzgerald's mosaic of habitats.

*E*roded spongolite cliff, Fitzgerald River National Park.

Native fauna also finds sanctuary in this largely unspoilt environment. In fact the Fitzgerald is regarded as having the most complete assemblage of mammal species in the entire southwest. This includes many rare species including the heath rat or Shortridge's native mouse (*Pseudomys shortridgei*) which is otherwise isolated to the Grampians in Victoria and was believed extinct until its recent rediscovery. The extremely rare dibbler (*Parantechinus apicalis*), a carnivorous dasyurid, has been located in the mallee heath of the north Fitzgerald. This particular habitat has shown itself to be very important for other rare species, most significantly the elusive ground parrot (*Pezoporus wallicus*) and western bristlebird (*Dasyornis longirostris*).

Given the great importance of these northern areas of the Fitzgerald, conservationists were delighted when, after a long battle against alienation to agriculture, a further 24 000 hectares were added to the park and another 24 000 hectares designated for conservation management. Conservationists are concerned that low budgets are hampering adequate management and also fear that dieback could increase if roadworks are enlarged. These issues should be addressed in a comprehensive management plan being developed in 1988.

The world heritage listing of the New South Wales rainforests provides a precedent for the declaration of non-contiguous sites. A nomination for southwest Western Australia could similarly comprise outstanding examples of each of the major vegetation communities. Full recognition of the value of this genetic storehouse is essential to ensure that it remains as part of the world's natural heritage.

PENELOPE FIGGIS

The Alps

The Alps

Morning in the Alps. The snow gums must withstand heavy loads of snow.

A prospect came in view the most magnificent. This was an immensely
high mountain covered nearly one fourth of the way down with snow,
and the sun shining upon it gave it a most brilliant appearance . . .

W. H. HOVELL near Tumut, on his journey from Gunning to Port Phillip, 1824

Previous pages
Sunset over Mt Feathertop and the Bogong High Plains in the Victorian Alps.

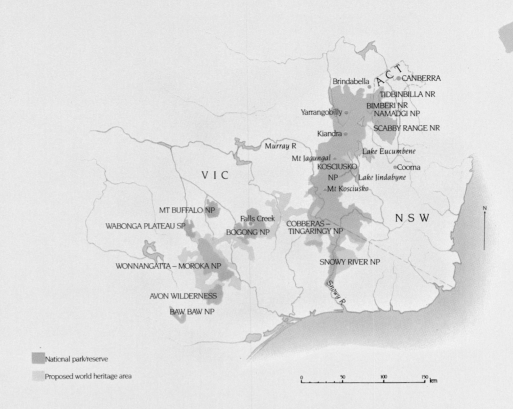

For such a great sprawling country as Australia it is a matter of surprise to the overseas visitor that its tallest mountains are tucked away in the southeast corner of the continent and that they have no sharp peaks, and no permanent ice and snow, the summits being for the most part the highest points of a series of rolling plateaus. In fact, it may seem that the name 'the Australian Alps' is a misnomer.

The name seems more appropriate, though, if one considers that in Switzerland the term 'alps' refers to the grassy areas between the treeline and the permanent snowline. Undoubtedly it is the treeless uplands covered with winter snow that form the most distinctive element in the landscape of the Australian Alps. But, as a regional term, 'the Australian Alps' is taken to include the mountainsides and deep valleys, and therefore the greater part of the area is forested.

The region is over 400 kilometres long and fifty to 100 kilometres wide. It starts in the mountains west of Canberra and finishes in the Baw Baw Plateau some 120 kilometres east of Melbourne. In shape it resembles a boomerang paralleling the coastline so that between the New South Wales–Victoria border the upland is aligned north to south and from the border to Baw Baw the orientation is northeast to southwest.

Sclerophyllous vegetation occupies the entire altitudinal range. This type of vegetation evolved in Australia as climatic conditions became more severe and is now found throughout the peripheral parts of the continent. But the vegetation has encountered such a high degree of diversity that the system of conservation reserves in the Australian Alps offers the world's best display of the adaptation of sclerophyll vegetation to a range of environments.

The alpine region is an outstanding example of a major stage in the earth's evolutionary history. This, combined with its superb natural beauty, makes it a strong candidate for inclusion on the world heritage list. As an area included to represent the eucalypts, it would make a worthy companion to the sites already included for their rainforests.

There are significant differences between the parts of the alpine region but it is altitude that everywhere is most important. This is not surprising when one considers that Mt Kosciusko, Australia's highest point, is 2228 metres while the lowest part of the Snowy River National Park is a mere sixty metres above sea level. The proposed world heritage area comprises twelve separate parks and reserves in New South Wales, Victoria and the Australian Capital Territory, covering over 1.6 million hectares. In most cases, the lower slopes as well as the tops are included.

The backbone of the region is the Snowy Mountains in the 646 893 hectare Kosciusko National Park. The highest points are on the western edge of the plateau around Mt Kosciusko, known as the Main Range, where the last glaciation sculpted a delicate landscape of cirques, small lakes and moraines. On the eastern side of the highest ridges the snowdrifts linger into late summer, reminding us that a drop of only

a few degrees in the mean temperature would see the return of permanent snow.

East of this area the land slopes gradually towards the Monaro Plateau. To the west the land drops away 1700 metres from Mt Townsend to Geehi Flats in a mere seven kilometres, and the view of this giant mountain slope is one of the most spectacular in Australia. The high ridge is maintained as far as Mt Jagungal (2061 metres), thirty kilometres to the north, but further north from here it becomes lower and flatter before rising again and forking into the granite uplands of the Bogong Mountains in the northwest and Brindabella Range in the northeast.

The latter forms the western edge of Namadgi National Park (94 000 hectares). Namadgi is dissected by the Goodradigbee, Cotter and Naas rivers and their tributaries into a series of valleys and ridges. Because of the lower elevation, only a small area is treeless. Adjoining Namadgi are three nature reserves — Bimberi and

*H*eath grows amid frost-shattered rocks in the Main Range, Kosciusko National Park.

Right

*S*ummer sun strikes the ridges of Mt Sentinel in the Snowy Mountains.

Overleaf

*S*now blankets the Main Range. In high summer the range is carpeted with flowers.

A filigree of ice thaws in the morning sun.

Scabby Range in New South Wales and Tidbinbilla in the Australian Capital Territory — totalling 16 000 hectares.

In the southeast of Kosciusko National Park the Snowy River occupies a spectacular gorge 100 kilometres long. Isolated from the main upland by the river is the Byadbo country. Popular interest in this district focuses on the wide sand-strewn rivercourse, and on the pure stands of white pine (*Callitris glaucophylla*) and white box (*Eucalyptus albens*) that cover the dry slopes. These semiarid features are continued over the border where the valley becomes part of Victoria's Snowy River National Park (41 300 hectares).

Victoria has five other alpine national parks — Cobberas Tingaringy, Bogong, Wonnangatta-Moroka, Baw Baw and Mount Buffalo. With the Snowy River National Park they cover 380 500 hectares. There is also the Wabonga State Park (21 200 hectares) and the Avon Wilderness (40 000 hectares). The proposed establishment of a Victorian Alpine National Park would incorporate most of the existing parks and add a further 332 300 hectares to link them together, creating a single park of 690 000 hectares.

*L*ichen-covered cirques, Snowy Mountains.

Above

*T*he Victorian Alps, more heavily dissected than those of New South Wales, are typified by a series of rolling, snow-capped ridges.

A granite tor in the Snowy Mountains. Tors are a distinctive feature of the alpine scenery of the Kosciusko National Park.

In contrast to the Snowy Mountains, the Victorian Alps are strongly dissected. The dissection is greatest around the Ovens and Kiewa valleys. Mt Bogong (1986 metres), Victoria's highest peak, is particularly impressive, while Mt Feathertop is distinguished in the spring by a plume of snow near its summit, a welcome landmark for approaching visitors.

In winter the mountains take on a new beauty. For sixty days the snow covers 1200 square kilometres, and for ninety days 400 square kilometres. In the high area of the Main Range it lasts for 120 days. The reliable snow and rolling plateaus make the Snowy Mountains and Bogong High Plains cross-country skiers' delights.

The questions of why and when the Alps were uplifted are not easily answered. Recent theories based on lava flow dating suggest that the uplift took place between 90 and 30 million years ago during the Cretaceous and Tertiary periods. What was uplifted was a landscape of folded Palaeo-

zoic sedimentary rocks with some igneous intrusions that had been reduced to a level plain during the Mesozoic era. The uplift was accompanied by warping, faulting and volcanic activity which, with subsequent erosion, created a more varied landscape. The remnants of the Mesozoic surface are obvious and the term 'high plains' is very appropriate.

Granite intrusions form the surface rock of 50 per cent of Kosciusko National Park, and the granite tors and boulders at the Ramshead, Mt Buffalo and Mt Baw Baw are characteristic of the alpine scenery. The smaller volcanic intrusions that occurred at two stages during the uplift appear as basalt at many places throughout the region. Their main legacies are the rich soils and flat-topped hills surrounded by dark cliffs at such places as Tabletop and Round Mountain in Kosciusko National Park and Mt Loch and Mt Jim in Bogong National Park.

The sedimentary rocks that form the main rock type in the western part of the Victorian Alps but also occur at Mt Gibbo and Watsons Crags have been eroded to form quite rugged landscapes. The escarpments of tilted strata at the Bluff, the Viking and the Razor, and the steep-sided gullies between Mt Hotham and Mt Feathertop, are all products of the sedimentary zone.

The effects of Pleistocene glaciation on the landforms of the region were limited to the higher areas and only the marks of the last glaciation (35 000 to 10 000 years ago) are evident. At the height of this last cold period, cirque glaciers merged to cover between ten and fifty square kilometres around Mt Kosciusko. These retreated to become smaller cirque glaciers that con-

The formations popularly known as 'ruined castles' are the hallmark of the granite country. Their formations are easily recognisable even under a heavy blanket of snow.

Overleaf
The expansive Bogong High Plains are the most extensive treeless area of the Victorian Alps.

*E*ucalypt-dominated forests show a remarkable adaptation to alpine conditions. A view of the rugged Watsons Crags from Olsens Lookout.

tinued to cut hollows into the south- and east-facing slopes of the highest areas. Four small lakes now occupy the floors of these hollows. It seems certain that it was the continued freeze–thaw action known as the periglacial process that was most influential in both the New South Wales and Victorian areas, creating a deep soil and generally rounding the topography.

Other evidence of the periglacial conditions are the solifluction terraces, earth hummocks and 'block streams'. The latter are steep rivers of frost-shattered basalt blocks which usually occur below volcanic outcrops. Stopped in their tracks by climatic change, these boulders once moved downward every thaw on a bed of frozen subsoil in a mixture of earth and melting

snow. Elsewhere in the outcrops of Silurian limestone at Yarrangobilly and Cooleman Plains, the turbulent melt-water created today's extensive cave systems. On a much reduced scale, in association with long-lasting snowdrifts, the periglacial processes are still operating.

The parks and reserves of the Australian Alps are a living museum of the adaptability of a uniquely Australian vegetation type — the eucalypt-dominated sclerophyll forest. The term 'sclerophyll' refers to plants having small leathery leaves with low rates of transpiration. They are relatively drought-resistant species which evolved in Australia from the closed rainforests as the climate became drier and the soils less fertile. In the Alps the vegetation has colon-

Mottled bark and twisted trunks are the most distinctive features of the snow gum.

ised environments that range from semiarid in the Snowy River valley to the cool temperate and alpine conditions of the higher areas of the region.

There are still uncertainties about the reason for the development of sclerophyll vegetation and the exact sequence of events, but it appears that the differentiation began at least in early Tertiary times within or on the edge of the rainforests. As the climate became drier and colder, the ancestors of the modern eucalypts, casuarinas, acacias and heaths gained a stronger foothold, eventually taking over. Increasingly, fire seems to have played a part, helping to eliminate the fire-sensitive rainforest species in favour of the eucalypts whose adaptations to fire include thick insulating bark and the production of woody capsules that release seeds after fire. The coming of the Aborigines almost certainly contributed to the increased incidence of fire.

As the climate of southeast Australia changed during the ice ages, the Alps provided a habitat for the development of a distinctive flora and fauna. The uplift of the Alps long before the building of the mountains of New Zealand and Papua New Guinea probably means that Australia's alpine flora is also more ancient. Today, except for the higher plateaus, the forest mantles the whole region, but the outward uniform appearance belies the existence of a complex mosaic of vegetation communities. Patches of warm temperate rainforest survive in gullies in the Snowy River, and at Baw Baw the oceanic influence is reflected in cool temperate rainforest species.

Everywhere the trees are zoned altitudinally, the sequence of the vegetation belts varying from the moist western side to the dry eastern slopes. Different elevations are reflected in different species of eucalypts. On the great slope west of Kosciusko the sequence starts with savannah woodland in the Geehi Valley, and passes upward into first dry sclerophyll and then wet sclerophyll. At about 1000 metres alpine ash (*E. delegatensis*) and mountain gum (*E. dalrympleana*) become the dominant association, but at about 1500 metres this vegetation gives way to snow gum (*E. niphophila*) woodland.

The snow gum is synonymous with the subalpine country which in the Snowy Mountains covers some 2250 square kilometres. Along with tussock, herbs and heathy shrubs, the snow gum extends some 300–500 metres to the upper limit of the trees. The creamy white blossom of this tree, its twisted trunk and its bark, which changes from white and grey to shades of red and pink in winter, make it a favourite with artists and photographers.

*T*he smooth branches of a snow gum emerge like antlers from the gnarled and variegated trunk.

*T*ubular ice encases a young eucalypt. Even saplings can withstand extremes of cold.

*S*now gums are found to an altitude of about 2000 metres. The trees are often stunted and irregular in shape, with short, thick trunks branching into stems at about a metre high.

Tree growth does not occur where the mean temperature of the warmest month is less than 10° Celsius but the height of the treeline is not always climatic. Drainage of cold air into 'frost hollows' has created pockets of treeless alpine vegetation in the subalpine zone and inverted the usual sequence of vegetation zonation on the surrounding slopes. Otherwise the height of the climatic treeline increases with distance eastward, from 1200 metres at Baw Baw to 1600 metres at the Bogong High Plains and 1800 metres around Kosciusko.

The alpine zone has its own vegetational complexity. Feldmark communities, characterised by dwarf prostrate plants, occupy the most exposed sites while stony, well-drained soils commonly support heaths, including the mountain plum pine (*Podocarpus lawrencei*), the only native conifer in the alpine areas. With increasing wetness the heath becomes sod tussock grassland.

Short alpine heath is found beneath semi-permanent snow patches. Sod tussock grassland covers more than half the alpine area and the other heaths a quarter. Out of approximately 200 alpine species in the Kosciusko area, twenty-one are endemic.

For the summer visitor the most wonderful feature is the masses of wildflowers, which on the slopes seem endless in their profusion. The silver snow daisy (*Celmisia* sp.), yellow billy button (*Craspedia* sp.) and twelve species of buttercups, including at Kosciusko the spectacular anemone buttercup (*Ranunculus anemoneus*), are but a few of the flowers that make this scene hard to match anywhere in the world.

Before the snow melts around Kosciusko a number of plants, such as the alpine marsh-marigold (*Caltha introloba*), will have already begun to flower. Even more surprising is the sight of the black and yellow striped corroboree frog (*Pseudophryne cor-*

335

roboree) emerging from beneath the snow. This endemic animal, which lives in sphagnum moss bogs under the winter snows, is one of several unusual members of the region's amphibian fauna.

More famous is the mountain pygmy possum (*Burramys parvus*) which, until it was discovered in a ski hut at Mt Hotham in 1966, was known only from fossil remains. Burramys has been noted at a number of places in the Bogong High Plains and Mt Kosciusko district and is believed to have a population of about twelve hundred. It lives in the boulder fields and block streams vegetated by trees and shrubs and is the only Australian mammal to be restricted to the alpine–subalpine environment.

The 'reverse oasis' of the Snowy River rain shadow has a fauna typical of the dry dusty plains of western Victoria. The common wallaroo (*Macropus robustus*), tree lizards and several skinks are at the eastern limit of their range. Also in the crags of the

Snowy River gorge and nearby hills are the last colonies of the brush-tailed rock wallaby (*Petrogale penicillata*) thought to have any chance of survival. Further east in the Rodger River area there have been finds of the long-footed potoroo (*Potorous longipes*), a terrestrial marsupial not scientifically described until 1980.

Many of the streams of the Alps are refuges for native fish elsewhere affected by changes to habitat and introductions of trout. The Cotter River, for instance, still supports river blackfish (*Gadopsis mamoratus*) and Macquarie perch (*Macquaria australasica*).

Among the insects are several colourful grasshoppers, including the Kosciusko grasshopper (*Kosciuscola tristis*) which can regulate its temperature by changing colour from dark bluish to light blue-green. These may delight the eye but it is the dowdy Bogong moth (*Agrotis infusa*) that is more likely to amaze by its habit of swarming in caves and under boulders. The moths travel

*T*he Cathedrals, Mt Buffalo. Fire has spread through the grass layer, killing much of the foliage.

*B*ogong moth (*Agrotis infusa*) feeding on grevillea.

*L*ong-footed potoroos (*Potorous longipes*) live in a proposed extension to the Snowy River National Park.

from as far afield as southern Queensland to spend the summer in the Alps.

With the possible exception of the Snowy River valley, the Aborigines used the Australian Alps only seasonally. However, there is plenty of evidence of their life in the fringing lowlands. At Cloggs Cave, near present-day Buchan, tools show that the Aborigines were in occupation from 17 700 years ago — the height of the last ice age — to 8500 years ago when the climate had become as warm as it is today. The richest area for Aboriginal remains is Namadgi where there are several rock art sites and stone arrangements.

Every year, for how long back no one is sure, the Aborigines of the surrounding lowlands trekked into the mountains to gather and roast the Bogong moths. The end came for the Aborigines with the arrival of the pastoralists, who moved into

the Monaro in the 1820s and by 1835 had reached Omeo. By the 1860s traditional group life had finished.

Most of the subsequent human use of the Alps has been either seasonal or ephemeral. Gold mining lasted for less than half a century and in the Snowy Mountains the summer grazing that had begun in the 1830s was terminated in 1969 to protect the catchment of the Snowy Mountains hydro-electric scheme, commenced in 1950. In preparation for this, the Kosciusko State Park was established in 1944. The logging industry was also shortlived. In the area of Kosciusko State Park it ended when the park was established. In Victoria it began to exploit the alpine ash stands after the Second World War; in a few years all the available timber will have been utilised.

Victoria was slow to act to conserve the area. Although a campaign for an alpine national park began in 1949, it was 1981 before parliament passed legislation authorising the first three national parks. In the

*F*ields of snow daisies (*Celmisia* sp.) are a summer delight, Kosciusko National Park.

Australian Capital Territory a reservation in the southern mountains was enlarged in 1984 to form Namadgi National Park.

In 1969 Sir Garfield Barwick, introducing the Australian Conservation Foundation *Viewpoint* on the High Country, said that thinking about the area was at a transitional stage. Although people were well aware of its value for water and there was growing recognition of its importance for recreation, inappropriate land use such as grazing and indiscriminate road building were still tolerated. There were, he said, no overall planning authorities to see that priority was given to the forms of land use for which an area was of greatest value and to achieve compatibility between use. The *Viewpoint* recommended that a national park authority should be given such responsibilities, as had already been done in the Snowy Mountains, and noted the advantages of a single national park incorporating areas in New South Wales, Victoria and the Australian Capital Territory.

Nearly twenty years later, public appreciation of the area's values has grown. At Kosciusko the situation has improved. There has been an effective management plan for fourteen years; wilderness areas have been protected; the road to Kosciusko summit has been closed; and the building of new accommodation for skiers has been diverted to villages outside the park. In the Australian Capital Territory, too, the national park approach has been introduced, although the legal basis of the park needs improving.

Victoria lags seriously behind. Cattle continue to graze on all except the highest peaks even in the Bogong National Park. This creates areas of bare ground, causing soil loss and more rapid runoff of water, and affects the composition of the vegetation. Some of the more spectacular plants such as the mountain celery (*Aciphylla glacialis*) are now rarely seen. Other effects include the trampling of moss beds and interference with the regrowth of snow gums. Cutting of the last stands of

*T*he Australian Alps: a heritage to preserve.

alpine ash is being allowed as logging is phased out. There are no national park management plans and therefore no official wilderness zones. The national parks that have been established are not contiguous and the alpine resorts are under the control of another body. Legislation that would link the parks into a single Victorian Alpine National Park has been blocked.

In spite of this setback, the Victorian government is preparing a management plan for the whole of the proposed national park and, while the concept of a joint three-state park seems even further away than the solving of the Victorian problems, in 1985 a Memorandum of Understanding was signed by Commonwealth and state ministers as the first step towards the preparation of an Australian Alps National Park Agreement. Even more effective than this would be the inscription of the Alps on the world heritage list which would require the removal of non-conforming uses and set a precedent for Australia in interstate cooperation for protection of the world heritage.

GEOFF MOSLEY

Left

*F*erns (*Dicksonia antarctica*), bracken, eucalypts and blackwood flourish in the moister alpine gullies.

The
Subantarctic Islands

The
Subantarctic Islands

*K*ing penguins (*Aptenodytes patagonicus*) on a rocky Macquarie Island beach.

If isolation and accessibility have hitherto been the great conserving forces in man's relations with wild nature, oceanic islands are the best examples we have of the catastrophic effects of the removal of these powerful constraints.

NIGEL WACE, 1982

Previous pages
*T*he treeless landscape of Macquarie Island's rugged west coast.

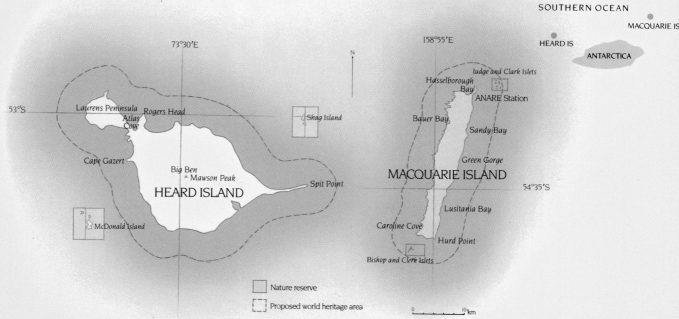

SOUTHERN OCEAN

MACQUARIE IS

HEARD IS

ANTARCTICA

73°30'E

53°S

Laurens Peninsula — Rogers Head
Atlas
Cove

Cape Gazert

Big Ben
Mawson Peak
HEARD ISLAND

Shag Island

Spit Point

McDonald Island

158°55'E

Judge and Clark Islets

Hasselborough
Bay   ANARE Station

Bauer Bay

Sandy Bay

Green Gorge

MACQUARIE ISLAND

54°35'S

Lusitania Bay

Caroline Cove

Hurd Point

Bishop and Clerk Islets

Nature reserve

Proposed world heritage area

0   10 km

I f you look at a map of the northern hemisphere, or better still a globe, you will see that about 70 per cent of the area between the latitudes of 50°N and 60°N is made up of land. By contrast, in the same latitude of the southern hemisphere, you will have to search hard for tiny specks of land in an ocean that completely encircles the earth. Two of these specks, Macquarie Island and the Heard–McDonald group, offer minute habitats on which the wildlife of this huge zone can cling and develop.

The Southern Ocean was created when the supercontinent Gondwana broke up, Antarctica moved to the pole, and the other continents drifted on their tectonic plates thousands of kilometres to the north. Until the eighteenth century geographers felt that there had to be a large continent in this area — an unknown southern land — to counterbalance the extensive landmasses of the northern hemisphere. In his voyages of 1773–76 Captain James Cook laid this theory to rest by crisscrossing the ocean without finding any sign of a large landmass. So extensive are the oceans that he missed Macquarie Island completely and did not actually sight either Heard or McDonald islands.

Macquarie and Heard islands are situated in a middle group of eight islands in the province that biogeographers call 'Insulantarctica', halfway between the more northerly islands, such as those near New Zealand, and those much closer to the Antarctic continent. The islands are 85 degrees of longitude apart. Their wildlife is linked by means of the west-wind drift but each island also has contacts with its northerly neighbours as well as with Antarctica. Macquarie Island lies south of Australia and New Zealand, and the Heard–McDonald islands are to the south of India.

There are three reasons why these subantarctic islands should be considered part of the world heritage. Firstly, they represent examples of land uplifted from the ocean floor. Secondly, as there is so little land in the area — a mere 12 000 square kilometres — they are breeding grounds for penguins, seabirds and seals. Thirdly, they are important for their plantlife.

Oceanic islands have simple ecosystems and limited species. Their plants are derived largely from long-distance dispersal by wind or from the plumage of birds. As terrestrial mammals have no means of crossing vast oceans, there were none on the subantarctic islands before humans arrived. When people did arrive, they brought with them species that had evolved in competitive situations on the major landmasses and the island species were in difficulty. Tussock grasslands that had never been grazed were vulnerable to grazing species such as the rabbit; birds that had no reason to fly quickly fell victim to predatory cats.

Macquarie Island suffered from human impact in full measure, but strong conservation actions are rescuing much of importance at the eleventh hour. Heard Island has a special scientific significance because, in spite of considerable contact, no exotic species have been introduced to the island, partly because of its more severe climate.

Macquarie Island is an excellent example of the elevation of part of a sea floor as a result of movement between tectonic plates; it is therefore critical for studying plate tectonics. Most of the subantarctic islands, including both Macquarie and Heard–McDonald, are of volcanic origin; a few, such as Heard and the South Sandwich islands, are still active. In the latitude they occupy they have borne the brunt of the last 2 million years of ice advance and retreat. Ice still dominates the Heard Island environment.

Macquarie Island is 1500 kilometres southeast of Tasmania, of which it has been politically a part since 1825. It lies 200 kilometres to the north of the Antarctic Convergence, the usually accepted boundary for the Antarctic. The island is thirty-four kilometres long and five kilometres wide at

A beach of volcanic rubble on Heard Island.

Right
*T*he afternoon light softens rugged Mt Haswell, near Caroline Cove, Macquarie Island.

its broadest point, and covers 12 785 hectares. Most of the island is an undulating plateau 100 to 300 metres above sea level. Mt Hamilton, the highest point, is 433 metres. The beaches are rocky and mainly narrow and the land rises steeply to the abrupt break of slope at the plateau edge. There are a number of raised beaches and many lakes, covering a total of 200 hectares. The sea bottom drops steeply close to the shoreline.

The climate is cool and wet with a very small seasonal and diurnal range, making it one of the most equable in the world. The mean daily maximum in January is 8.6° Celsius and in July 4.8° Celsius. Personnel of the ANARE station at North Head can be forgiven for wanting more variety because the equability includes strong winds that blow on average twenty-eight days in the month. Rain, hail or snow can be expected to fall on 312 days every year, but the snow does not lie permanently and the surface water is too warm for sea ice.

A giant crevasse on Heard Island.

Macquarie Island is located on Macquarie Ridge, the boundary of the Indian–Australian tectonic plate with the Pacific plate, which further to the northeast in New Zealand becomes the Alpine Fault.

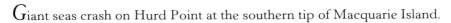

*G*iant seas crash on Hurd Point at the southern tip of Macquarie Island.

Left
*M*acquarie Island cabbage (*Stilbocarpa polaris*) on the slopes of North Head. It was once eaten by sealers to prevent scurvy.

A lone albatross chick among the tussock at the protected breeding site near Caroline Cove.

The island is the product of faulting along the lines of the two plates which has elevated part of the ocean crust (thought to be 15–22 million years old) above sea level. Such mid-ocean ridges are characteristically basalt, and lavas and basaltic dykes cover four-fifths of the island.

The extent to which Macquarie Island was glaciated during the last glaciation is hotly debated but it seems that only about half was ice-covered. Examination of plant samples collected on Wireless Hill suggests that over the last 5500 years the island has risen by seventy metres. The plateau is covered by glacial gravels but there are deeper acid peat soils in low-lying bogs.

Not surprisingly, in view of its persistence, wind is the dominant factor influencing the island vegetation. There are no trees and much of wind-exposed areas are bare or occupied by tundra-like feldmark. Herbfields cover the more sheltered parts of the plateau. The cushion plant *Azorella selago*, which forms terraces aligned parallel to the prevailing wind, is one of the main plants in this zone.

The tallest vegetation on the island is wet tussock grassland (*Poa foliosa*). It occurs in sheltered areas, mainly on the east side and particularly on steep slopes, well-drained valleys and raised beaches, and provides cover for nesting petrels and prions. Although there are no trees, the luxuriance of the vegetation of some of the valleys makes a welcome relief from the often bare windswept plateau. Two plants have conspicuous flowerheads. One of them, the Macquarie Island cabbage (*Stilbocarpa polaris*), which was eaten by the sealers to prevent scurvy, has a beautiful yellow flower. There are forty-five species of liverworts, 100 species of lichens (some endemic) and many freshwater algal plants.

The most memorable image that any visitor takes away from Macquarie Island is the scene of hundreds of thousands of penguins and seals crowding the beaches during the summer breeding season. This imposing assembly reflects the productivity of a vast area of ocean, for in its huge expanse the island is a convenient place for breeding and moulting.

*A*ntarctic prion (*Pachyptila desolata*), one of tens of thousands of petrels that breed on Macquarie Island.

Right
*T*he rugged terrain and wet misty climate of Macquarie Island combine to create waterfalls such as this one on the east coast.

With half a million birds, the colony of macaroni penguins (*Eudyptes chrysolophus*) at Hurd Point is the largest in the world. In addition, the island supports over 200 000 king penguins (*Aptenodytes patagonicus*), as well as smaller populations of gentoo penguins (*Pygoscelis papua*) and rockhopper penguins (*Eudyptes crestatus*).

Among the seventy-two species of birds recorded on Macquarie Island there are four species of albatross, all with small breeding populations. The number of breeding pairs of wandering albatross (*Diomedea exulans*) has declined to about fourteen and is considered to be at risk. Other birds of note include an endemic subspecies of cormorant, the king shag (*Phalacrocorax albiventer purpurescens*), and the great skua (*Stercorarius skua lonnbergi*), which during the breeding season defends its territory vigorously and aggressively. In fact, one person from the ANARE base was savagely attacked by a skua after he lay injured following a fall.

Sharing the beaches with the penguins are large numbers of elephant seals and three species of fur seals. The southern elephant seal (*Mirounga leonina*) reached a population of some 110 000 in the mid-1950s but has since declined in number.

*L*ight-mantled sooty albatross (*Phoebetria palpebrata*).

*L*ate afternoon light in rare fine weather bathes the tussock-clad slopes near Cape Star, Macquarie Island.

350

*S*outhern elephant seals (*Mirounga leonina*) recovered rapidly from exploitation, but populations are now declining worldwide.

The populations of fur seals were decimated by sealers in the early nineteenth century. No one knows what species they were but they have been replaced by New Zealand fur seals (*Arctocephalus forsteri*) and the Antarctic and subantarctic fur seals (*A. gazella* and *A. tropicalis*).

Although the submarine shelf around the island is narrow, it is very rich in marine life. The giant bull or Antarctic kelp (*Durvillaea antarctica*) provides a highly productive habitat for fish and plankton, which in turn support the seals and birds.

Ironically, Macquarie Island, with its vast populations of seals and penguins, was discovered accidentally by a sealer. Captain Frederick Hasselborough of the brig *Perseverance* was en route to the Campbell Islands in 1810 when storms drove him well to the west of his course and to Macquarie Island. One can imagine his elation at the find. Over twenty thousand fur seals were taken for their skins in the first eighteen months; so thorough were the sealers that by 1822 there were none to take. The sealers then turned their attention to the oil of the elephant seals, then to the king penguins and finally to the smaller macaronis. Their boilers and digesters, which eventually replaced the simple try pots, could process 2000 penguins at a time. They remain today as lasting memorials to a rapacious attitude to wildlife.

All but the fur seals have made a good recovery, but unfortunately some of the effects of the sealing era and several shipwrecks were more insidious. Rats and cats, and the Stewart Island weka (*Gallirallus australis scotti*), which was introduced as a food source, take young nesting birds from their burrows; rabbits, introduced in 1870, have reduced the area of tussock grassland and therefore the area suitable for nesting by small burrowing birds. The Macquarie Island parakeet (*Cyanorhamphus novaezelandiae erythrotis*) and the Pacific banded rail (*Rallus philippinensis macquariensis*) have both fallen victim to these pressures and are now extinct.

Several scientists visited the island with the New Zealand sealers and more systematic studies began with the setting up of a station at the north end of the island by the Australasian Antarctic Expedition between 1911 and 1914. On his return the expedition leader, Dr Douglas Mawson, began to lobby for the area to be declared a wildlife sanctuary. The sealing licences were revoked in 1916 and the area became a sanctuary in 1933. A 1958 proposal for a resumption of sealing met strong public opposition. In 1948 the Australian National Antarctic Research Expedition (ANARE) meteorological and research station was

*W*hen the fur and elephant seals had been decimated, digesters and boilers were used to extract oil from penguins.

Right

*T*he colony of macaroni penguins (*Eudyptes chrysolophus*) at Hurd Point is the largest in the world.

established on the flat isthmus between Buckles Bay and Hasselborough Bay and this has been manned ever since. At present there is a wintering party of about twenty people.

Mawson's views about the seals and penguins did not extend to concern for the other biota, and both he and the ANARE party of 1948 put sheep and other livestock ashore. They have long since been rounded up. The main turning point came in the 1970s when the Tasmanian National Parks and Wildlife Service (since May 1987, the Department of Lands, Parks and Wildlife) took control. The status of Macquarie Island was upgraded to state reserve in 1972. It became a UNESCO Biosphere Reserve in 1977 — the only one in the Southern Ocean — and, to make clear the management orientation, it was declared a nature reserve in 1978.

A feral cat among king penguins. They have a disastrous effect upon small indigenous birds.

Most importantly, the Parks and Wildlife Service instituted management programs, including the control of the introduced plants and animals. The European rabbit flea was introduced in 1968 to provide a vector for the myxoma virus. In 1978 the

*S*outhern elephant seals (*Mirounga leonina*) on a rocky kelp-strewn beach on the north coast of Macquarie Island.

*B*ig Ben, with its thick cap of ice, dominates the Heard Island landscape.

flea populations provided a suitable biting host for the virus and rabbit control became feasible. In the ten years since then rabbit numbers have been reduced from some 150 000 to between 15 000 and 17 000 and the herbfield and tussock have made a good recovery. The effect on all aspects of the environment is being monitored. There are doubts, though, as to the practicality of complete removal on the island because the tussocks also provide the rabbits with cover. Cat and weka eradication programs were also started in the 1970s. A management plan has been prepared and a suggestion has been made, but rejected, that a marine reserve be established in the territorial sea zone of three nautical miles around the island.

The vast number of penguins and seals that occupy the beaches is one of the great wildlife sights in the world. Although entry to the island is by permit only and the welfare of the reserve has priority, tourists who are prepared to accept the conditions are not discouraged. The small but still pristine islets of Bishop and Clerk and Judge and Clerk are excluded from entry as is the habitat of the wandering albatross at Caroline Bay during the island's summer breeding season.

Heard and McDonald islands were the last of the subantarctic islands to be discovered. An external territory of Australia, they are situated 4100 kilometres to the southwest of Perth. The islands are raised sections of the extensive Heard–Kerguelen submarine plateau. Heard Island is forty-two by twenty-five kilometres in extent. The main part of the island is roughly circular, being formed around the conical Big Ben massif whose highest point, Mawson Peak (2745 metres), contains the crater of an active volcano. The McDonald Island group lies forty kilometres to the west. McDonald Island itself covers 260 hectares and is also volcanic.

*A*lthough ice covers most of Heard Island, the glaciers are currently in retreat.

The main icecap that blankets the volcanic features of Heard Island is about 150 metres thick. The ice is carried rapidly from the Big Ben massif in the centre by some fifteen glaciers which flow between steep basalt buttresses and terminate at the sea in high ice cliffs. This makes movement around the island very difficult. Travellers have to pick their way through a maze of crevasses. Elsewhere there are grey volcanic sand beaches. Cliffs also make it difficult to land on McDonald Island and, as far as is known, the island has been visited only twice (in 1971 and 1980).

The islands have a cool moist maritime climate which is colder and wetter than Macquarie Island and less equable. In August the minimum temperature at sea level is $-0.6°$ Celsius. Most days have either snow or rain, the amount of precipitation being influenced by the height of Big Ben which causes the westerly air to rise and deposit large amounts of snow on the high ground. Although further north than Macquarie Island, Heard and McDonald islands lie 180 kilometres to the south of the summer boundary of the Antarctic Convergence, the northern limit of the cold Antarctic water. Aerial photographs taken in 1947 and 1980 show that between these dates the ice underwent a marked overall retreat, but the majority of glaciers still reach the sea.

*T*he vent of Mawson Peak on Big Ben, Australia's only active volcano.

Left

*L*ooking down Stephenson Glacier to Spit Point, once a centre of sealing operations.

*H*eard Island has a very simple flora, with only eleven vascular plant species.

Most of the basal limestone rocks of Heard and McDonald islands are covered by glacial till and volcanic lavas. They contain foraminifera, pointing to marine origins in the late Tertiary and to the uplift that has created the foundations of the islands. However, it has been volcanic activity which has created the additional elevation, perhaps occurring when the tectonic plate of which the islands are a part was passing over a 'hot spot'.

Not surprisingly, in view of the scouring effect of the ice, the soils of Heard and McDonald islands are poorly developed and the flora is even simpler than that of Macquarie Island. There are only eleven species of vascular plants. A naturalist with the *Challenger*, J. H. Moseley, who landed on Heard Island in 1874, noted that it was 'miserably poor in flora even for the higher latitudes of the Southern Hemisphere'.

Tussock, herbfield and feldmark are the main vegetation communities below 200 metres. These include cushion plants (*Colobanthus kerguelensis* and *Azorella selago*) and the Kerguelen cabbage (*Pringlea antiscorbutica*). Above 200 metres ice-free areas support only mosses and lichens. Around the coastline kelp (*Macrocystis antarctica*) is abundant and plays an important role in supporting the extensive seal and penguin breeding colonies.

Right

*A*zorella selago, a cushion plant, and *Poa cookii* in old southern elephant seal wallows, Heard Island.

A blue-eyed shag (*Phalacrocorax atriceps nivalis*).

The subantarctic fur seals which were virtually exterminated on Heard Island are steadily recolonising the island, evidently from McDonald Island which remained inaccessible to the sealers. In 1980 some 4300 fur seals were on the island. The island is visited by a large number of leopard seals (*Hydrurga leptonyx*) in September when the sea ice is at its maximum.

The most abundant penguin species is the macaroni (*Eudyptes chrysolophus*). A rookery on McDonald Island is estimated to have 160 000 pairs. There are also

breeding populations of the gentoo, rockhopper and king penguins. Among the other birds recorded from Heard Island, one of the most interesting is the lesser sheathbill (*Chionis minor nasicornis*), an endemic subspecies of a bird which on other subantarctic islands has been wiped out by rats and cats. There are also about 100 pairs of the endemic Heard Island shag (*Phalacrocorax atriceps nivalis*), an example of the capacity of the island fauna to evolve in isolation.

Heard Island appears to have been first sighted by British sealer-explorer Peter Kemp who was on his way to Antarctica, but it was named after John Heard, the captain of an American vessel on a voyage from Boston to Melbourne, who published his 1855 sighting of the island. The McDonald Islands were discovered by a British sealer, Captain McDonald, in 1854. It was on the basis of Peter Kemp's prior sighting that the British claimed the area, which was annexed to Australia in 1947.

The first landing on Heard Island was in 1855 and sealing gangs were continuously in residence on the island from 1857 to 1887, and then sporadically until the 1930s. When the *Challenger* called in 1874, forty sealers were living on the island in wretched conditions. Today, grave markers, a few wooden barrels and the foundation stones of old huts are among the tangible forms of evidence of this era.

*F*ur seal, Heard Island. The fur seals are still recovering from the depradations of the sealing era.

*K*erguelen cabbage (*Pringlea antiscorbutica*) grows inside the remains of a Heard Island oil barrel.

*W*eighted drums secure an expedition tent in the high winds of Atlas Cove, Heard Island.

Concern to establish a continuing 'presence' on Heard Island because of American non-recognition of the Australian claim was a major reason for the establishment of an ANARE base at Atlas Cove from 1947 to 1954 and for a number of subsequent visits. There have been several private expeditions in recent years and ANARE makes intermittent summer visits.

The Territory of Heard and McDonald Islands is subject to the laws of the Australian Capital Territory. In 1983 it was listed on the register of the National Estate. A draft environmental protection and management ordinance and a draft plan of management have been drawn up. If implemented, the plan would determine the areas for tourist visitation and protection, control waste disposal, and lay down measures to prevent the introduction of exotic plant and animal species.

There are other more difficult problems relating to the effect on the island wildlife of fishing and potential oil drilling on the Kerguelen Plateau. Considering the concern that has caused the Australian government to send parties to Heard Island to strengthen its claim, it is strangely slow to move on conservation policies.

As Nigel Bonner has pointed out, the uniqueness of the environment of the oceanic islands demands 'continuing vigilance and discipline', but the lesson of Macquarie Island suggests that prevention may be a lot easier than cure. Efforts to eliminate introductions and protect the island ecosystems would be spurred throughout the subantarctic if some or all of the islands were nominated for the world heritage list. Australia is well placed to show the way to the rest of the world.

GEOFF MOSLEY

Antarctica

Antarctica

*U*nusual fractures of ice on Lake Vanda, Ross Dependency.

*For sheer utter magnificent desolation it is the most
magnificent thing in the world.*

LAURENCE M. GOULD, Antarctic Scientist

Previous pages
A breeding colony of gentoo penguins (*Pygoscelis papua*) at midnight.

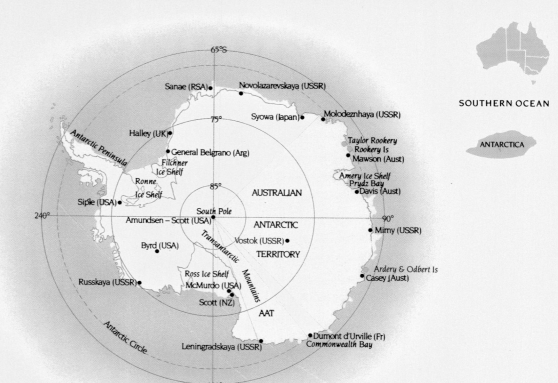

Specially Protected Area

The Antarctic continent is almost certainly the single most important part of the world's heritage. It covers 10 per cent of the earth's surface, and plays a critical role in the world's atmospheric and oceanic circulation systems. Its icecap contains 90 per cent of the world's 'permanent' ice and 68 per cent of its fresh water. If it were to melt — and there is evidence to suggest that much of it did some 3.3 million years ago — global sea level would be raised by some sixty metres.

For most people the Antarctic, like the oceans and the atmosphere, is something that belongs to the world community. The World Conservation Strategy called it a 'global common'; many Third World nations refer to it as 'the common heritage of mankind'. To a certain extent this international status is recognised in the Antarctic Treaty of 1959. Judged against the specific criteria for inclusion of natural properties on the world heritage list, the case for the Antarctic becomes overwhelming.

As a major example of much of the earth's evolutionary history, its merit is obvious. Nature recorded in the ice the evidence, not only of the build-up of the ice sheets, which had significant impacts on world climate, but also of events in the rest of the world. Today's scientists are reclaiming the information to find out what happened in earth history and to make predictions about the future.

The Antarctic is also an immensely dynamic place where all the processes of glaciation can be studied. A visit to Antarctica is like a walk back in time to the Pleistocene era, when great ice sheets occupied the northern parts of Europe and North America and created a lesser icecap over central Tasmania. Among the ice phenomena are floating ice shelves that cover about 2 million square kilometres and are a major source of huge tabular icebergs, and the sea ice which fluctuates in extent from 2.6 million square kilometres in September to 19 million square kilometres in February, when the total area of ice in the Antarctic is doubled.

Although the extreme cold and strong winds make conditions very trying for humans, the beauty of Antarctica and the feeling of being 'out of this world' make it all worth the effort. Apart from the breath-taking grandeur of the ice and the mountain landforms, which either poke through the ice or are exposed near the coast, there is the wonder of the wildlife, particularly the large populations of emperor and Adelie penguins that have adapted to the severe Antarctic climate.

While each facet of the environment has an individual interest and fascination, it is the total environment, and the sense of wilderness that derives from the vast pristine ice features, that give the Antarctic continent a unique dimension.

With the exception of the bases, which provide accommodation for several thousand people, this continent, twice the size of Australia, remains unblemished. None of its resources have ever been exploited. The ocean scenery, which is ever-changing as sea ice forms or breaks up and thousands of icebergs make their stately processions, is undoubtedly part of the wilderness scene. To experience this, and to gain some idea of the remoteness of Antarctica, it is best to travel there by sea. Any seasickness suffered in the 'roaring forties' and the 'furious fifties' is amply compensated for by the enthralling scenes of icebergs, the sea ice and its wildlife.

The commonly accepted boundary for the region is known as the 'Antarctic Convergence'. This is the point where cold water from the continent meets and flows below warmer water from the north. South of this line, which varies in position but is between 50° and 60°s, temperatures drop and wildlife changes considerably. The area to the south of the convergence covers about 49 million square kilometres, of which 14 million square kilometres is the continent of Antarctica.

*A*delie penguins (*Pygoscelis adeliae*) breed on the mainland but obtain all their food from the sea.

Right
*S*ea ice near Davis base. In winter it completely bars the sea route to Antarctica.

Mt Erebus (3794 metres), seen beyond the fantastic forms of ice pressure ridges.

The Australian Antarctic Territory, encompassing 109 degrees of longitude between 45°E and 160°E (but excluding the land between 136°E and 142°E, which is claimed by France), covers 6 million square kilometres, an area three-quarters the size of Australia. It has been administered by Australia since 1936. It would be easy to imagine that this huge area, 98 per cent of which is ice-covered, has a simple geography. In fact the terrain is very varied, at least along the 7500 kilometre coastline where there are islands, ice shelves, glaciers and ice cliffs as well as ice-free areas.

All of the Australian Antarctic Territory (AAT) is part of the dominant east, or greater, Antarctica, whose western boundary is the Transantarctic Mountains. Here the ice is 2000 metres thicker than in the west Antarctic and the overall height of the surface is also considerably greater. In fact Antarctica is the world's most elevated continent. In Wilkes Land the base of the ice is 1400 metres below sea level and reaches a maximum thickness of 4776 metres. So great is the pressure that there are several large lakes underneath the ice.

The coastal zone is the most dynamic because it is here that the ice separates or 'calves' from the icecap. Outlet glaciers and ice shelves remove about 80 per cent of the ice. Included in the AAT is Lambert Glacier, the world's largest, 400 kilometres long and forty kilometres wide. Most glaciers flow either out into the ocean, forming floating tongues, or into ice shelves. The Lambert flows into the Amery Ice Shelf. The icebergs that break off from these glaciers and shelves can be up to 150 kilometres long. They are carried around the continent by the east-wind drift and are sometimes trapped for some time in bays or against islands until freed by the wind. Eventually they move into the westward drift and after about four years of movement, disintegrate and finally melt.

Antarctica is one of the fragments of the former supercontinent Gondwana which, until 150 million years ago when it began to break up, included all the other southern hemisphere continents. Palaeomagnetic evidence suggests that Antarctica was in its present polar position between about 87 and 65 million years ago.

Between about 225 and 65 million years ago the climate was warm and dry and Antarctica supported an evergreen vegetation. At the beginning of the Tertiary (65 million years ago) the climate began a long irregular slide into glaciations which culminated in the development, about 26 million years ago, of ice sheets at sea level in the Ross Sea area. The separation of South America and the full opening of the Drake Passage 23.5 million years ago had allowed the deep west-wind circumpolar current to isolate the continent from contact with the warm ocean water from the north, thus making conditions more favourable for the build-up of the ice sheets.

There are differing scientific opinions on whether the west or the east Antarctic ice sheets formed first, but by 10 million years ago they had united. The ice had built up even more quickly than the uplift of the Transantarctic Mountains. These mountains, which are along a major rift line between the Weddell and Ross seas, started to rise some 20 to 15 million years ago. There is recent evidence, still controversial, of a warmer period about 3.3 million years ago, when the east Antarctic ice sheet may have disappeared.

The climate cooled again and about 2 million years ago major ice sheets formed in the northern hemisphere and the ice in west Antarctica began to fluctuate cyclically. The last major expansion of Antarctic ice was 18 000 years ago during the height of the Pleistocene glaciation.

The Antarctic climate is a key factor in current geomorphological processes. Because of its polar location the Antarctic receives little solar radiation. Even during

*T*he tranquillity of a summer evening belies the potential fury of the Antarctic climate.

*A*ntarctica's outlet glaciers, like this one off King George V Land, float to the ocean.

the nightless days of summer, when incoming radiation is high, the whiteness of the ice and snow reflects most of it back. Therefore it is altitude that most determines differences in temperature. While even in the short summer only a small part of the Antarctic peninsula has a mean annual temperature greater than 0° Celsius, most of the high plateau falls within the −40° Celsius isotherm in winter and the −20° Celsius isotherm in summer. The world's lowest recorded temperature is −89.6° Celsius, at Vostok, 1300 kilometres inland from Casey station.

The great amount of ice suggests the presence of considerable moisture, but Antarctica is actually the driest continent. Over the whole of the continent average precipitation is only ten centimetres per annum. All of this precipitation falls as snow — relatively little melts — and the icecap is the product of hundreds of thousands of years of steady accumulation. The snow-free oases appear to have been created mainly by dust, blown on to the snow by the wind and, by absorbing radiation, causing it to melt and expose the bare rock. Snow that falls is soon blown away, and an oasis like the Bunger Hills is usually snow-covered for a shorter period than are the Australian Alps.

*M*t Erebus, Ross Island, is Antarctica's only active volcano.

370

*T*abular icebergs are carved from ice shelves
and generally survive for about four years.

Much of the research carried out since
people first set foot on the continent in
1895 has been directed towards studying
the history and mechanisms of the ice. Sea
ice research is particularly valuable since
the sea ice will be the first to go if the
world's climate warms up; the removal of
the reflective shield will mean that the
increase in temperature will be greatest,
relatively, in the polar areas. Cores taken

from ice drill holes contain air bubbles to a
considerable depth, and the gases, dust and
pollen that are trapped in these bubbles
yield information about past events and
allow trends to be predicted.

The natural absence of local sources of
dust and smoke makes Antarctica an excellent place to carry out global monitoring of
the atmosphere. Industrialisation of the
region would obviously reduce its value for
this purpose. Even more insidious is the
threat to the existence of the Antarctic ice
from the effect of activities outside the
region. Nature's role in changing climate is
being taken over by the human production
of 'greenhouse gases', which cause temperatures to rise. It has been calculated that the
ice shelves of west Antarctica will begin to
melt if the offshore water temperature
increases by as little as 1.5° Celsius during
the Antarctic summer.

Millions of years of glaciation have
stripped away virtually all trace of soil in
Antarctica, and the lack of available moisture and the chilling cold and wind make
conditions very hard for plant and animal

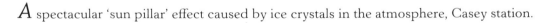

A spectacular 'sun pillar' effect caused by ice crystals in the atmosphere, Casey station.

Right
*A*urora Australis over sea ice, Wilkes Land.

Magnetic Island near Davis station. Ice-free areas are limited and sought out by birds and seals.

life. As a result the only plants that occur outside the Antarctic peninsula are mosses, lichens and algae.

Pick up a quartz rock in one of the ice-free areas and you will swear that the bright green lines are paint marks. Actually they are algae in minute fissures in the rock — a symbol of the desperate search for niches in the harsh climate. The full plant complement of east Antarctica comprises 125 species of lichen, thirty mosses, hundreds of species of land and freshwater algae and one liverwort, *Cephaloziella exiliflora*, which occurs near Casey station. The richest plant life is in the lakes and ponds where there are dense mats of algae and small aquatic animals known as rotifers and tardigrades.

Occasionally, careless people from the northern hemisphere use a polar bear as a symbol of the animal life of Antarctica. In fact a microscope would come in handy for the examination of the continent's largest permanent land animal — a wingless midge about four millimetres in length! In addition there are arthropods, mites, nema-

todes and other invertebrates living in the mosses, guano beds and ponds.

In contrast to the biologically poor continental environment, the ocean is rich in life. The basic building block of the marine food chain is the phytoplankton, including algae, some of which live in the ice and can be detected by a conspicuous pink stain. This is grazed by krill (*Euphausia superba*), a shrimp-like crustacean four or five centimetres long and a key species because it in

Green algae near a penguin colony.
Algae are among the few plants of Antarctica.

turn is eaten by penguins, fish, baleen whales and seals.

There are about 700 000 baleen whales — comprising blue, humpback, sei and minke whales — in Antarctica. The blue whale, the largest mammal on earth, spends about four months of the southern summer feeding close to the edge of the ice.

The true symbols of Antarctic wildlife are the Adelie (*Pygoscelis adeliae*) and emperor (*Aptenodytes forsteri*) penguins, which are the only penguins that breed on or close to the shores of the continent. The Adelie penguins breed on windy rock outcrops. The one-metre-tall emperors incubate their eggs in winter, mainly on the stable sea ice. Of the other birds only the Antarctic petrel (*Thalassoica antarctica*) does its breeding solely on the Antarctic continent and the offshore islands. The total bird population has been put at 188 million.

Antarctica bears a few marks of the impact of humans in the form of the bases but it remains essentially a wilderness. The marine environment, on the other hand, while it seems completely virginal, has been dealt a severe blow from which it will recover only with the passing of time.

When James Cook returned to England in the *Resolution* in 1775 he brought news of the large number of fur and elephant seals in the southern oceans. Ten years later the first sealing in the subantarctic islands had begun and in fewer than four decades the fur seals had been exterminated. The sealers then turned for oil, first to the lumbering elephant seals and then to the plentiful supply of penguins.

The whales suffered a similar fate. In the last decade of the nineteenth century, after the whaling stocks of the northern oceans had been fished to the point of exhaustion, the whalers, armed with steam-driven catchers and explosive harpoon guns, turned their attention to the Southern Ocean. By the 1960s the blue and the humpback had been reduced to fewer than 5000 individuals.

*E*mperor penguins (*Aptenodytes forsteri*), weighing thirty kilograms, breed on the sea ice from March to May.

Overleaf

*T*he Transantarctic Mountains are a distinctive landform in the Antarctic continent.

*W*hen the sea ice breaks, it often fractures into regular shapes.

The tragic destruction of the great whales is not yet matched by any similar event on the Antarctic continent. In fact the huts of the 'heroic age' of the early years of this century are recognised as historic monuments. Mawson's huts at Commonwealth Bay, which formed the base of the first Australian expedition between 1911 and 1914, have been placed on the register of the National Estate and restoration work is taking place.

The events in the Southern Ocean were so starkly tragic that even those who participated in the slow-moving Antarctic Treaty system resolved that something should be done. The Convention on the Conservation of Antarctic Marine Living Resources, which was negotiated under the aegis of the Antarctic Treaty in 1980 (and came into force in 1982), introduced a concept which takes into account the impact of fishing on other parts of the ecosystem. The weakness of this largely voluntary approach is, however, highlighted by the overfishing, near South Georgia, of the Antarctic cod.

The main instrument for trying to achieve conservation on the continent is the Agreed Measures for the Conservation of Antarctic Fauna and Flora of 1964. As these are only recommendations and depend on the goodwill of countries involved

A visiting southern elephant seal (*Mirounga leonina*) outside one of Mawson's huts.

*A*ttempts are being made to preserve Mawson's huts, erected in 1912 at Commonwealth Bay.

in Antarctica, they do not offer much protection to the environment. The Agreed Measures give priority to the establishment, supply and operation of stations. There are several 'Specially Protected Areas' (SPAs), or nature reserves, but these have been kept to a minimum in number and size and there are none in marine areas. Australia, despite its vast area in the Antarctic, has only three SPAs, all of them important as breeding areas for small birds.

Another defect of the Agreed Measures is that they do not provide for positive management. The treaty itself has no staff and the resulting mishmash of national ordinances and regulations creates a piecemeal system of conservation.

'Act only when there is a problem' could be the watchword of the Antarctic Treaty system, but the threat to wilderness is not recognised by the treaty members. The treaty was designed to ensure continued scientific cooperation and maintain the Antarctic for peaceful purposes. It banned military activities, nuclear explosions and the dumping of nuclear waste, but it said nothing about the exploitation of resources. Mining was regarded as a 'peaceful purpose', and references to 'conservation' in the treaty have been used to justify the regulation of mineral exploitation. A policy of voluntary restraint has applied since 1978 but the negotiation of a minerals convention is almost completed.

*M*uch of the Antarctic coastline is made up of ice, seen here at John O'Groats, Commonwealth Bay.

*E*mperor penguins (*Aptenodytes forsteri*). The chicks are brooded during the height of the Antarctic winter.

The severe climatic and ice conditions are likely to make mining in the Antarctic a risky business and the general opinion among mining interests is that mineral extraction is not likely to be commercially viable until well into the next century. However, once applications can be made, it seems likely that some companies, for a variety of reasons, will want to be 'first in'.

The threat of contamination by oil is of particular concern since recent experiments show that it would take spilled oil 580 years to decompose in the Antarctic. The effect of this on the relatively simple Antarctic food chain, and on scientific studies, can easily be imagined, as can the impact of industrial activities on the value of Antarctica for monitoring changes in the atmosphere. Integral to these specific losses is the loss of the opportunity to create a system that would optimise the scientific, recreational and fishing benefits, and that would be more likely to maintain peacefulness in the region.

It is clear that those who support mining want to profit from access to the area's non-living resources; but they also argue that if there were no minerals regime unregulated mining would take place and cause even more environmental damage. This of course is an admission of the weakness of the present system of control.

*D*ry valley landscape from Asgard Range.

The clear option is to make Antarctica and parts of the surrounding seas into a national park with a strong system of administration. It would be the first 'world park' and its creation would ensure that priority was given to conservation, that mineral activity was banned, and that management was improved.

Better planning is obviously needed because, although Antarctica is huge, human and wildlife activity is focused on the ice-free areas which together occupy an area no larger that the state of Victoria. Waste disposal, transport facilities, tourism and scientific research all require a planned approach. Although a world park, established under the Antarctic Treaty, would entail no change in jurisdiction, there would for the first time be a management body. Properly developed, this also would be the best means for keeping the area free from future international disputes. Unfortunately, as the Antarctic Treaty parties have never considered the establishment of a world park, it is essential that the moratorium on mineral activity be continued until this option is considered.

The inclusion of the Antarctic on the world heritage list would give formal international recognition to the values that are so obvious to those who have been to Antarctica and would increase the moral imperative for protection. Claimant states

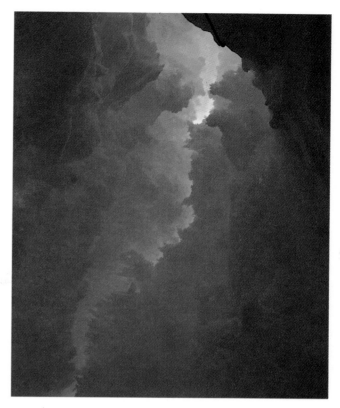

A view upward to the roof of a deep crevasse.

such as Australia could nominate their territories, either separately or together, perhaps after gaining the concurrence of the treaty parties. It would be up to the World Heritage Committee to judge whether there were responsible authorities capable of protecting the world heritage. The best formula for the Antarctic would be a combination of world park and world heritage listing.

Antarctica was the last of lands to be discovered. Miraculously it has survived intact into an era where naturalness is now appreciated. In spite of this, sustainable land management plans do not exist for most areas on earth and the fate of the Antarctic as wilderness hangs by a slim thread. The chance to be involved in the heroic age of exploration has gone but not so the opportunity to take on an equally difficult challenge — the fight to save our last great wilderness. In that fight we will also perhaps discover the cooperation required to save the planet.

GEOFF MOSLEY

A modern glacier — the rubbish dump near Casey station. Refuse is now being shipped back.

Left

*A*delie penguins (*Pygoscelis adeliae*) on brash ice.

A Wealth
of Possibilities

A Wealth of Possibilities

Part of the vast wilderness that is the Nullarbor Plain.

The humanising gifts of Nature are necessary for our interest, education, adventure, romance and peace of mind. They constitute the antidote for the evils of our semi-artificial existence. As we destroy our bushland environment we destroy just so much of ourselves. The balance of Nature is finely adjusted; upset it, and there will be a desert at our doors.

Myles Dunphy, *Katoomba Daily*, 24 August 1934

Previous pages
Sunset over the Cape Range Peninsula, Western Australia.

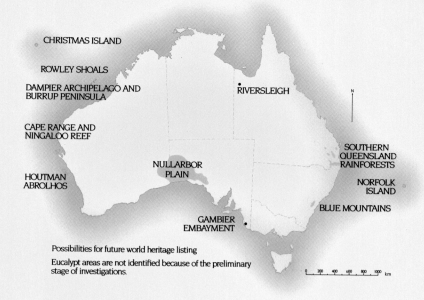

CHRISTMAS ISLAND

ROWLEY SHOALS

DAMPIER ARCHIPELAGO AND
BURRUP PENINSULA

RIVERSLEIGH

CAPE RANGE AND
NINGALOO REEF

SOUTHERN
QUEENSLAND
RAINFORESTS

NULLARBOR
PLAIN

HOUTMAN
ABROLHOS

NORFOLK
ISLAND

BLUE MOUNTAINS

GAMBIER
EMBAYMENT

Possibilities for future world heritage listing

Eucalypt areas are not identified because of the preliminary
stage of investigations.

0   200   400   600   800   1000 km

The survey of Australia's world heritage in this publication has important qualifications. It has taken a broad-brush approach in identifying areas; it has not tried to define boundaries. The maps and text simply seek to describe substantial areas that contain known characteristics of world class. While some featured areas have been thoroughly investigated for their world heritage values, others have been little, or only partly, evaluated. Therefore actual world heritage proposals may be substantially different — larger, smaller or with an emphasis other than that our chapters have indicated. This leaves aside the complex politics frequently involved in determining the details of a proposal.

Other regions, particularly those discussed below, have great potential but have not been accorded the status of a full chapter in this publication because of space limitations and sometimes because of the lack of detailed data. Time may show that some of the areas which we have covered in only a few paragraphs are of equal or greater importance than those that were accorded chapters. Although we have tried to identify Australia's key natural sites of international importance, it is also possible that the text may not acknowledge an area whose importance becomes evident in the future. In this varied and ancient land there really is a wealth of possibilities.

The vast Nullarbor Plain, which occupies a third of a million square kilometres of the continent's underbelly, symbolises the perceptions of both Australians and non-Australians about this land — remote, arid and creating a 'tyranny of distance'. Surprisingly, perhaps, many scientists regard it as having high potential for world heritage listing. The Nullarbor is one of the world's largest limestone areas and by far the largest in an arid region. There are many surface limestone (karst) features of interest and over a hundred caves, some of which are very large and contain spectacular underground lakes and rare cave decorations of great beauty. One of the caves, Koonalda Cave in South Australia, was used as a flint mine up to 22 000 years ago. The rock art found there is possibly the oldest in Australia and comparable with the Palaeolithic cave art of Europe.

*T*he edge of a continent: the Great Australian Bight.

The region is rich in other archaeological sites which illustrate the remarkable adaptability of humans to an inhospitable environment. Apart from its scientific and archaeological values, the Nullarbor has its own aesthetic appeal, particularly when the great plain abruptly and dramatically ends in high cliffs that plunge into the turquoise waters of the Great Australian Bight.

Another cave region, the Gambier Embayment in southeast South Australia and southwest Victoria, is also considered of international significance. The principal cave area around Naracoorte contains some of the most important fossil sites in the southern hemisphere. Within the rich deposits scientists have found the remains of giant Pleistocene animals. Huge kangaroos, a large echidna, a wombat-like species the size of a hippopotamus and a marsupial 'lion' are among the many extinct species found. Other still living species have been identified from the remains in the chambers. The quantity and excellent state of preservation of the deposits afford outstanding opportunities for the study of animal populations.

Australia is rich in important fossil sites apart from Naracoorte. The Australian Heritage Commission has identified more than fifty palaeontological sites of national and international importance. Chief among these is Riversleigh in northwest Queensland's Gulf Country, a site widely acknowledged as one of the most significant in the world. Located in unspectacular spinifex-covered low hills between the comparatively lush oases of Lawn Hill Gorge and the Gregory River, the region has yielded a huge find of superbly preserved fossils of this continent's extraordinary animals. The fossil deposits date from between 15 million years ago (Miocene) and 50 000 years ago (Pleistocene); most of them are between 10 and 15 million years old.

Although the site has been known for many years, the deposits were explored in detail only in 1983. Since then, more than two hundred new vertebrate species have been recognised by the research teams. They include a giant seven metre python, a cow-sized wombat-like species, a tiny ancient koala, and a carnivorous pouched 'lion' which probably dwelt in the trees.

Scientists believe that these ancient animals were supported by dense wet sclerophyll forests and rainforests. Many of the descendants of these creatures are still found in today's remaining rainforests; others are found in arid and semiarid environments. This raises the very real possibility that the majority of our land-based fauna originated in rainforests and have evolved and adapted as the climate changed. Such fossil evidence underlines the urgency of protecting what remains of the rainforests.

Riversleigh offers science a remarkable opportunity to study the evolution of Australia's fauna and an opportunity for Australia to take a lead in international palaeontological and evolutionary studies. Its discovery has caused enormous excitement in international scientific circles and the area's acknowledgment by world heritage listing would be universally applauded.

*T*he island territory of Christmas Island.

*N*aracoorte caves, Gambier Embayment.

Far from the arid landscapes of the Nullarbor and Riversleigh is Australia's remote territory of Christmas Island. Located 2300 kilometres northwest of Perth, the island has long been celebrated by both amateur and professional scientists as a place of unique ecology. It is one of the world's great seabird islands with breeding rookeries for a number of rare and endangered species. These include the endemic Christmas Island hawk-owl (*Nonix squamipila natalis*), the Christmas Island frigatebird (*Fregata andrewsi*), Abbot's booby (*Sula abboti*) and the lovely golden bosun (*Phaethon lepturus fulrus*) and large colonies of more common seabirds.

This tiny island is rich in species that exist nowhere else on earth; apart from the seabirds, there are seven land birds, twenty-one plants, five reptiles, two bats and a number of insects. Many of these species breed in the rainforest which has found a niche above the sheer cliffs that ring the island on stepped terraces that rise to a central forested plateau. A diverse and interesting marine fauna thrives in the coral reefs that fringe this beautiful island.

The phosphate industry, which has mined the island for nearly a century, is now closing down. This should mean an end to the disastrous clearing of rainforest that has threatened its heritage. With proper management the island could be an outstanding destination for the naturalist.

Norfolk Island, another island territory of Australia, is considered by many to be the best preserved example in the world of the European penal settlements that were established in remote locations in the first half of the nineteenth century. The island combines its interesting cultural heritage with exceptional natural values. It possesses magnificent coastal scenery, major seabird breeding areas and remnants of endemic flora and fauna in the subtropical rainforests, including groves of the famous Norfolk Island pine (*Araucaria heterophylla*).

A far-flung archipelago of outstanding forested areas could be nominated for listing if an initiative begun by the major non-government conservation organisations in 1987 is successful. The preliminary study into the world heritage value of eucalypt forests concludes that 'there are good prospects that a group of substantially undisturbed eucalypt forest sites, representing a range of vegetation communities, would be of world heritage quality'. The study argues that Australia's substantially undisturbed eucalypt forests are among the few forests in the world that remain essentially unmodified by human activities. The declaration of these forests could incorporate or extend several of the areas described in this book; for example, southwest Western Australia and the Alps are both regarded as prime eucalypt areas.

There appears to be a *Eucalyptus* species for virtually every environment on this large continent, from snow-blasted mountaintops to swamps and the better watered arid areas. As a result, the genus provides an excellent example of the processes of speciation and evolution. Its adaptability, including the ability to survive fire, grow on soils with very low fertility and tolerate salt,

means that Australian eucalypt forests have international value as a gene pool of species which may well prove vital in other parts of the world in controlling erosion and providing wood products on degraded land. In addition, the great variety of eucalypt forests provides extremely beautiful landscapes while sheltering a range of unique plants and animals.

A first step towards the achievement of world heritage listing for Australia's prime eucalypt-dominated forested areas has been taken with the announcement by the Victorian government in late 1987 that it will seek world heritage listing for the Alps and the national parks of East Gippsland. The struggle to protect some of these outstanding forests has been one of Australia's

*E*ucalypts flourish on the sandstone plateau and in the gorges of the Wollemi National Park.

longest conservation efforts. The nomination would include the Rodger Bowen wilderness area, which contains one of the few pristine catchment areas left in Victoria and rare undisturbed stands of the lofty mountain ash (*Eucalyptus regnans*). The diverse vegetation, rich wildlife and scenic beauty of the Errinundra Plateau would also be acknowledged for its international significance.

Eucalypt forests are an important feature of the Blue Mountains region of New South Wales. Extending from the Hunter Valley in the north to Wombeyan Caves in the south, the mountains are acclaimed for their outstanding scenery. The plateaus have been eroded into deep valleys with sheer cliffs of beautiful coloured sandstone.

Both the plateaus and valley floors harbour a rich sandstone flora with many local endemics. The mountains also encompass the state's two largest wilderness areas, the wild Colo and Kowmung rivers and many sites of cultural importance to both Aboriginal and European cultures.

The acceptance of the New South Wales rainforests and the nomination of the wet tropics in the north of Queensland have given the wet forests a lead over the eucalypts in world recognition. However, a gap remains where the rainforests of southern Queensland have not been adequately recognised. These forests include splendid areas of subtropical rainforest like the Lamington National Park and the Conondale Ranges west of Brisbane.

*T*he Burrup Peninsula near Dampier in Western Australia has an
unspoiled marine environment of scientific importance. Its low hills
shelter Aboriginal rock art galleries of undoubted international significance.

Australia's largest state, Western Australia, has always lent itself to superlatives. It is not surprising therefore that Western Australian scientists argue vehemently for the inclusion of several of their many valuable areas. Houtman Abrolhos, for instance, is a collection of low islands and reefs some 500 kilometres north of Perth. The area has an interesting cultural history as the site of early contacts with European explorers and the resting place for numerous wrecks, including the famous *Batavia* of 1629. The ecological significance of the region arises from the reef's location as the most southerly coral reef in the Indian Ocean and one of the most southerly in the world. As the reef lies at the boundary of the southern temperate marine province and the tropical zone, it gives rise to a rich environment with many overlaps of species.

The islands support huge rookeries of seabirds, including probably the world's most important breeding colony for the beautiful lesser noddy (*Anous tenuirostris*) and populations of mammal species like the tammar wallaby (*Macropus eugenii*) which is rare on the mainland.

At the point where the great northwestern curve of Western Australia turns northeast lies the Cape Range Peninsula and offshore Ningaloo Reef. The range is notable for its rugged arid beauty, as the ages have dissected its limestone layers into often deep and colourful canyons. Lying off

*T*he subtly coloured limestone hills and canyons of
Cape Range are rich in fossils.

*T*he reefs and islands of the Houtman Abrolhos
have historical and ecological significance.

the Cape, Ningaloo Reef is one of only two places in the world where a coral reef exists on the western side of a continent.

Another 400 kilometres to the northeast lie the Burrup Peninsula and Dampier Archipelago. The marine environment is of great beauty and interest, but its chief claim to world heritage status is that the peninsula is regarded as having one of the finest galleries of rock art in the world. The strange low boulder hills of the peninsula are covered in countless rock engravings or petroglyphs, many of which are believed to date from the ice age. The engravings depict the rich fauna of the region, including some species which are now extinct like the Tasmanian tiger. The scenes are considered to be more complex and animated than any other engravings in Australia.

A further Western Australian site is a group of remote coral atolls perched on the edge of the continental shelf at its widest and one of its deepest points. The Rowley Shoals are nearly perfect examples of atoll geomorphology, while their unusual location adds scientific interest. They are among the few reefs in the world affected by a high tidal range. The dramatic five metre tides pouring massive volumes in and out of the coral framework have created a most unusual structure of strong aesthetic appeal. Their remote location gives the shoals a marine wilderness status while their pristine condition makes them an important resource for scientific research.

In the world of economics nations must evaluate where they have particular strengths over other nations; in the jargon of the discipline, this becomes their 'comparative advantage'. It is clear from this book that Australia has a significant comparative advantage in possessing a wealth of magnificent natural areas, at least some of which remain in wilderness condition. This heritage is unique because of the continent's ancient isolation and the relatively recent arrival of non-Aboriginal people. But Australia's comparative advantage goes beyond the actual treasures that its people hold in trust and extends to their ability to safeguard them. Australia is a comparatively affluent country whose citizens are not forced by the need to survive from day to day to forgo the future and exploit the land to exhaustion. It is also an educated land. Australians are increasingly acquiring an understanding of the values of these areas and a knowledge of how to manage them so that their precious qualities remain to be passed on to future generations.

PENELOPE FIGGIS

THE MAKING OF AUSTRALIA'S WILDERNESS HERITAGE

THE PHOTOGRAPHER

LEO MEIER is undoubtedly one of Australia's leading wildlife photographers. He gained his technical expertise from training in printing, graphic arts, scientific and process photography. This background brings superb craftsmanship to the range of natural subjects which Leo photographs. At the same time, his profound affinity with nature adds an emotional depth and sensitivity to his work.

Leo's photographs have been published in many books and magazines, both in Australia and overseas. His major nature books have been *Australia the Beautiful Wilderness*, *Wilderness Blooms*, *Small Creatures of the Australian Wilderness*, *Daintree*, *Rainforests of Australia* and, most recently, *Kakadu: a Heritage for the Future*. As a dedicated conservationist, Leo hopes his photography will contribute to the better protection of the Australian environment by awakening his fellow Australians to the beauty of their land.

To obtain the images used in this publication, Leo Meier travelled almost 50 000 kilometres. He drove, alone, for over 45 000 kilometres in a specially converted four-wheel-drive truck through some of the toughest and loneliest areas of the continent. He covered another 2000 kilometres by plane and helicopter in order to photograph areas whose special qualities can best be appreciated from the air. He investigated coastal and inland waterways by boat and trudged 1200 kilometres on foot through areas that were otherwise inaccessible.

In the course of this mammoth expedition Leo had to face difficulties of sometimes epic proportions and was often exposed to danger. Extreme weather conditions caused discomfort and illness, and sometimes played havoc with the complex and extremely sensitive equipment needed to undertake his task. At Khancoban in the Australian Alps he was blocked in for three days by heavy snowstorms, while in the north his four-wheel-drive vehicle was frequently bogged as a result of monsoonal rains. In the Ormiston Ranges of central Australia he experienced nausea and dizzy spells while lugging a forty-four kilogram pack in the 39° Celsius heat, and in Kakadu he suffered severe pain and partial paralysis for several days as a result of a scorpion bite. At Victoria Downs he became lost at night in desert conditions. Cut and bruised and relying on the stars, he found his way back to camp after almost seven hours. At Gosse's Bluff in the Northern Territory his radio failed while he was lost among unmarked bush tracks and a police alert was instituted when he remained out of contact for several days.

Leo's commitment and skill have been well justified. These volumes are a tribute to his undoubted dedication and talent.

THE AUTHORS

PENELOPE FIGGIS is a vice-president of the Australian Conservation Foundation and serves on the Board of Management of Uluru National Park as the appointee of the Commonwealth minister for the environment.

An honours graduate in political science, Penny has been an active campaigner for the environment for over a decade. She contributed to the successful New South Wales campaigns to protect the Wollemi wilderness and remaining rainforests, and went on to defend the environment at Commonwealth level as the national liaison officer of the Australian Conservation Foundation from 1982 to 1984. Her work involved lobbying on issues such as the Franklin Dam, the Daintree rainforest and Kakadu.

After moving to central Australia in late 1984, Penny became a Northern Territory councillor for the foundation and was elected its first woman vice-president. She has written and published many articles and papers, and is the editor of *Rainforests of Australia* (Weldons, 1985).

GEOFF MOSLEY, as director of the Australian Conservation Foundation from 1973 to 1986, was a leader of the campaigns to save many of the areas described in this book. His interest in conservation developed from an upbringing in the Peak District, England's first national park, and his training as a geographer.

From 1981 to 1988 Geoff was Australia's representative on the Council of the International Union for Conservation of Nature and Natural Resources (IUCN), and helped this body assess Australia's nominations for the world heritage list. His chief conservation ambition for the future is to help realise a world park in Antarctica, the subject of his latest book, *Antarctica: Our Last Great Wilderness* (Australian Conservation Foundation, 1986). He now works as an environmental consultant.

C. WARREN BONYTHON has had wide-ranging experience of the eastern arid region for nearly forty years. While working professionally in the chemical industry he carried out scientific studies of outback Australia in such disciplines as geography, geology, geochemistry, meteorology and hydrology. He has been researching Lake Eyre since 1950 in its ever-changing environmental roles.

His walks across the Simpson Desert, round Lake Eyre and through parts of the Tirari and Sturt's Stony deserts, and several off-road traverses through the region by motor vehicle, consolidated his knowledge of and love for the area.

DAVID DALE is a Perth-based scientific consultant whose major interests are environmental protection and development planning. He originally qualified as a physical chemist and has experience as an academic, public servant, city councillor and businessman.

David was born and raised in Zimbabwe. Since migrating to Australia in 1962 he has lived in the eastern states and Papua New Guinea for several years but has spent most of his time in the west. He visits the Kimberley and Shark Bay regularly, sometimes as a tour leader for groups.

He organised a major Kimberley conservation seminar for the Western Australian government in 1987 and a Shark Bay seminar in 1986.

ROBERT COUPE is a freelance writer. For a number of years he was a high school teacher and since 1973 has worked in the publishing industry. He has been involved in the publication of numerous books, both for children and adults, on aspects of natural history, has written articles for reference works and is the author and co-author of five books.

The Consultant Editors

TIM FLANNERY is the zoological consultant to the project. He is a leading authority on rainforest mammals and has also a particular interest in fossils. He has named and classified many of the extinct kangaroo species discovered at Riversleigh and other sites and has made a particular study of the evolution of mammals in Melanesia and the Pacific Islands. Recently Tim discovered the world's largest rat, a previously unknown species, in a remote area in New Guinea. He is a research scientist with the Australian Museum in Sydney.

TONY RODD is the botanical consultant to the project. For eighteen years Tony was a horticultural botanist at the Royal Botanic Gardens in Sydney, in charge of record keeping, labelling and preparing informational material about the plants growing in the gardens. More recently, Tony has built up a reputation as a botanical photographer and writer. He is the co-author of a major work, *Palms* (Angus & Robertson, 1981), and has acted as botanical consultant to the *Macquarie Thesaurus*, the *Macquarie Dictionary of Trees and Shrubs* and the *Australian Encyclopaedia*.

BIBLIOGRAPHY

KAKADU AND ARNHEM LAND

Australian National Parks and Wildlife Service. *Kakadu National Park: Plan of Management.* The Service, Canberra, 1986

Australian National Parks and Wildlife Service. *Nomination of Kakadu National Park for Inclusion in the World Heritage List.* The Service, Canberra, 1980

Balderstone, S. and Meier, L. *Kakadu: a Heritage for the Future.* Weldons, Sydney, 1987

Christian, C. S. and Aldrick, J. M. *Alligator Rivers Study: a Review Report of the Alligator Rivers' Environmental Fact-finding Study.* AGPS, Canberra, 1977

Cooper, D. and Gunn, B. 'Kakadu's Stage III: Aboriginal Art Treasures in Danger'. *Habitat* 15, 4, August 1987, 16–19

Fox, A. 'Kakadu is Aboriginal Land'. *Ambio* 12, 3–4, 1983, 161–66

Fox, R. W. et al. *Ranger Uranium Environmental Inquiry Second Report.* AGPS, Canberra, 1977

Gillespie, D. (ed). *The Rock Art Sites of Kakadu National Park: Some Preliminary Research Findings from their Conservation and Management.* (Australian National Parks and Wildlife Service Special Publication, 10) The Service, Canberra, 1983

Jones, R. *Archaeological Research in Kakadu National Park.* (Australian National Parks and Wildlife Service Special Publication, 13) The Service, Canberra, 1985

Neidjie, W. et al. *Kakadu Man.* Mybrood, Queanbeyan, NSW, 1985

Ovington, D. *Kakadu: a World Heritage of Unsurpassed Beauty.* AGPS, Canberra, 1986

THE GREAT BARRIER REEF

Bennett, I. *The Great Barrier Reef.* Lansdowne, Sydney, 1971

Gillet, K. *Coral Wonderland.* Reed, Sydney, 1980

'The Great Barrier Reef'. *Habitat* (Special issue) 3, 4, October–November 1975

Great Barrier Reef Marine Park Authority. *Nomination of the Great Barrier Reef for Inclusion in the World Heritage List.* The Authority, Townsville, January 1981

McGregor, C. *The Great Barrier Reef.* Time–Life, Amsterdam, 1974

Wright, J. *Coral Battleground.* Nelson, Melbourne, 1977

WILLANDRA LAKES

Australian Heritage Commission. *Nomination of the Willandra Lakes Region for Inclusion in the World Heritage List.* The Commission, Canberra, 1980

Mulvaney, D. J. and Bowler, J. M. 'Lake Mungo and the Willandra Lakes', in *The Heritage of Australia: the Illustrated Register of the National Estate.* Macmillan, Melbourne, 1981

National Parks and Wildlife Service of New South Wales. 'Draft Regional Environmental Study for Willandra Lakes World Heritage Region'

WESTERN AND CENTRAL TASMANIA

Angus, M. *The World of Olegas Truchanas.* The Olegas Truchanas Publication Committee, Hobart, 1975

Banks, M. R. (ed). *Lake Country of Tasmania.* Royal Society of Tasmania, Hobart, 1972

Binks, C. *Explorers of Western Tasmania.* Mary Fisher Bookshop, Launceston, 1980

Brown, R. *Lake Pedder.* Wilderness Society, Hobart, 1986

Dombrovskis, P. *Wild Rivers.* The Author, Hobart, 1983

Gee, H. and Fenton, J. *The South West Book: a Tasmanian Wilderness.* Australian Conservation Foundation, Melbourne, 1978

Jones, R. 'Ice-Age Hunters of the Tasmanian Wilderness'. *Australian Geographic* 8, October–December 1987, 26–45

Siseman, J. and Chapman, J. *Cradle Mountain National Park.* Alhona, Melbourne, 1984

Southwell, L. *Mountains of Paradise.* The Author, Melbourne, 1983

Tasmania. Lands Department. *Handbook: the Central Plateau of Tasmania.* The Department, Hobart, 1982

Tasmanian Conservation Trust. *The Forest*

Book: Photographs of Tasmania's Endangered Forests. The Trust, Hobart, 1984

Wilderness Society. *The Franklin Blockade: By the Blockaders.* The Society, Hobart, 1983

LORD HOWE ISLAND

Australian Heritage Commission. *Nomination of the Lord Howe Island Group by the Commonwealth of Australia for Inclusion in the World Heritage List.* The Commission, Canberra, 1981

Edgecombe, J. and Bennett, I. *Discovering Lord Howe Island.* Pacific Maps, Sydney, undated

Hutton, I. *Lord Howe Island: Discovering Australia's World Heritage.* Conservation Press, Canberra, 1986

Lord Howe Island Board. *Lord Howe Island Regional Environmental Plan.* The Board, Sydney, 1986

Murray, C. 'Lord Howe Island', in *Australia in Trust.* Collins/Australian Council of National Trusts, Sydney, 1985

National Parks and Wildlife Service of New South Wales. *Plan of Management: Lord Howe Island Permanent Park Preserve.* The Service, Sydney, 1986

New South Wales State Planning Authority. *Report of the Chairman of the Lord Howe Island Board on the Future Land Use and Management of Lord Howe Island.* The Authority, Sydney, 1975

Recher, H. F. *A Report to the Lord Howe Island Board on an Environmental Survey of Lord Howe Island.* Department of Environmental Studies, Australian Museum, Sydney, 1974

NEW SOUTH WALES RAINFORESTS

Adam, P. *New South Wales Rainforests: the Nomination for the World Heritage List.* National Parks and Wildlife Service (NSW), Sydney, 1987

'The Border Ranges' *Habitat* (Special issue) 4, 3, August 1976

Figgis, P. (ed). *Rainforests of Australia.* Weldons, Sydney, 1985

Goldstein, W. (ed). *Rainforests.* National Parks and Wildlife Service (NSW), Sydney, 1977

Serventy, V. and Raymond, R. *Rainforests of Australia.* Hamlyn, Sydney, 1980

'Terania' *National Parks Journal* (Special issue) 24, 2, April 1980

Werren, G. L. and Kershaw, A.P. (eds). *Australian National Rainforest Study, Vol I.* Australian Conservation Foundation, Melbourne, 1984

THE WESTERN ARID REGION

Australian National Parks and Wildlife Service. *Nomination of Uluru (Ayers Rock–Mount Olga) National Park for Inclusion on the World Heritage List.* The Service, November, 1986

Chippendale, G. M. 'Ecological Notes on the Western Desert Area of the Northern Territory'. *Proceedings of the Linnean Society of New South Wales.* 78, 1, 1963

Davey, K. *Our Arid Environment.* Reed, Sydney, 1983

Figgis, P. 'The Magnificent Macdonnell Ranges: a Conservation Disgrace'. *Habitat* 14, 4, August 1986

Kenneally, T. *The Outback.* Hodder and Stoughton, Sydney, 1983

Latz, P. K. et al. 'A Biological Survey of the Kings Canyon Area of the George Gill Range'. Internal Report to the Wildlife Research Section, Conservation Commission of the Northern Territory, September 1981

Moffit, I. *The Australian Outback.* Time–Life, Amsterdam, 1976

Northern Territory National Parks Association. 'Wilderness, Parks and Conservation Areas in Central Australia: Future Possibilities'. Draft Position Paper, November 1987

'Pukulpa pitjaria anangaku ngurakuta: Welcome to Aboriginal Land'. A series of pamphlets produced by the Mutitjulu Community on the history, lease and environment of Uluru National Park, 1985

Roff, D. *Ayers Rock and the Olgas.* Ure Smith, Sydney, 1979

Uluru Katatjuta Board of Management. *Uluru (Ayers Rock–Mount Olga) National Park Plan of Management.* Australian

National Parks and Wildlife Service, 1986

Walton, P. *Red Centre.* Currey O'Neil, Melbourne, 1984

THE WET TROPICS

'Australia's Tropical Rainforests'. (Habitat Education Supplement, 4) *Habitat* 15, 2, April 1987

Borschmann, G. *Greater Daintree: World Heritage at Risk.* Australian Conservation Foundation, Melbourne, 1986

Habitat 12, 4, August 1984

Keto, A. 'Last Glimpse of an Ancient Era'. *Habitat* 15, 2, April 1987

Keto, A. 'Tropical Rainforests', in Figgis, P. (ed). *Rainforests in Australia.* Weldons, Sydney, 1985

Parker, P. and Callahan, S. 'Daintree: Rainforest or Real Estate'. *Habitat* 15, 2, April 1987

Rainforest Conservation Society of Queensland. *Tropical Rainforests of North Queensland: Their Conservation Significance.* (Australian Heritage Commission Special Publication, 3). AGPS, Canberra, 1986

Russell, R. *Daintree: Where the Rainforest Meets the Reef.* Kevin Weldon/Australian Conservation Foundation, Sydney, 1985

THE GREAT SANDY REGION

Baverstock, F. *Fraser Island: Sands of Time.* Australian Broadcasting Corporation, Sydney, 1985

Cato, N. *The Noosa Story.* Jacaranda, Brisbane, 1979

Hemmings, L. and Sinclair, J. *Nomination of the Great Sandy Region for Inclusion in the World Heritage List.* Report Prepared for the Australian Conservation Foundation, Melbourne, 1984

'Incredible Fraser Island'. *Habitat* (Special issue) 2, 4, October 1974

Miller, G. and Coster, J. *Cooloola: Queensland's Unique Coastal Wilderness.* Milcos Associates, Queensland, 1979

Sinclair, J. *Discovering Cooloola.* Pacific Maps, Sydney, 1978

Sinclair, J. *Discovering Fraser Island.* Australasian Environmental Publications, Sydney, 1987

CAPE YORK PENINSULA

Australian Conservation Foundation. *Cape York Peninsula: a National Parks and Land-Use Plan.* The Foundation, Melbourne, 1979

Breeden, S. and Breeden, K. *Tropical Queensland.* Collins, Sydney, 1970

Flood, J. 'The Rock Paintings of Cape York', in *Australia in Trust.* Australian Council of National Trusts/Collins, Sydney, 1985, 238–45

Henry, D. and Reeders, P. 'What Future Eastern Cape York?' *Habitat* 15, 2, 1986

Roberts, J. P. (ed). *The Mapoon Story by the Mapoon People.* International Development Action, Melbourne, 1975

Stanton, J. P. *National Parks for Cape York Peninsula.* Australian Conservation Foundation, Melbourne, 1976

Stevens, N. C. and Bailey, A. (eds). *Contemporary Cape York Peninsula.* Royal Society of Queensland, Brisbane, 1980

Trezise, P. J. *Quinkan Country.* Reed, Sydney, 1969

Wright, J. et al (eds). *Reef, Rainforest, Mangroves and Man: a Focus on Cape York Peninsula.* Wildlife Preservation Society of Queensland, Cairns, 1980

THE KIMBERLEY

Burbidge, A. A. et al. 'Nature Conservation Reserves in the Kimberley, Western Australia'. Submission to the Kimberley Region Planning Study. Department of Conservation and Land Management, Perth, 1987

Conservation Through Reserves Committee. 'Conservation Reserves for Western Australia: System'. Report to the Environmental Protection Authority, Perth, 1978

Davies, R. J. P. *Conservation Priorities in North-Western Australia.* Australian Conservation Foundation, Melbourne, 1985

Environmental Protection Authority. *Conservation Reserves for Western Australia: System 7.* The Authority, Perth, 1980

SHARK BAY

Conservation Through Reserves Committee. 'Conservation Reserves for Western Australia.' Report to the Environmental Protection Authority, Perth, 1974

Environmental Protection Authority. *Conservation Reserves for Western Australia: Systems 4, 8, 9, 10, 11, 12.* The Authority, Perth, 1975

Environmental Protection Authority. 'Implications of the Shark Bay Region Plan for Conservation in System 9'. Report and Recommendations of the Environmental Protection Authority, Perth, 1987

Lawrence. R. 'Shark Bay: the Best in the West.' *Wildlife Australia* 2, 2, 1985, 8–13

Nevill. J. and Lawrence. R. 'Conservation Issues in the Shark Bay Region'. Research Report. Australian Conservation Foundation, Melbourne, and Fund for Animals, Sydney, 1985

Shark Bay Action Group. *A Sustainable Future For Shark Bay: a Response to the Shark Bay Region Plan.* Australian Conservation Foundation and Conservation Council of WA, Perth, 1987

THE EASTERN ARID REGION

Bonython, W. C. *Walking the Simpson Desert.* Rigby, Adelaide, 1980

Fraser, A. S. (ed). *The Great Filling of Lake Eyre in 1974.* Royal Geographical Society of Australasia, South Australian Branch, Adelaide, in press

Greenslade, J. et al. *South Australia's Mound Springs.* Nature Conservation Society of SA, Adelaide, 1985

Jessop, J. 'Vegetation of Northeastern South Australia', in Foale, M. R. (ed). *The Far North East of South Australia.* Nature Conservation Society of SA, Adelaide, 1975

Kotwicki, V. *Floods of Lake Eyre.* Engineering and Water Supply Department, Adelaide, 1986

National Parks and Wildlife Service. *Draft Management Plan for Simpson Desert Conservation Park.* Department of Environment and Planning, Adelaide, 1983

Parker, S. 'Birds and Conservation Parks in the North-East of South Australia'. *South Australian Parks and Conservation* 3, 1980, 11–18

Reader, P. A. 'Lake Eyre, the Mound Springs, Cooper Lakes, Related Drainage System and Adjoining Desert Wilderness: World Heritage Area.' Proposal by Conservation Council of SA and Australian Conservation Foundation for an Eastern Aridlands World Heritage Area, 1985

Wopfner, H. and Twidale, C. R. 'Geomorphological History of the Lake Eyre Basin', in Jennings, J. N. and Mabbutt, J. A. (eds). *Landform Studies from Australia and New Guinea.* Australian National University Press, Canberra, 1971

SOUTHWEST WESTERN AUSTRALIA

Beard, J. S. *Vegetation Survey of Western Australia: Swan.* University of Western Australia Press, Perth, 1981

Chittleborough, R. G. and Keating, F. M. *Western Australian Environmental Review 1986.* Department of Conservation and Environment, Perth, 1986

Conservation Council of Western Australia et al. *Karri at the Crossroads.* Perth, 1982

'The Forests of South Western Western Australia'. *Habitat* (Special issue) 4, 6, May 1977

Hopkins, A. J. M. 'A New Reserve for the Mt Lesueur Area'. *Swans* 13, 3, 1983

Hopkins, A. J. M. et al. 'Species-rich Uplands of South Western Australia'. *Proceedings of the Ecological Society of Australia,* 12, 1983

Jenkins, C. F. H. *The National Parks of Western Australia.* National Parks Authority of Western Australia, Perth, 1980

Keighery, G. J. 'Rediscovering Mountain Bells'. *Landscope* 1, June 1985

Pate, J. S. and Beard, J. S. (eds). *Kwongan, Plant Life of the Sandplain.* University of Western Australia Press, Perth, 1984

Schmidt, W. and Kimber, P. 'The Lane-Poole Jarrah Reserve', *Landscope* 1, June 1985

THE ALPS

Barlow, B. A. (ed). *Flora and Fauna of Alpine Australasia: Ages and Origin.* CSIRO,

Melbourne, 1986

Flood, J. *The Moth Hunters: Aboriginal Prehistory of the Australian Alps.* Australian Institute of Aboriginal Studies, Canberra, 1980

Frawley, K. J. (ed). *Australia's Alpine Area: Management for Conservation.* National Parks Association of the ACT, Canberra, 1986

Hancock, W. K. *Discovering Monaro: a Study of Man's Impact on the Environment.* Cambridge University Press, Cambridge,1972

Johnson, D. *The Alps at the Crossroads: the Quest for an Alpine National Park in Victoria.* Victorian National Parks Association, Melbourne, 1974

Land Conservation Council, Victoria. *Report on the Alpine Study Area.* Two vols. The Council, Melbourne, 1977; and supplementary report, 1982

McDougall, K. *The Alpine Vegetation of the Bogong High Plains.* Victorian Ministry for Conservation, Melbourne. 1982

McDougall, K. and Totterdell, C. J. *Bogong High Plains Vegetation Map and Guide to Alpine Flora.* Four sheets. Victorian Conservation Trust/Soil Conservation Authority, Melbourne, 1982–85

Nankin, H. *Victoria's Alps: an Australian Endangered Heritage.* Australian Conservation Foundation/Collins, Sydney, 1983

National Parks and Wildlife Service of New South Wales. *Plan of Management, Kosciusko National Park.* The Service, Sydney, 1982

Williams, R. J. *Shrub–Grassland Dynamics on the Bogong High Plains.* Botany School, University of Melbourne, 1985

THE SUBANTARCTIC ISLANDS

Clark, M. R. and Dingwall, P. R. *Conservation of Islands in the Southern Ocean: a Review of the Protected Areas of Insulantarctica.* International Union for Conservation of Nature and Natural Reasources, Gland, Switzerland, 1985

Cumpston, J. S. *Macquarie Island.* (NARE Scientific Reports Series A1) Antarctica Division, Department of External Affairs, Melbourne, 1968

Keage, P. L. *The Conservation Status of Heard and the McDonald Islands.* (University of Tasmania Environmental Studies Occasional Paper, 13), University of Tasmania, Hobart, 1981

Laws, R. M. (ed). *Antarctic Ecology.* Two vols. Academic Press, London, 1984

National Parks and Wildlife Service of Tasmania. *Macquarie Island Nature Reserve Visitors' Handbook.* The Service, Hobart, 1987

Royal Society of Tasmania. 'Proceedings of Macquarie Island Symposium 11–15 May 1987, University of Tasmania'. *Proceedings of Royal Society of Tasmania* 122, 1988

Temple, P. *The Sea and the Snow: the South Indian Ocean Expedition to Heard Island.* Cassell, Melbourne, 1966

ANTARCTICA

Antarctic Division, Department of Science. *A Visitor's Introduction to the Antarctic and its Environment.* AGPS, Canberra, 1986

Antarctica: Great Stories from the Frozen Continent. Readers Digest Services, Sydney, 1985

Barnes, J. *Let's Save Antarctica.* Greenhouse Publications, Melbourne, 1982

Harris, S. (ed). *Australia's Antarctic Policy Options.* Australian National University, Canberra, 1984

Hosel, J. *Antarctic Australia.* Currey O'Neill, Melbourne, 1981

Laws, R. M. (ed). *Antarctic Ecology.* Two vols, Academic Press, London, 1984

Mosley, G. *Antarctica: Our Last Great Wilderness.* Australian Conservation Foundation, Melbourne, 1986

Mosley, G. *Protected Area Options for the Antarctic: Report to the International Union for Conservation of Nature and Natural Resources.* Australian Conservation Foundation, Melbourne, 1987

Shapley, D. *The Seventh Continent: Antarctica in a Resource Age. Resources for the Future,* Washington, 1985

Zumberge, J. H. (ed). *Possible Environmental Effects of Mineral Exploration and Exploitation in Antarctica.* Scientific Committee on Antarctic Research, Cambridge, 1979

PHOTOGRAPHER'S ACKNOWLEDGMENTS

The creation of this book was made possible by the generous help of many people. First and foremost, I wish to express deep gratitude to my wife, Irene, for her love, friendship and support. Her contribution has been vital.

Grateful recognition and thanks go also to the National Parks and Wildlife Services throughout Australia, with special mention of the following people: Dr Tony Press, Ian Morris, Greg Miles, Mike Williams, Wayne Dornbush, Russell Knutson, Peter Ingram, David Smith, Chip Morgan, Con Boekel, Gary Shearsby, Peter Stanton, Graham Burst and Val Storey.

I obtained considerable help from many non-government organisations, including the Australian Conservation Foundation, the Total Environment Centre and the Cairns and Far North Environment Centre. I would particularly like to thank the following conservationists: Milo Dunphy, Bill and Yvonne Cunningham, Gregg Borschmann, Peter Reeder, Alan Tingay, Klaus Uhlenhut, John Sinclair, Keith Bradby, Mike Graham, Rosemary Hill and Roli Haly. Penny Figgis provided support and guidance beyond her role as author.

I would also like to thank the following people for their assistance: Steve and Janette Trezise, Chris de Podolinsky, Marcel Grubenmann, Lotti Maser, the management and staff of Four Seasons Cooinda Hotel (Corrie Kelly, Phillip Burt and Joan Sutton) and the Yellow Waters Cruise tour guides. Very special thanks are due to Rolf Gerig from Gerig Electronics for his electronic wizardry which made possible the special equipment needed for my task; and to Sheena Coupe, the project's managing editor.

Very important also was the professional support and back-up I received from many people in the photographic industry. Special thanks are due to the management and staff of Maxwell Optical Industries, especially Ken Forbes, the management and staff of Sam Lewis, and the management and staff of Baltronics.

Finally, I would like to salute the outstanding talent and sensitivity of John Bull, the book's designer, whose skill is so vividly displayed in this publication, and to thank him for the monumental unseen work he contributed under relentless deadline pressures. His dedication was an inspiration.

PHOTOGRAPHIC CREDITS

Key t: top; b: bottom; c: centre; l: left; r: right

page 16 Dennis Harding/Wilderness Society; **21** Kathie Atkinson; **33** b, John Cann/Australasian Nature Transparencies; **35** t, A. S. Weston; **42-3** Leo Meier/Weldon Trannies; **44** Kathie Atkinson; **45** Leo Meier/Weldon Trannies; **46-7** Dean Lee; **48** Ron & Valerie Taylor/Australasian Nature Transparencies; **50-1** Leo Meier/Weldon Trannies; **51** tl, Weldon Trannies; **51** tr, Dean Lee/Weldon Trannies; **52** t, Australian Picture Library/Volvox; **55** tl, Ron & Valerie Taylor/Australasian Nature Transparencies; **55** cl, Australian Picture Library; **56** t,b, **56-7** t Dean Lee; **56-7** b, **58** t Ron & Valerie Taylor/Australasian Nature Transparencies; **58** b, Dean Lee; **59** t, Reg Morrison/Weldon Trannies; **59** b, Ron & Valerie Taylor/Australasian Nature Transparencies; **60** t, Dean Lee; **60** b, **61** t, Ron & Valerie Taylor/Australasian Nature Transparencies; **61** b, Kevin Deacon/Auscape; **62** Australian Picture Library/Volvox; **63** tl, Ron & Valerie Taylor/Australasian Nature Transparencies; **70, 71** t,c, Promotion Australia/Australian Heritage Commission; **71** b, Peter Clark; **74** Reg Morrison/Weldon Trannies; **80** Frank Park/Australasian Nature Transparencies; **82-3** Dennis Harding/Wilderness Society; **84** Ted Mead/Wilderness Society; **86** Grant Dixon/Wilderness Society; **87** Kathie Atkinson; **88** Ted Mead/Wilderness Society; **89** Dennis Harding/Wilderness Society; **90** t,b, Ted Mead/Wilderness Society; **91** Dennis Harding/Wilderness Society; **92** t, Rob Blakers/Wilderness Society; **92** b, Ern Mainka/Australasian Nature Transparencies; **93** Dave Watts/Australasian Nature Transparencies; **94** t, Dave Watts/Wilderness Society; **94** b, Ted Mead/Wilderness Society; **95** Dennis Harding/Wilderness Society; **96** Grant Dixon/Australasian Nature Transparencies; **96-7** Dennis Harding/Wilderness Society; **98** t,b, John Brownlie/Australasian Nature Transparencies; **99** Jean-Paul Ferrero/Auscape; **100** t, Dave Watts/Australasian Nature Transparencies; **100** b, Kathie Atkinson; **101** Dennis Harding/Wilderness Society; **106** John & Valerie Butler/Lochman Transparencies; **108** Ian Brown; **110** tl, Ian Hutton; **110** tr, E. Gaffrey; **112** t, Graham Robertson/Auscape; **114** Ian Hutton; **120-1** Leo Meier/Weldon Trannies; **126** Ian Brown; **128** br, Glen Threlfo/Auscape; **131, 132, 133** t, Leo Meier/Weldon Trannies; **133** b, J. Cancalosi/Auscape; **134** D. & V. Bagden/Australasian Nature Transparencies; **136-7, 138,** Ian Brown; **139, 164-5, 166, 170, 171** b, Leo Meier/Weldon Trannies; **171** t, G. E. Schmida; **175** C. & D. Frith; **176** Jean-Paul Ferrero/Auscape; **178** G. A. Wood/Australasian Nature Transparencies; **179, 183, 191** Leo Meier/Weldon Trannies; **195** J. Burt/Australasian Nature Transparencies; **199** G. E. Schmida/Australasian Nature Transparencies; **200** H. & J. Beste/NPIAW; **203** c, Dave Watts/Australasian Nature Transparencies; **203** b, D. Parer/Australasian Nature Transparencies; **224** C. & D. Frith; **236, 238-9, 246, 248** tl, Leo Meier/Weldon Trannies; **252** tl, Jiri Lochman; **254** Richard Woldendorp/Photo Index; **255** Jiri Lochman; **258** Reg Morrison/Weldon Trannies; **260** tl, Ralph & Daphne Keller/Australasian Nature Transparencies; **260** r, Richard Woldendorp/Photo Index; **260** bl, Paddy Ryan/Australasian Nature Transparencies; **267** tr, Richard Woldendorp/Photo Index; **268** tl, D. Parer/Australasian Nature Transparencies; **271** t, Otto Rogge/Australasian Nature Transparencies; **273** J. Weigel/Australasian Nature Transparencies; **278-281** Leo Meier/Weldon Trannies; **282-3** Natural Images/Australasian Nature Transparencies; **283** tr, Leo Meier/Weldon Trannies; **283** cr, NPIAW; **283** br, **284** Natural Images/Australasian Nature Transparencies; **285** G. E. Schmida/Australasian Nature Transparencies; **286** tl, Leo Meier/Weldon Trannies; **286** tr, Ted Hutchison/Australasian Nature Transparencies; **286-7, 287** t, J. Burt/Australasian Nature Transparencies; **288, 288-9,** Leo Meier/Weldon Trannies; **290** t, Ted Hutchison/Australasian Nature Transparencies; **290** b, J. Burt/Australasian Nature Transparencies; **291** Leo Meier/Weldon Trannies; **295** Grenville Turner/Wildlight; **298** Jean-Paul Ferrero/Auscape; **303** Graeme Chapman/Auscape; **308-9** Jiri Lochman; **315** Leo Meier/Weldon Trannies; **318-9** Harry Nankin; **320** Leo Meier/Weldon Trannies; **322** Rob Blakers; **326-7** Harry Nankin; **333** b, Esther Beaton/Auscape; **336** Harry Nankin; **337** t, Jean-Paul Ferrero/Auscape; **337** c, G. & R. Wilson/Australasian Nature Transparencies; **337** b, Jean-Paul Ferrero/Auscape; **340-1** Chris Bell/Australasian Nature Transparencies; **342** Michael Mallis/Australasian Nature Transparencies; **344** Jonathan Chester/Wildlight; **345-6** Chris Bell/Australasian Nature Transparencies; **347** t, Jonathan Chester/Wildlight; **347** b, Graham Robertson/Auscape; **348** t, Chris Bell/Australasian Nature Transparencies; **348** b, Graham Robertson/Auscape; **349** Chris Bell/Australasian Nature Transparencies; **350** Michael Mallis/Australasian Nature Transparencies; **350-1** Chris Bell/Australasian Nature Transparencies; **352** t, Jean-Paul Ferrero/Auscape; **352** b, Michael Mallis/Australasian Nature Transparencies; **353** Graham Robertson/Auscape; **354** t, Nigel Brothers; **354** b, Graham Robertson/Auscape; **355** D. Pemberton & Gales; **356, 357** t, Jonathan Chester/Wildlight; **357** b, D. Pemberton & R. Gales; **358** Jonathan Chester/Wildlight; **359, 360** t, Jonathan Chester/Australasian Nature Transparencies; **360** bl, Jonathan Chester/Wildlight; **360** br, **361** D. Pemberton & R. Gales; **362-3** Jean-Paul Ferrero/Auscape; **364** Colin Monteath/Auscape; **366** Jonathan Chester/Wildlight; **367** D. Pemberton & R. Gales; **368** Colin Monteath/Auscape; **369** Gordon Claridge/Australasian Nature Transparencies; **370** Jutta Hosel; **370-1** Jean-Paul Ferrero/Auscape; **372** t, Jutta Hosel; **372** b, **373** Gordon McInnes/Australasian Nature Transparencies; **374** t, D. Pemberton & R. Gales; **374** b, H. Marchant; **375** John Béchervaise/Australasian Nature Transparencies; **376-7** Jean-Paul Ferrero/Auscape; **378** t, b, Jonathan Chester/Australasian Nature Transparencies; **379** t,b, **380** t, Jonathan Chester/Wildlight; **380-1** Colin Monteath/Auscape; **382** Jean-Paul Ferrero/Auscape; **383** t,b, Jonathan Chester/Australasian Nature Transparencies; **384-5** Robert Karri-Davies/Photo Index; **389** t, John Hicks/Australasian Nature Transparencies; **389** b, J. Burt/Australasian Nature Transparencies; **392, 393** l,r, Richard Woldendorp/Photo Index

PHOTOGRAPHIC NOTES

For the images in this book Leo Meier used the following equipment and films: Nikon F3 and FA 35mm cameras and Nikkor lenses from 18mm to 600mm; Mamiya RZ 6 x 7cm cameras and lenses from 50mm to 500mm; Kodachrome PKM 25 and PKR 64; Fujichrome 100 RDP.

INDEX